Working-Class Mobilization and Political Control

Working-Class Mobilization and Political Control

Venezuela and Mexico

CHARLES L. DAVIS

THE UNIVERSITY PRESS OF KENTUCKY

Scholarly publisher for the Commonwealth,
serving Bellarmine College, Berea College, Centre
College of Kentucky, Eastern Kentucky University,
The Filson Club, Georgetown College, Kentucky
Historical Society, Kentucky State University,
Morehead State University, Murray State University,
Northern Kentucky University, Transylvania University,
University of Kentucky, University of Louisville,
and Western Kentucky University.

Editorial and Sales Offices: Lexington, Kentucky 40506-0336

Library of Congress Cataloging-in-Publication Data

Davis, Charles L., 1943-
    Working-class mobilization and political control : Venezuela and
Mexico / Charles L. Davis.

    p. cm.
    Bibliography: p.
    Includes index.
    ISBN 0-8131-1670-8
    1. Labor and laboring classes—Venezuela—Political activity.
2. Labor and laboring classes—Mexico—Political activity.
3. Political participation—Venezuela.   4. Political participation
—Mexico. I. Title.
HD8368.D38   1989
322'.2'0987—dc19   88-23314

Contents

278342

Tables

Figures

Acknowledgments

This book would not have been possible without the assistance of others. It is largely based on interviews in late 1979 and early 1980 with over 1,000 workers in various locales throughout Mexico and Venezuela and numerous local union leaders who were interviewed in 1981. More so than library or archival research, survey research depends on the support and cooperation of others. This assistance is particularly vital in the case of cross-national research.

The data presented in this study were collected under grants from the National Science Foundation and the University of Kentucky Research Foundation. Without this financial assistance, the data collection would not have been possible. The collection of survey data in Mexico and Venezuela would not have been possible without the assistance of marketing research firms in the host countries. Fortunately, firms with academic survey research experience were located in Mexico and Venezuela. In Mexico City the survey was carried out by the firm Tecnía. The assistance of Manuel Cosio, the director, and Juana Figueroa in all phases of the data collection is gratefully acknowledged. In Venezuela the survey was conducted by the marketing research firm Multianalisis, then headed by Dr. Fausto Izcaray. Dr. Izcaray and his staff, particularly Oly Lozada de Izcaray, provided essential supervision in all phases of the data collection. The assistance of the Venezuelan and Mexican interviewers who administered the questionnaire is also gratefully acknowledged. Finally, the many workers and union leaders who gave of their time in order to tell their story and to present their views ought to be mentioned.

The assistance of sociologist Dr. Francisco Zapata was essential. Dr. Zapata, of the Colegio de México in Mexico City, supervised the data collection in Mexico. In addition, he gave extensively of his time to provide his own expertise on labor relations in Latin America and to refine the theoretical basis of the study.

The following individuals provided very useful comments on the style and substance of various chapters in this manuscript: Jennifer McCoy, David E. Blank, and, in particular, Philip A. Greasley, the director of the University of Kentucky Center. Mitchell Seligson and Kevin Middlebrook provided valuable comments on an earlier version of the manuscript. I was also helped by the comments of reviewers for the University Press of Kentucky. Finally, the assistance of the staff at the University Press of Kentucky is acknowledged. Also, I would like to thank Kim Hayden for typing an earlier version of the manuscript.

Two individuals deserve special mention. Sandra Lusk, the business manager for the University of Kentucky Center at Fort Knox, typed and retyped this manuscript. Her work was exemplary despite her multiple responsibilities in managing the Fort Knox Center.

The other individual is Dr. Kenneth M. Coleman, who is an associate professor of political science at the University of Kentucky. Dr. Coleman was the original principal investigator for this project and participated in the interviewing of all union leaders in Mexico and Venezuela. He also participated in writing an earlier version of this book but dropped out of his project because of increasingly heavy administrative responsibilities. His involvement was particularly helpful in the preparation of chapters 2 and 9 and in co-authoring chapter 3.

As my former mentor, longtime research colleague, and constant friend, I dedicate this book to him. I am sure that my wife, mother, and kids will understand why I am not doing the usual.

Chapter One

State Capitalism and Mass Mobilization

Richard Couto coined the phrase "political silence" to characterize the political behavior of the impoverished masses in Appalachia.[1] The point that Couto emphasized is that these people have every reason *not* to remain silent in the face of environmental destruction, inadequate public services, extreme concentration of land ownership, regressive taxation, and lack of economic opportunity.[2] The focus of this study is also on political silence—the silence exhibited by industrial workers in the state-capitalist regimes of Mexico and Venezuela. The study will show that workers in these two countries also have every reason not to remain politically silent yet tend to do so. The consequences of political silence in Latin America are much the same as in Appalachia—the perpetuation of social injustice and inequity. It is hoped that this study will contribute to a greater understanding of why the lower classes in Latin America remain politically silent though not necessarily inactive.[3]

Before examining in more depth the major theoretical issues to be addressed in this study, let us discuss why political silence is detrimental to the interests of the lower classes in the late industrializing countries of Latin America, though functional for state-capitalist economic development in these countries.

Most late industrializing nations in contemporary Latin America have opted for a strategy of economic development that has been labeled *dependent state capitalism*. The term *dependent* indicates the crucial role that foreign investment and multinational corporations have come to play in the economic development of the capitalist nations of the third world. These links to the outside world sometimes imply constraints on developmental possibilities.[4] For that reason development is construed as "dependent" rather than "autonomous." The latter term, *state capitalism*, underscores the vital role that the state has come to play in capitalist expansion in late industrializing nations.[5] This strategy is predicated on the state promoting an attractive climate for private investment, both domestic and foreign. In addition to various direct incentives to private economic activity, such as cheap credit, subsidies, regressive taxation, and infrastructural develop-ment, public authorities often support public policies that sacrifice immediate improvements in living standards and in the social welfare of the working population in order to maximize long-term economic growth. Wayne Cornelius has described very aptly the public policy choices that political elites in late industrializing countries often make in order to promote dependent capitalist development. Referring to the policy debate over allocation of Mexico's petroleum revenues in the late seventies, he writes:

The basic operating premise of Mexican government policy seems to be that the country's employment problems can only be solved in the long run (i.e., in the next generation), and only as a result of urban-industrial development. The overriding goal, in the medium-to-long run, is to turn today's peasants, and their offspring, into factory operatives with more secure, better-paid em-ployment. In this policy context, the "oil bonanza" must not be squandered on temporary make-work projects, income transfer programs, and other kinds of "welfare schemes" (*subsidios a la miseria*) for the rural and urban poor. Rather, the revenues must be used to build up a much larger base of per-manent employment in the urban-industrial sector. Thus, massive, short-term job creating programs are not in the cards.[6]

Comprehensive socioeconomic reforms that seek to bring about widespread immediate improvement in mass living standards are in-consistent with the economic logic and priorities of dependent capi-talist development.[7] Reforms such as higher minimum wage laws, increased public sector employment, progressive taxation, or social welfare programs pose a potential threat to capital formation as scarce resources are diverted from investment into consumption. Addition-ally, the increased purchasing power of the popular sector generated by such policies raises the specter of runaway inflation. A plethora of economic reforms could also lead to capital flight if investors, fearful of the need to tax to support new social welfare programs, decide to move their funds to safer markets. For these reasons political elites committed to conventional capitalist development[8] often shy away from economic reform unless there is a compelling political logic to do otherwise. In that case their response to pressures for reform is often little more than rhetoric, limited to preemptive reforms designed to regenerate popular support.[9]

Alain de Janvry's analysis of the relationship between capital ac-cumulation in late industrializing countries and restricted internal consumer markets provides further insight into structural pressures on political elites to limit redistributive socioeconomic reforms.[10] In the "socially disarticulated economies" of the third world, capital accumulation depends on (1) the containment of labor costs and the extraction of oligopolistic rents and (2) the expansion of exports and of luxury goods for a restricted internal market. By contrast, capitalists in the "socially articulated economies" of early industrializing countries profit when *internal markets* expand via the growth of real wages and social benefits for workers. Socioeconomic reform is, therefore, consistent with logic of capital accumulation in early industrializing countries; it is inconsistent with capital accumulation in the "socially disarticulated" economies of the late industrializing nations.

"Socially disarticulated economies" clearly "reflect the imposition of the values and interests of some groups to the exclusion of others."[11] Those with investable capital stand to benefit far more than do those who must sell their labor and only hope for a trickle-down effect. As James Malloy puts it, "The latter (labor) literally pay the costs of development, simply because they are forced to do so."[12] The social costs can be further exacerbated during periodic crises related to recession in the world capitalist economy, inflation, international debt, trade imbalances and currency devaluations, and International Monetary Fund (IMF) austerity programs. In these circumstances the working classes have often been asked to absorb cuts in real wages and in access to public services as a way to regenerate and to stabilize economic growth.[13]

The allocation of social costs to the working class would seem to be sufficient incentive for political mobilization. Only by organizing for political activity could workers hope to shift the social costs of development policies to privileged classes and to obtain a more equitable distribution of economic and political resources. However, working-class mobilization represents a potential threat to the income and control rights of capital and thus to the underlying logic of capital accumulation in "socially disarticulated" economies.[14] Therefore, political elites in state-capitalist regimes often seek to limit working-class mobilization that might challenge existing developmental policies.

One solution to working-class mobilization that has been tried in Latin America is political exclusion of the lower classes. To use Charles Anderson's terminology,[15] *power contenders* linked to the lower classes who had previously gained entry into the political arena are formally excluded. This technique has typically been tried in the bureaucratic-authoritarian regimes[16] of the sixties and seventies that sought to deactivate the popular sector. The early eighties, however, have seen many of these regimes unravel because of their failure to deliver on the promises of economic stabilization and superior growth rates. Their legitimacy eroded since military or authoritarian elites could not deliver on their promises. Other bases of legitimacy such as a revolutionary ideology or popular consent were simply not available.[17]

Not all state-capitalist regimes in Latin America opted for a bureaucratic-authoritarian solution during the turbulent sixties and seventies. Countries such as Colombia, Costa Rica, Venezuela, and Mexico maintained inclusionary political systems while experiencing severe economic crises and massive social problems linked to delayed dependent development and to crises in the international economy.[18] In these countries formal exclusion of lower-class organizations and political parties from the political arena has not been attempted in recent times. The reason is simply that elites perceived no threat to long-term goals of capital accumulation and political stability from mass mobilization. Lower-class mobilization has served neither to strengthen significantly the left nor to increase alarmingly the incidence of destabilizing, unconventional participation.

The point is well illustrated by the 1983 presidential race in Venezuela where the two ruling centrist parties (Acción Democrática [AD] and the Christian Democratic Party [COPEI]) gained 91.3 percent of the vote[19] or by the 1982 presidential race in Mexico where the winning candidate of the ruling Partido Revolucionario Institucional (PRI) received 71.6 percent of the vote.[20] These totals were gained during a time of severe economic crisis in both countries. In both countries parties on the political left have failed to harvest great electoral support, nor have there been any serious threats to the long-term political stability of either regime.

In both Mexico and Venezuela, hegemonic parties that dominate the electoral arena have emerged. In Mexico's semicompetitive electoral system, the PRI has never lost a gubernatorial or presidential election nor control of the national or state legislatures since its inception in 1928 until the legislative elections of 1985. By contrast, a two-party system emerged in Venezuela—with AD and COPEI becoming the dominant parties. In the last three presidential races (1973, 1978, and 1983), they have managed to garner over 80 percent of the vote, while minor parties on the right and left combined have not gained over 15 percent of the vote.[21]

A fundamental objective of this study is to explore how these parties in Mexico and Venezuela have managed to secure working-class electoral support. To understand this phenomenon, the commitment of these hegemonic parties not only to state-capitalist development but also to populism must be examined. As Malloy states, "An explicit assumption of all populist approaches has been that regimes could simultaneously spur development, incorporate many sectors of the society in the political system, and broadly distribute the surplus."[22] Chapter 3 will examine more closely how hegemonic parties in Venezuela and Mexico have sought to achieve these diverse objectives. Some of the general features of populism in these two countries will be noted here.

First, incorporation of any given sector is achieved through either ties with hegemonic parties or ties with the bureaucratic state. In both cases incorporation is based on explicit or implicit bargains (or pacts) by which the state or party agrees to provide economic benefits or other privileges in exchange for political support. Generally, goods and services are distributed through patron-client networks.[23] The nature of the bargain negotiated by various groups depends on its political power and control over investable capital.[24] More privileged groups can negotiate with the state more favorable bargains than the less privileged. In the case of the lower classes, blue-collar workers in the urban industrial sector generally fare better than either the peasants or the urban workers in the informal sector.[25]

Second, the resource scarcity and recurring economic crises that dependent capitalist countries confront create difficulties in achieving simultaneously continuing economic growth and a large surplus that can be distributed broadly to all sectors of society. The petroleum bonanza of the seventies gave both Mexico and Venezuela a brief respite from this dilemma. Still, elites in both countries have confronted difficult choices between investment and consumption goals and between the interests of labor and capital. As noted, elites generally side with the interests of capital hoping that sustained economic growth might eventually expand the surplus available for distribution to incorporated groups.

Third, the long-term political stability of these two inclusionary regimes, Venezuela and Mexico, depends on the continuing capacity of hegemonic parties to retain lower-class support. Consider the alternative. If the lower classes were to switch their loyalty to parties of the left, as found in many Western European countries,[26] such parties might then challenge the hegemony of the ruling populist parties. The state-capitalist model of economic development could then be put in jeopardy with the consequence of unraveling the social pacts with more privileged groups. Furthermore, if lower-class ties to hegemonic parties were to break down, then more radical socio-political movements could recruit more effectively among the lower classes. Such social fissions could conceivably generate the climate for a military coup or a regime breakdown, similar to what has occurred in other Latin American countries.

This study examines why the urban working class in Mexico and Venezuela has generally supported hegemonic parties and remained politically silent. Subsequent chapters explore how these behavioral patterns are shaped by mechanisms of political control. The data analysis utilizes national samples of around 500 blue-collar workers who were interviewed in 1979 and 1980. The focus of the study is the most privileged stratum of the lower class in Mexico and Venezuela, workers employed in the urban formal sector of the economy.[27]

The focus on urban labor is significant for two reasons. While this sector of the working class is less numerous than the peasant or informal sector, it is a potentially more powerful actor in the political arena. It is likely to be less atomized socially and thereby more capable of resorting to collective action. Furthermore, this sector of the working class is more likely to be organized by labor unions. Thus, the industrial work force possesses a greater potential to challenge government priorities than do either unorganized peasants or urban workers in the informal sector.

An empirical study of industrial workers in Mexico and Venezuela is useful because of the paucity of survey data on this sector of the Latin American working class. Most previous survey research conducted in Latin America has focused on either the rural peasantry or the urban informal sector.[28] While industrial workers and labor unions in Latin America have received considerable attention recently from scholars,[29] there has been relatively little systematic investigation of working-class political attitudes and behavior.[30] The survey data set used for this study should allow for a more systematic assessment of the capacity of industrial workers in Venezuela and Mexico to mobilize politically.

Before proceeding to a discussion of the major theoretical issues to be addressed, one thing must be emphasized. The purpose here is not to advance another "lap dog" interpretation of industrial labor in Latin America.[31] Noting quiescent behavioral patterns or relative political inactivity does not necessarily imply that workers are either necessarily content with state-capitalist development or too politically immature for active mobilization. Even though the working class has generally remained quiescent, there have been pockets of lower-class resistance to the prevailing sociopolitical system in both countries throughout the postwar period. Control of working-class mobilization has proved to be problematic for elites in both Mexico and Venezuela and has not always come easily.[32] The recent *Coordinadora* movement in Mexico and the *nuevo sindicalismo* in Venezuela during the eighties illustrate how pockets of working-class resistance develop in both countries.[33] To examine modal patterns of restrained political mobilization does not imply that exceptions to these patterns are not to be found.

Alternative patterns of working-class political mobilization can now be examined. First, it should be noted that mobilizational patterns exhibited by lower-class populations are not permanently fixed. Workers may be prone to quiescence and to support for hegemonic parties at time "x" but not necessarily at time "y."[34] Furthermore, variation in lower-class mobilizational patterns can be found across different contexts. Cornelius, for example, found significant variation in participant activity across different squatter settlements in Mexico City.[35] Patterns of differential mobilization can be observed from a cross-national perspective as well.[36] It is useful, therefore, to construct a typology of alternative patterns of political mobilization that a working-class population might exhibit.

It is important to note that ideal types of mobilization patterns are being identified. In the real world, there is not likely to be a perfect fit with any of the types identified. Also, a definition of political mobilization needs to be provided. It has been defined "as the process through which subordinate groups increase their capacity to pursue collective goals."[37] This definition suggests three possible types of working-class mobilization: (1) autonomous political mobilization, (2) demobilization, and (3) controlled mobilization. These patterns are defined by certain behavioral and attitudinal syndromes that working-class populations might exhibit. Each one of the above-mentioned mobilizational patterns will be considered, focusing first on autonomous mobilization.

Autonomous mobilization occurs (1) when subordinate groups come to define their collective interests as being in conflict with those of other groups or with the state and (2) when such groups actively pursue their collective interests as they have so defined them. Autonomous political mobilization is most likely to occur in state-capitalist regimes when opportunities to exercise political influence are widely available. In those contexts in which the working class is extended ample opportunities to pursue collective interests, one would expect to find a relatively high awareness of conflicting class interest (*concientización*) and psychological involvement in politics. That is, workers acquire participatory motivations that equip them for self-directed political participation. Furthermore, autonomously mobilized workers should be prone to support left-wing, working-class parties and to be politically active beyond periodic voting.

Karen Remmer's discussion of mass political mobilization in Chile before 1973 illustrates these patterns of autonomous mobilization.

Prior to 1973 Chile experienced an exceptionally rapid process of political mobilization. In fact, Henry A. Landsberger and Tim McDaniel have characterized the growth in political awareness and activity, which was initiated during the Christian Democratic government of Eduardo Frei and accelerated under the Allende administration as "hypermobilization."

. . . On a comparative basis, the process of political mobilization was not only rapid; it produced an exceptionally high level of subordinate group organization and participation in politics. . . . The estimated level of union organization in Chile by the end of the Allende period compared favorably even with that of Argentina, whose trade union movement is typically regarded as the largest and most powerful in Latin America. Taking into account as well participation in political parties and the proliferation of non-union lower class organization, for which no comparative data are available, the level of popular involvement in politics by 1973 probably exceeded that of any country in Latin America, with the possible exception of Cuba.

. . . Most evidence does suggest that lower class organization and political consciousness in Chile were strong by Latin American and Mediterranean standards. First, Chile had a relatively lengthy tradition of lower class organization and militancy. The labor movement developed comparatively early and was historically organized under Marxist leadership. In contrast to countries such as Argentina, Spain, Brazil, and Mexico, the union movement also achieved a relatively high degree of autonomy from state control and, particularly after 1953, an unusual level of unity with the formation of the Communist dominated national trade union central, the *Central Unica de Trabajadores* (CUT).[38]

Certainly, the case of the working class in Chile during the Frei and Allende years does not provide the optimal illustration of autonomous political mobilization.[39] As chapter 5 will show, working-class political mobilization in Chile during this era was more controlled than in certain Western European countries. Still, the case of the working class in Chile as well as the cases of Jamaica during the Manley years (1972-80)[40] and, to a lesser extent, Brazil during the Goulart years (1960-64)[41] illustrate far more autonomous political mobilization than what this study found among workers in Venezuela and Mexico. The point to be emphasized is that working-class populations in Latin America do not exhibit uniform levels and styles of political mobilization. One can find significant variation in the political mobilization patterns manifested by lower-class populations in Latin America. Before 1973 Chile illustrates relatively autonomous mobilization; the other extreme is represented by the suppressed mobilization patterns found in bureaucratic-authoritarian regimes.

Autonomous working-class mobilization poses a potential threat to the hegemony of populist parties as well as to social pacts with privileged groups. While such mobilization patterns undoubtedly tend to create more equitable distributional patterns, they can also generate social fissions and strains on existing distributive mechanisms as the aforementioned case of Chile illustrates. It is this type of mobilization that the politically stable regimes of Latin America suppress or contain, though generally at the cost of a more equitable development strategy.

Demobilization represents the opposite end of the spectrum from autonomous mobilization. In this case opportunities for political mobilization by subordinate groups are effectively eliminated. Political activity, if at all, is limited to particularized contacting for specific benefits and public goods and perhaps to problem-solving action within local communities. Such activities did occur in various bureaucratic-authoritarian regimes of the southern cone.[42] A primary goal of these regimes was to demobilize various sectors of the population—that is, to exclude them altogether from the political arena so that political decision making could become a monopoly of selected military officers and technocrats.[43] These regimes came into existence largely to contain the threat of autonomous political mobilization by the popular sector.[44]

In the case of *controlled mobilization*, subordinate groups are not demobilized, but rather their capacity to pursue collective goals is limited by effective political controls. Political control can be asserted through either structural or cultural mechanisms that limit the mobilizational capacity of a group. If political control is effectively asserted, targeted groups are likely to disengage from politics except for periodic voting as directed by hegemonic parties. If there is effective control over political mobilization of a given working-class population, one should find (1) a high level of electoral support for hegemonic parties, (2) a low level of support for leftist and other system-challenging parties, (3) a low level of psychological involvement in politics and of awareness of conflicting class interests (*con-*

cientización), and (4) a low level of political activity except for periodic voting.

Moreover, controlled mobilization is likely to be characterized by externally mobilized rather than by self-directed political participation. Self-directed as opposed to externally directed mobilization requires that individuals acquire some knowledge of the political process as well as motivations to participate. In the absence of such motivations and knowledge, workers are likely to lack the capacity for political activism unless externally mobilized by political parties or interest groups.[45] As Ronald Inglehart notes, external mobilization "may not reflect the translation of public preferences into elite decision, so much as the effective mobilization of the public by elites, in pursuit of goals largely chosen by the latter."[46] External or elite-directed mobilization, Inglehart also points out, produces "only a relatively low qualitative level of participation—generally not going much beyond mere voting."[47] Such transient, vertically directed mobilization clearly favors ruling parties that have a larger base of supporters to mobilize than do opposition parties.

The concept of controlled mobilization implies that the participatory motivations as well as choices of individuals can be systematically manipulated. Control mechanisms allow elites to influence the participatory motivations and decisions of individual citizens. For example, the capacity of a hegemonic party to control the flow of economic benefits might discourage workers from voting for the left. Similarly, the dispossessed in American society are often discouraged from radical political action because of a pervasive "individualist ethos" in the American political culture.[48] In both cases controls (cultural in the latter, structural in the former) serve to limit and to discourage political mobilization. Thus, controlled political mobilization in the case of the working class protects elite autonomy in decision making and social pacts with more privileged societal actors.

We now turn to a theoretical discussion of alternative mechanisms that might be utilized to control political mobilization.

Unfortunately, data are not available on a wide array of political systems that would provide cross-systemic variation in patterns of political mobilization. If such data were available, it would be possible to assess the relationship between alternative system-level controls and patterns of political mobilization. Within the limitations imposed by a two-country sample, it is still possible to assess how various structural and cultural controls affect the capacity of industrial workers for political mobilization. Additionally, useful comparisons between Mexican and Venezuelan workers can be drawn as control structures are more fully developed in Mexico than in Venezuela (see chapter 4). The intent of the data analysis in chapters 6 to 8 is to gain a better understanding of how control mechanisms affect working-class mobilization in Venezuela and Mexico. The purpose is to determine which structural or cultural control mechanisms best account for observed patterns of controlled mobilization.

Let us now examine four possible structural control mechanisms beginning with *corporatist interest intermediation*.

As defined by Philippe Schmitter, *corporatism* is a system of interest intermediation in which "constituent units are organized into a limited number of singular, compulsory, noncompetitive, hierarchically ordered and functionally differentiated categories, recognized or licensed . . . by the state and granted a deliberate representational monopoly . . . in exchange for observing certain controls on their selection of leaders and articulation of demands and supports."[49]

Schmitter separates corporatist systems of interest intermediation into two subtypes: *state corporatism* and *societal corporatism*, corresponding essentially to a distinction between forms of "guided" intermediation imposed from above versus forms of "self-limited" intermediation that evolve from below. It is state-corporatist arrangements that tend to characterize interest intermediation in Latin America.

Unlike in the early industrializing nations where political parties developed out of preexisting socioeconomic, ethnic, and religious cleavages,[50] multiclass political parties in Latin America were sometimes formed by elites to preempt the emergence of societal cleavages. The labor movement was often initiated or preempted by political parties and consequently became dependent on sponsoring political parties. To use Kay Lawson's typology of party-interest group linkages, the ties established between political parties and the union movement are often "directive" rather than "participatory" or "policy-responsive."[51] The nature of "directive" or state-corporatist linkages is well illustrated in John Corbett's discussion of how interest groups relate to the PRI in Mexico.

There is a strong tendency in the conceptual literature on political parties to emphasize linkage upward through the system, from masses to elites or from the grass roots to upper echelons. Such a notion is implicit in the idea of parties as "specialized aggregation structures" or sometimes explicit as "the organization called the party is expected to organize public opinion and to

communicate demands to the center of governmental power and decision."
But in the Mexican context the emphasis on mobilizing support for the *status
quo* suggests that attention should be directed to the downward linkages or
to those aspects of the party system that facilitate communication and control
from the top down.[52]

Kevin Middlebrook has shown that corporatism is generally institutionalized in two ways by Latin American states: (1) through
"social corporatist organizations" by which interest groups are linked
to political parties and (2) through "state administrative structures,"
which are "those governmental administrative mechanisms that represent the formal integration of societal interests and the state."[53] In
this study the focus is on social corporatist organizations. The point
is to assess whether workers belonging to labor unions affiliated with
dominant parties exhibit different patterns of political mobilization
than do workers belonging to unions that have achieved a degree of
autonomy from control by dominant parties. The former type of union
will be referred to as an *incorporated union*; the latter type as an *autonomous union*. The former type of union presumably operates as a
mechanism to control working-class political mobilization, while the
latter type of union might facilitate more autonomous political mobilization on the part of the working class.

The literature on corporatism and clientelism helps one to understand why incorporated unions might be effective devices for controlling working-class political mobilization. Like hegemonic parties,
incorporated unions can utilize patronage resources to mobilize clients
for political activities. On the other hand, autonomous unions, like
leftist parties, frequently lack patronage resources because of lack of
control over public sector distributional systems. Hence, they must
rely more on symbol manipulation as a device for external mobilization. Particularly in the case of the poor and the working class,
symbol manipulation is not likely to be as powerful a resource as the
distribution of material goods. Hence, hegemonic parties can utilize
their control over incorporated unions to thwart efforts by the left or
other opposition parties to make inroads among the working class.
Furthermore, patronage resources can be used to discourage large-
scale political activation on the part of the working class. As Robert
Kaufman notes, the intent of corporatism is to "coopt new social forces
and defuse their revolutionary potential."[54]

If corporatist interest intermediation in Mexico and Venezuela
provides an effective control over working-class mobilization, one
should find (1) that the level of psychological involvement in politics

and *concientización* should be lower among workers in incorporated unions than among other workers; (2) that the level of electoral support for hegemonic parties should be greater among workers in incorporated unions; (3) that electoral support for the left and other opposition parties should be less among workers in incorporated unions; and (4) that incorporated unions should exhibit a greater capacity to turn out voters than do autonomous unions.

Limitation of partisan competition is the second control mechanism. First, one should note that electoral systems, in general, provide a mechanism not only for popular expression but also for control of political mobilization. As Benjamin Ginsberg explains:

The fundamental difference between voting and rioting is that voting is a socialized and institutionalized form of mass political expression. The peasant uprising or urban riot is usually a spontaneous affair, sparked by some particular event or grievance. Though riots may have been commonplace, each was itself a unique event. . . . Voting, however, is far from spontaneous. Elections provide routine institutional channels for the expression of demands and grievances. They thus transmute what might otherwise take the form of sporadic, citizen-initiated activity into a routine public function. When, where, who, and how individuals participate in elections are matters of public policy rather than questions of spontaneous public choice. . . . By establishing an institutional channel of political activity and habituating citizens to its use, governments reduced the danger that mass political action posed to the established political and social order. Elections contain and channel away potentially violent and disruptive activities and protect the regime's stability.[55]

Still, alternative electoral systems vary in their capacity to limit system-challenging mobilization by opposition parties. Representational multiparty systems reflect one extreme in which there is virtually no disincentive to partisan mobilization by opposition parties. Exclusionary authoritarian systems represent the other extreme in which all opposition partisan activity is repressed. In a two-party aggregative system as found in Venezuela or an inclusionary authoritarian system as found in Mexico, partisan opposition is permitted, but the "mobilization of bias" favors dominant parties or what will be referred to as hegemonic parties. The hegemony of dominant parties is protected both by the "rules of the game" that political elites determine and by their quasi-monopoly of power resources.

The nature of the party system determines in fact whose interests will prevail in the electoral arena. If parties favoring development strategies other than state capitalism are put at a competitive disadvantage to the dominant parties, electoral challenges to the dominant pattern of development are less likely. As we shall see in Chapter 4, the political left in Mexico and Venezuela find themselves in this situation. However, as that chapter will show, leftist parties have greater opportunities to gain power in Venezuela than in Mexico. Furthermore, the incumbent party is periodically defeated in national elections in Venezuela, unlike in Mexico. Thus, the Venezuelan and Mexican regimes provide a useful contrast in the degree of partisan competition. This contrast provides an opportunity to assess how restricted partisan competition contributes to controlled political mobilization.

Restricted partisan competition might affect the acquisition of participatory motivations and subsequent capacity for self-directed participation as well as the electoral choice. Self-directed participation depends on citizens acquiring participatory motivations that might be difficult to acquire under conditions of restricted competition. Restricted partisan competition might impede workers from becoming attentive to politics and from developing a critical consciousness of the existing sociopolitical order. (The nature of these two participatory motivations will be examined more closely in chapter 6.)

Under conditions of restricted partisan competition, a hegemonic party (or incorporated unions) ought to be better able to suppress active attentiveness to politics on the part of their working-class supporters, while leftist parties (or autonomous unions) might confront difficulty in sustaining attentiveness. The reason is that workers, like other citizens, are likely to face difficulty in sustaining interest in politics when election results are predictable. Restricted competition might also facilitate the hegemonic party or incorporated unions in suppressing *concientización*[56] among their followers by allowing them to propagandize more effectively among working-class supporters. By contrast, hegemonic parties or unions in a less restrictive electoral system might not be able to propagandize effectively because of competing messages from rival parties. Restricted competition might also lead opposition leaders to conclude that there is little to be gained by radicalizing their base of working-class supporters since the ruling party is not going to be dislodged from power. By contrast, opposition leaders in a more competitive electoral system might see more utility in promoting a more radicalized base of working-class support if they believe that they can share or win political power. In sum, workers in a more restricted electoral system might be less prone to acquire participatory motivations that facilitate self-directed political participation. Thus, hegemonic parties and incorporated unions might be able to guide electoral mobilization more easily in a context where partisan competition is more restricted.

Restricted partisan competition might also affect electoral choice. Weak partisan competition should decrease the "floating" vote that is created by long-term partisans of the ruling party switching their vote to opposition parties. The only "floating" voters in the context of restricted partisan competition should be long-term partisans of opposition parties who decide to vote for the ruling party. Rational choice theory suggests why the floating vote in the context of one-party dominations should tend to gravitate toward the ruling party rather than toward opposition parties. Opposition parties might be viewed as providing no viable option from which to choose. The only options might be seen as voting for the ruling party or abstention. Therefore, long-term supporters of the ruling party who become disenchanted might abstain rather than vote for opposition parties that cannot win. By contrast, such voters in more competitive electoral systems should perceive greater utility in voting for opposition parties if, in fact, the opposition can gain political power.

Similarly, leftist parties might better capitalize on working-class discontent with incumbent performance if workers believe that the left can gain political power. Conversely, if workers believe that the left cannot realistically gain power, then they might eliminate the left as a viable electoral option. Thus, a past history of failure on the part of the left might well lead discontented workers to turn away from the left even though sympathetic to its message. Therefore, the less the opportunity for the left to win power, the less discontented workers ought to vote for leftist parties.

In like manner, restricted partisan competition might limit the capacity of autonomous labor unions to influence the voting behavior of workers. Leaders of incorporated unions might find the task of persuading workers to vote for a hegemonic party to be easier if there is no meaningful competition. Similarly, leaders of autonomous unions might be better able to convince workers to support opposition parties if such parties have a realistic chance of gaining power. Therefore, the capacity of labor unions to influence voting behavior might be related to the degree of partisan competition. Weak competition should facilitate the task of incorporated unions and weaken the capacity of autonomous unions to promote the left. Conversely, meaningful electoral competition should enhance the capacity of autonomous unions to promote leftist voting.

In sum, if restricted partisan competition accounts for controlled political mobilization, one would expect to find the following differences between Venezuelan and Mexican workers: (1) Mexican workers identifying with the PRI or belonging to an incorporated union ought to exhibit less attentiveness to politics than Venezuelan workers identifying with COPEI or AD or belonging to such a union; leftist workers or members of autonomous unions in Venezuela ought to exhibit greater attentiveness to politics than their counterparts in Mexico; (2) leftist parties and autonomous unions are more likely to foster *concientización* among their supporters in Venezuela than in Mexico; (3) incorporated unions and hegemonic parties can more effectively mobilize electoral participation among Mexican workers than among Venezuelan workers; (4) self-directed electoral participation is more likely to occur among Venezuelan workers than among Mexican workers; (5) deviations from long-term loyalty to a hegemonic party are more likely to occur among Venezuelan workers than among Mexican workers; (6) conversely, loyalists of opposition parties are more likely to deviate and vote for a hegemonic party in Mexico than in Venezuela; (7) discontent with the performance of hegemonic parties is more likely to be converted into electoral support for the left among Venezuelan workers than among Mexican workers; (8) incorporated unions are more likely to influence the electoral choice of workers in Mexico than in Venezuela; (9) autonomous unions are more likely to influence the electoral choice of workers in Venezuela than in Mexico.

The third control mechanism rests in the capacity of a regime to generate *satisfaction with performance*. As noted, state-capitalist regimes in the third world are generally willing to sacrifice the short- or intermediate-term interests of the lower classes to improve capital formation. This condition does not necessarily mean that these regimes cannot generate short-term satisfactions for the lower classes. Periods of sustained economic expansion may permit the real wages of labor to increase even if not at the rate of management and technicians.[57] Such periods of expansion might also enable elites to extend public services to marginal populations and, thereby, to solidify pacts with these elements of the population.[58]

Industrial workers in contemporary state-capitalist systems are likely to acquire far better wages, benefits, and job security than are peasants or workers in the urban informal sector.[59] For this reason some scholars have suggested the "labor aristocracy thesis" to explain why industrial workers in late developing countries tend to exhibit patterns of controlled political mobilization. Such workers are presumably coopted and are not likely to be attracted to backing opposition parties or movements. To the contrary, their relative affluence allows them to enter the consumer society and even the privatistic world of the middle class. Thus, the 'labor aristocracy thesis' provides a plausible explanation for patterns of controlled political mobilization observed among industrial workers in Mexico and Venezuela. Privileged workers might see little reason to give attention to the world of politics or to engage in opposition politics against a sociopolitical order that has served them reasonably well.[60]

If performance satisfaction explains how political elites in Mexico and Venezuela have maintained *political* control over working-class mobilization, one would expect to find (1) that levels of satisfaction with government performance are relatively high among workers who were interviewed for this study and (2) that performance satisfaction accounts for patterns of controlled mobilization. Specifically, one would expect to find that performance satisfaction leads to lower psychological involvement in politics and *concientización*, less self-directed electoral participation, and greater electoral support for hegemonic parties.

The discussion thus far has considered how structural constraints might limit the capacity of workers to pursue collective goals. The next point to examine is how a cultural control might limit the capacity of workers to mobilize. According to the working-class culture thesis, the political culture of workers weakens their capacity for self-directed mobilization. Presumably maladaptive for "participant citizenship," lower-class political culture is often characterized as "subject" or "parochial" rather than as "participant."[61] It leaves workers ill-prepared for self-directed participation; therefore, they must depend on cues from external organizations in order to participate in politics.

Working-class culture, thus, provides a possible explanation for low psychological involvement in politics and receptivity to external guidance by hegemonic parties and incorporated unions. Also, it provides an explanation as to why a lower-class population might not be attracted to leftist or working-class parties. Such parties rely on ideological appeals that may not be comprehended by the politically unsophisticated lower classes.[62] Similarly, a lack of political sophistication could contribute to low *concientización*.

Finally, the fourth control mechanism consists of *vertical patterns of political decision making*. Susan Purcell has described how decision-making processes differ in democratic and authoritarian systems. "The authority flow in an authoritarian system is the reverse of what supposedly characterizes democratic politics. Instead of responding to and reflecting demands, pressures, and initiatives that originate at lower levels, the executive in an authoritarian regime shapes and manipulates demands emanating from below while enjoying sub-stantial leeway in the determination of the goals that the regime will pursue."[63] Purcell's characterization suggests that elites in democratic regimes confront far more constraints from below in decision making than do elites in authoritarian regimes. Conversely, elites in authori-tarian regimes are more insulated from popular pressures and de-mands than their counterparts in democratic regimes. Closure of political decision-making processes from linkages with the masses creates disincentives for mass political mobilization. While the masses in more authoritarian regimes may be able to *"pursue* their collective goals," they have less assurance that they can *obtain* goals. Corpo-ratism and limited party competition contribute to elite insulation from below. As chapter 4 will show, the powerlessness of repre-sentative institutions, elite consensus, and high repressive capability can also increase elite autonomy in decision making.

Unfortunately, the impact of elite autonomy in decision making on political mobilization cannot be directly assessed. However, it can be shown that elite autonomy is more fully developed in Mexico's semiauthoritarian regime than in Venezuela's competitive democracy. This factor ought to be taken into account in explaining differences in mobilizational patterns found between Mexican and Venezuelan workers.

Data for this study were collected in two phases. The first phase involved interviewing of Venezuelan and Mexican workers in late 1979 and early 1980. These surveys were conducted by marketing research firms with previous experience in social scientific research.[64] In the spring of 1981, interviews were conducted with leaders from the unions from which workers were sampled.[65]

The research design is intended to move the study of lower-class political behavior in Latin America and elsewhere in the third world beyond the modernization paradigm to a focus on variant political environments as determinants of political behavior. Severe criticism has been leveled against the modernization paradigm on both theo-retical and empirical grounds for its near-exclusive focus on cultural and socioeconomic determinants of behavior.[66] A primary objective of the research design, therefore, is to facilitate comparison of the political behavior of workers situated in variant political environ-ments. This study seeks to determine how differing political locations, or structural settings, affect working-class political mobilization. Spe-cifically, cases were selected so as to assess the effects of four varia-tions in structural settings: (1) unionization versus nonunionization;

Table 1. Original Sampling Design and Final Sample Sizes

Type of polity	Nonstrategic Industries			Strategic Industries	
	Non-union Workers	Incorp. Unions	Auto. Unions	Incorp. Unions	Auto. Unions
More competitive regime— Venezuela	n = 100 (85)[a]	n = 100 (128)	n = 100 (99)	n = 100 (72)	n´ = 100 (100)
Less competitive regime— Mexico	n = 100 (100)	n = 100 (100)	n = 100 (100)	n = 100 (100)	n = 100 (100)

[a]For some analyses an additional 35 cases of nonunionized workers in unionized plants are employed. Those cited above are nonunionized workers employed in small shops in nonstrategic industries.

(2) membership in incorporated unions versus membership in autonomous unions; (3) employment in industries strategically important to national economic life versus employment in industries that are less important to national economic life; and (4) type of political system, that is, competitive versus semicompetitive polity.

Variation in type of union membership and type of party system enables one to examine corporatist interest intermediation and limited partisan competition as control mechanisms. The other two structural variables—unionization and strategic location in the economy—might also help in explaining patterns of controlled mobilization. For example, it may be that unions, whether incorporated or not, provide an effective mechanism of control. In like manner, it may be that incorporated unions only in strategically important industries affect political participation. Thus, these latter two variables may help to refine further the explanations as to how political control is asserted over working political mobilization in Mexico and Venezuela.

The original intention was to select subsamples of 100 Venezuelan and Mexican workers located in the following work settings: (1) nonunionized industries, (2) incorporated unions in nonstrategic industries, (3) incorporated unions in strategic industries, (4) autonomous unions in nonstrategic industries, and (5) autonomous unions in strategic industries. That would have produced national samples of 500 workers in each country. The original sampling design and final sample sizes are shown in table 1.

It would have been ideal to draw random samples from all workers in both Mexico and Venezuela situated in each structural setting.

Unfortunately, problems of cost and access often preclude using the most scientifically ideal sampling procedure in survey research. In lieu of using representative national samples of workers located in each structural setting, particular unions that provided specific macro-characteristics were selected for the study.

The logic of case selection was to select workers who were clearly *exposed to variant structural settings*. Therefore, the selection of these unions was done only after careful consultation with experts in the field. The goal was to guarantee that structural settings did vary. Follow-up interviews were conducted in 1981 with the leadership in each union so as to collect further information on the nature of each work setting. While it cannot be said with certainty that workers in each structural setting are "representative" of a generic type on a national scale, it can be asserted that the samples contain workers who are indeed exposed to differing structural environments. Those characteristics of the structural setting that differentiate one setting from another can be identified. Thus, it is possible to assess whether different structural settings affect working-class political behavior and opinion formation.

In analyzing the data, one also needs to remove confounding variation introduced by compositional differences in the samples.[67] To do so, certain demographic traits can be held constant. Some potential compositional differences in the samples were eliminated by decisions made about whom to sample. The sample is comprised almost entirely of male,[68] blue-collar employees. Hence, gender and type of employment are held constant.

Other variables are "held constant" via statistical manipulation of the data. As the study will demonstrate, differences between national samples on key socioeconomic and personal characteristics are minimal. There is variation in these characteristics across work settings within both national samples, but that variation is theoretically comprehensible. Nonetheless, where appropriate, statistical controls have been used to minimize the confounding effects of these personal variables. Thus, it is possible to assess more accurately the effects of key structural variables on dependent variables.

Where it was possible to obtain accurate lists of workers, random samples drawn from the union membership were used. Often, access to lists could not be obtained. In some cases the *tabulador*[69] was used to approximate representative samples. In other cases information on number of workers in each section of the plant was obtained and then used to approximate representative samples. In a few cases, such information was not available. Again, it is important to emphasize representative samples of the unions are not necessary to assess the effects of exposure to structural variables. What must occur is that sampling must guarantee that workers confront variant structures. Analysis can focus directly on the consequences of such "exposure" while holding constant other confounding sources of variation in the dependent variable.

The next chapter will provide profiles of the unions used for this study and descriptive data on the workers who were interviewed. The following chapters (chapters 3 and 4) provide useful background for understanding working-class politics in Mexico and Venezuela. In chapter 3 the historical emergence of an industrial working class in these countries and its incorporation into the political system are discussed. Chapter 4 discusses the Venezuelan and Mexican regimes as systems of control designed to limit the power and political influence of the lower classes. Chapter 5 begins the data analysis with descriptive data to show evidence of controlled political mobilization among Venezuelan and Mexican workers who were interviewed. Chapter 6 examines how previously discussed control mechanisms affect the level of psychological involvement in politics as well as the level of *concientización* exhibited by workers. This analysis will enable one to probe how working-class motivations to participate are controlled in the Mexican and Venezuelan regimes. Chapter 7 focuses on how voter turnout is controlled, and chapter 8 looks at how electoral choice is manipulated. Chapter 9 provides a general overview of the findings and returns to the question of labor's role in societal development.

Chapter Two

Demographic Characteristics of Unions

In this chapter the reader is introduced to profiles of the work settings from which samples of workers were drawn and provided an overview of the personal and socioeconomic characteristics of workers who were interviewed. In addition to its intrinsic interest, this information on the immediate context and characteristics of workers in the sample is vital for interpretation of results. Workers as a class do not respond uniformly to political stimuli. Factors such as age, region, or intraclass variation in socioeconomic status can account in part for differences in political attitudes and behavior among workers.[1] Furthermore, there is evidence to suggest that the everyday context in which workers live out their lives affects political attitudes and behavior.[2] This chapter provides profiles of each work setting from which workers were sampled and then characteristics of the workers who were interviewed.

Ayotla Textiles, a parastatal enterprise that employed about 1,850 workers in late 1979, provides the setting for an incorporated union in a nonstrategic industry. One of the largest textile firms in Mexico,[3] Ayotla Textiles was not always a state-owned enterprise. Founded in 1946 with private capital, the company could not survive the death of the original owner in 1949 and passed into state ownership at that time. From 400 workers in 1949, the company's labor force expanded considerably in 1956 and 1957 and grew slowly thereafter, until contractions began in the early eighties. The Mexican textile industry no longer plays a major role in the Mexican manufacturing sector. It now employs less than 10 percent of the industrial workers and produces less than 6.5 percent of the value added in manufacturing.[4] Consequently, it is no longer a strategic industry capable of eliciting the attention of state elites.

The labor history of Ayotla Textiles has always been troubled. Formally, the Ayotla sections (Sections 11 and 38) of the Union of

Textile and Similar Workers from which workers were sampled were affiliated with the official Confederation of Mexican Workers (CTM) at the time of interviewing (1979-80). This affiliation is reflected by the fact that the infrequent meetings of Sections 11 and 38 are held at No. 8 Vallarta Street in Mexico City, the national headquarters of the CTM; the Ayotla workers must be bused to Mexico City, where they meet in imposing surroundings not conducive to rebellion. Rebellion, nonetheless, has occurred over the years. In 1970 600 workers were dismissed as they supported a union leader who wanted to take Sections 11 and 38 out of the CTM. Police "protection" was provided in a bitter twenty-three-day strike that ultimately was resolved by the secretary of labor, who authorized dismissing the strikers and the reimposition of strong control by the officialist CTM. Such tactics continued up to and beyond the time of interviewing; a unit comprising 300 workers was closed in 1980, ostensibly to protect the safety of the workers. However, it is more likely that the introduction of labor-saving (and conflict-saving) machinery was the real motivation of management. The secretary-general of Section 11 and another member of the union directorate were among those dismissed. No alternative employment was found for these individuals. It is quite plausible to assume that these dismissals were politically motivated.

The "Antonio M. Amor" Refinery is located at the eastern edge of the pleasant provincial city of Salamanca. It provides the setting of the incorporated union in a strategic industry. The location is convenient, for the Salamanca refinery can supply not only Mexico City but also various rapidly growing industrial cities of the North Central Zone. A small city of 100,000, Salamanca is dominated by the refinery that employs at least 5,450 workers, a significant portion of whom live in small but pleasant private dwellings in a residential area near the refinery. Rarely do as many workers from a single Mexican plant live as well as do those of the petroleum refinery at Salamanca. These workers have acquired their small, single-family dwellings by virtue not only of the high salaries they receive but also by the intervention of union leaders with credit-granting agencies to provide low-interest loans to the workers. The import of working in petroleum does not end with the personal dwellings, however. Nestled among the private dwellings are (1) an imposing building with a large auditorium (used for such things as community concerts and films) that contains the offices of Section 24 of the Sindicato de Trabajadores Petroleros de la República Mexicana (STPRM); (2) a cooperative market where subsidized foodstuffs are sold; (3) a recreational complex encompassing a swimming pool, bowling alley, and nightclub; and (4) an "Article 123" public school bearing the legend that this educational facility was a gift of Petroleos Mexicanos. All this is pleasant and, given the standards of Mexican working-class communities, very well maintained. To be a petroleum worker living in this zone is to be a privileged Mexican worker. Yet it is to be *a worker*, for in a fenced-off area closer to the refinery live the Pemex managers. In this zone the homes rival those of a North American suburb, complete with a golf course.

Being treated well is one reason that Section 24 of the stprm has never gone out on strike. However, that is not the only reason. Section 24 is run by a well-oiled political machine that is intimately linked with the ctm national headquarters and the regional pri apparatus. Section 24 does no negotiation of contracts on its own; all contract negotiations are handled by the national staff of the stprm, to whom the Section only sends a delegate. The atmosphere at union headquarters was secretive and defensive. Perhaps, this was because an individual described by other members of the executive committee of the local union[5] as "the spiritual leader" of Section 24, Ramón López Díaz, had recently been accused of having killed a twenty-two-year-old female worker in a predawn drunken orgy at union headquarters.[6] Whatever the depths of degradation to which leaders of this section had fallen, union proceedings in Section 24 are far from democratic. The Grupo Unificador Mayoritario (gum) dominates union affairs, compiling the slate of candidates that is *always* elected in union elections. The fact that the union elections employ raised-hand voting procedures in an open assembly probably discourages most workers from being bold enough to buck the tide. Not surprisingly, turnout at union elections is modest. But the "bodyguards" whom López Díaz maintains on Pemex payrolls at an alleged cost of two million pesos a month (roughly U.S. $90,000 in 1980) also dissuade those inclined to rebel.[7]

A political machine exists not only in Section 24 of the stprm at Salamanca but up to the highest levels of the union.[8] The machine blends the very effective distribution of material benefits and the occasional use of violence so as to create a docile work force dedicated to keeping the refined petroleum flowing. Since there is so much to lose, were one expelled from the union via the *clausula de exclusión*,[9] most workers at Salamanca "go along" with their leaders so as personally to "get along."

Recent studies of Mexican labor have emphasized the varying degrees of external control over incorporated unions. Uniformly strict control is not imposed over all unions incorporated into the CTM or other PRI-dominated labor confederations. Clearly, the PRI can live with internal democracy and industrial military in some unions but not in others.[10]

Section 24 of the STPRM at Salamanca and the textile union at Ayotla provide examples of contrasting degrees of external control. A degree of internal democracy is tolerated in the Ayotla union, although it is limited as seen by the fact that unions could not freely choose to exit from the CTM. Strikes have occurred as well as rebellion from below against the CTM. By contrast, there is no internal democracy in the STPRM oil workers' union, and strikes have never occurred. It represents the essence of controlled unionism in Mexico.

The next work setting is an autonomous union in a nonstrategic industry. For over a century, the shoes that most Mexicans wear have been made in León, Guanajuato. Located between the highly fertile agricultural area of the Bajio and the more arid cattle-raising zones of northern Mexico, León is well located to acquire the leather needed for shoe production. The 3,500 business establishments in this city of 700,000 encompass a striking array of work settings, most of which pertain to leather and shoes but which range from the automated modern factories that "use up and discard" workers by age forty to the *picas* (small shops) that assemble portions of shoes on a piece-rate basis. The *picas* utilize the nonunionized labor of children, homebound females, the elderly, and the discarded factory workers. Often hidden away from the streets to avoid inspectors from the Department of Labor, the *picas* allow evasion of the national labor laws and lower cost of shoe production for the large distributors that market products of the *picas* under their own brand names. Botas Doble Equis,[11] the plant sampled for this research, began as a family-operated *pica* employing 5 artisans in 1950 and expanded to factory status with an assembly line in 1962. The current owner, a college-educated son of the founder, is a Mexican citizen who has acquired two other shoe factories in León. Unionization at Botas Doble Equis came easily, compared to other instances in León. A collective contract was signed in 1964 with the autonomous Frente Auténtico de Trabajo (FAT) confederation, after little resistance by the owner.

Most other unions of leather workers in León are affiliated with the CTM (11 out of 14 in 1978). In 1978 only three unions were affiliated with FAT; only 11 percent of the total unionized work force belonged to the independent confederations. Efforts by the FAT to organize large shoe factories in the sixties had generally failed because of direct CTM intervention.[12] Thus, FAT unions in Leon, few in number, operate in a precarious, hostile environment, not particularly receptive to unionization by independent confederations.

The FAT is affiliated with the Central Latinoamericana de Trabajadores (CLAT) that seeks to promote a Christian Democratic ideology among workers in Latin America. The leadership of FAT seeks to promote not only greater union democracy and autonomy but also greater *concientización* of workers consistent with Christian Democratic ideology. It advocates alliances with other progressive organizations and greater worker participation in economic and political decisions that affect the welfare of workers.[13] The union makes available to workers various pamphlets and other materials on labor relations and also conducts training sessions on union rights under the Federal Labor Law.[14] But it does not encourage political action by the labor force.

The "5 de Mayo" Union seems to bargain well on behalf of the workers at Doble Equis. Contract renewals occur every two years; strikes were undertaken in 1974, 1976, and 1978, but none have been especially bitter. No strike has lasted more than a week; indeed, the factory owner has been known to carry coffee to the workers while the strike is going on. Violence has never occurred in these strikes. The internal life of the union seems highly democratic with frequent meetings, rotation occurring in the leadership positions and competition between slates being the norm in union elections.

The owner of Doble Equis resists unionization of two other plants and threatens routinely in each contract negotiation to close Doble Equis, moving his operations to the other plants. There seems to be an implicit bargain here: the PRI-linked public authorities will not repress the "independent" FAT local as long as it does not press to make dramatic inroads in organizing other workers in León. The factory owner will play ball with "5 de Mayo" as long as the other plants are left undisturbed. For its part "5 de Mayo" leaders report having received offers of support from opposition political parties but reject such offers, saying that "to politicize labor relations can only harm the workers." Such is the degree of union "autonomy" that is tolerable in León. However, even this modest degree of autonomy is unavailable to most unionized workers in León.

The other autonomous union in Mexico used for this study is located in a strategic industry. It is found in historic Cuautla, where Emiliano Zapata once led the *agraristas* during the Mexican Revolution. A centerpiece of a modern industrial park is the Nissan Motors plant, where Datsuns have been assembled since 1965. Beginning as

a union affiliated with the CTM, the auto workers at Cuernavaca successfully disaffiliated in 1972 from the official CTM confederation. Organized factions developed around workers sympathetic to the locally
more militant FAT and around workers sympathetic to the Unidad
Obrera Independiente (UOI). In addition, a minority conservative faction sympathetic to the CTM still existed. These three factions have
since structured union politics in this plant.[15]

In 1976 the Nissan workers went on a long and bitter strike. The
more militant FAT faction controlled the executive committee at the
time. Management as well as the more conservative factions used the
opportunity to discredit the militants in the eyes of the rank-and-file
workers. Consequently, the executive committee was recalled, and
the UOI soon gained control of the executive committee. These events
led to "the implantation of firm UOI control within the union leadership."[16]

The Unidad Obrera Independiente, Mexico's largest independent
labor confederation, is headed by a controversial labor lawyer, Juan
Ortega Arenas. The UOI accepts the rules of the game in Mexico's
authoritarian politics and is very careful to stay within permissible
limits.[17] Rabidly anticommunist, the UOI accepts the existing state-
capitalist economy and is primarily concerned with maximizing labor's share of profits.[18] The confederation eschews all partisan
involvement and tries to remain apolitical.[19] Nevertheless, it advocates greater union democracy, although the UOI leadership has been
known to use available repressive mechanisms to limit opposition
once it gains control of a union.[20] Eight tumultuous years of UOI
control ensued in which competitive union elections produced frequent turnover in union leadership, as well as the midterm destitution
of others. Ultimately, the workers at the Nissan factory withdrew from
the UOI and continued to reject affiliation with either the CTM or the
FAT. This rejection of all existing major confederations may reflect,
curiously, the lack of consensus among organized factions within the
union. Autonomy from all national confederations may not have been
desired by a majority of the autoworkers in Cuernavaca, yet it seems
to have emerged as a way to keep political peace among factions that
would prefer different affiliations.

With that kind of intraunion fragmentation, it is conceivable that
union leaders would have produced little for their members. But the
troubled Cuernavaca *sindicato* has indeed generated material benefits;
in 1980 wages at the Datsun factory were the highest paid to manual
laborers in Cuernavaca. An impressive series of fringe benefits was

made available to workers, including a life insurance policy that was respectable by Mexican working-class standards.[21] Payments were also made to all unionized workers for work clothes, transportation, and the noon meal, with payment of a traditional "thirteenth month" (the *aguinaldo*) and "profit sharing" (an additional ten workdays' worth of pay) guaranteed by contract. Some workers received a one-time payment for getting married, scholarships for the education of their children, bonuses for punctuality and attendance, while others were "lucky winners" of household appliances donated by the company to a union raffle. Collectively, the enterprise contributed U.S. $1,300 for a Christmas party, as well as the use of a union headquarters building and U.S. $670 a month for union operations.

These gains, while modest by external standards, were attained at least in part because of union combativeness. The Nissan workers went out on a twenty-day strike in 1974 and on a forty-seven-day strike in 1976, not to mention the turbulence of 1972 surrounding the decision to exit from the CTM. The union leaders noted with pride that in the late seventies they had succeeded in negotiating contracts that surpassed the wage guidelines preferred by labor authorities in Mexico City. However, the Nissan workers retained the vulnerability of an isolated union; they had no external patrons and in conflict situations found themselves exposed to repression by public authorities operating on behalf of the Nissan management, which is presumably Mexicanized.[22]

So union autonomy was, once again, a mixed blessing. As the automobile workers were among the most highly paid workers in Mexico, the Mexican state did not have to devote extensive public resources to coopting them. As long as they were not coherently unionized across the whole industry, the state would permit an element of autonomy to workers at selected plants. That autonomy could be used to negotiate better contracts, even to affiliate with opposition labor confederations, but not to challenge the structure of Mexican state capitalism. Thus, the Nissan union often exhibited militance in negotiating with management but remained officially apolitical and avoided all partisan affiliation.[23]

In sum, these two autonomous unions appeared to be rather typical of most other autonomous unions in Mexico that have forged no ties with leftist parties.[24] They affiliated with independent labor confederations that avoided direct and formal ties with political parties and remained strictly nonpartisan and apolitical. Avoidance of partisan politics may be a price that they had to pay for their autonomy. Autonomy had at least brought a high degree of internal democracy and effective collective bargaining as evidenced by the *prestaciones* (benefits) that these unions had acquired for their workers.

Last, nonunionized workers used for this study are described. The southern rim of the central zone of Mexico's capital city contains a series of *colonias* (neighborhoods) of working-class character. Some are oriented toward the production of goods and services of a functionally specific nature, such as automobile parts, body work, and repairs. Others include small shops providing different kinds of services, but most contain some poorly capitalized, labor-intensive production facilities. The working-class nature of such neighborhoods is apparent in a variety of ways, from the quality of the (generally ill-maintained) dwellings to the type of Spanish spoken, to the nature of the nightclubs and bars that dot the streets. A total of 100 workers from five such *colonias* were interviewed: Tepito, Obrera, Asturias, Doctores, and "El Centro."[25] Filter questions were employed to select only nonunionized employees of small shops (up to 20 employees) or manual laborers who participate as members of small work teams. The workers so chosen tend to be employed, for example, as electricians, automobile mechanics, machinists, carpenters in small furniture factories, body repairmen, plumbers, and painters.

These nonunionized workers may well be considered as individuals experiencing an unmitigated "state of nature" in a developing-country market economy. Their relations with their employers are unmediated by the protection of any union, be it corrupt or honest, militant or passive. The most important consequence of the absence of unions is a more complete exposure to expansion and contraction of the economy, as those who employ workers will respond to the logic of the market, expanding production and the use of wage labor when demand is high but restricting production and the use of wage labor when demand is low. The nonunionized workers are highly subject to insecurity of employment, having no unions interceding to protect jobs. If the nonunionized workers do not lose jobs in economic recessions, they may suffer a diminution of the number of hours of *salaried* employment they can find, or, if employed on a piece-rate basis, they may find that they have to work more hours to produce equivalent or lower income. The nonunionized workers tend to look favorably on unions.[26] These are not atomistic, wholly self-centered individuals incapable of participating in union organizations. Rather they are individuals located in a sector of the economy where small enterprises operate with rather fixed, marginal technologies, generating very small economic surpluses. Such economic activities tend not to expand but rather to survive. Unionization of such small shops is further impeded by the legal requirement of twenty members before a union can be officially registered.

In Venezuela workers living in a smaller but essentially comparable range of cities were sampled. The important sampling criterion was not city-size; instead, the criteria of industry type (strategic versus nonstrategic) and degree of "union incorporation" (autonomous versus incorporated) were invoked. In Venezuela certain obstacles to access led to selecting multiple unions representative of a single structural environment.[27] In the strategic petroleum industry, however, all workers studied came from two major refineries in Punto Fijo, even though six separate unions were sampled.

The sample of workers in incorporated unions of nonstrategic industries came from AD- or COPEI-dominated unions in Barquisimeto. Venezuela's fourth largest city, Barquisimeto is the center of economic growth in the west-central area of Venezuela.[28] Capital of the state of Lara and center of population reception for cityward migrants, the population growth rate of 5.7 percent annum experienced by Barquisimeto between 1950 and 1971 made it one of the fastest growing cities in the country. By the mid-seventies it was calculated that roughly 60 percent of the sizable yearly population increases (25,000 per year) were coming from migrants to Barquisimeto. By the time of the fieldwork in 1979 through 1981, the population of Barquisimeto was officially 542,000, perhaps even higher.[29] Typical of cities receiving such an influx of population, few workers were absorbed in industry, in spite of a government plan to foment industrial decentralization. In 1976, for example, demographers associated with the Municipal Planning Office estimated that 72.6 percent of total employment was in the service sector, while 12.2 percent was in manufacturing. By early 1980 the percentage of industrial employment may have crept upward by a few percentage points, but the dominance of service sector activity would have remained. Much of that (1976) service sector activity was in commerce and banking (34.2 percent). Excluding construction firms, Barquisimeto had a total of 756 industrial establishments in 1977, which would have meant that most were very small, averaging 20 workers each. These small industries were often in traditional areas, such as food processing plants, leather goods, and paper firms. However, some larger manufacturing firms began to locate in a new industrial park to the west of the city in the late seventies.

The incorporated unions included a small textile firm (n = 24 workers sampled of 80 unionized workers) where AD and COPEI jointly

control the union directorate, a dairy where 47 workers were interviewed (of 150 unionized workers in a COPEI-dominated union), a
metalworkers' union where another 47 workers were interviewed
(again controlled jointly by AD and COPEI, plant size circa 400), and
two smaller plants (a bottler and a graphic arts shop) where very few
workers were sampled (n = 6 and n = 4, respectively). The former
was an "apolitical" white union, and the latter was an AD-dominated
union.

The leaders of these unions tend to accept a social democratic
bargain of peace between labor and management and to play down
the ideological rhetoric. One such leader (of a graphic arts union)
went to the heart of this viewpoint when asked to define the meaning
he ascribed to the phrase "class conflict." He said, "We simply don't
use this phrase; it is a hollow expression." Other leaders of incorporated unions in Barquisimeto defined the phrase in terms of the
struggle to achieve immediate economic benefits for workers. Illustrative of the temper of incorporated unions in Barquisimeto is the
fact that three of these unions had not been out on strike in the past
decade. A fourth had experienced two one-day strikes. The graphic
artists had experienced a two-week strike but could not in any sense
be considered a radical union since their focus had been on enterprise-
level grievances.

For the sample of workers belonging to incorporated unions of
strategic industries, we interviewed petroleum workers living in the
port city of Punto Fijo in the state of Falcón. There are two major
refineries there. The first refinery was established by Creole Petroleum
in 1949. Since the nationalization of the oil industry in 1976, it has
been operated as the state company, Lagoven. The other refinery was
established by Royal Dutch Shell. Since 1976 it has been operated
under the aegis of Maraven. Were it not for its two major petroleum
refineries, Punto Fijo would be a small port city, not the growing
metropolis that it has become. But because of petroleum, population
growth in the sixties and seventies was substantial. Based on a population of 34,457 in 1961 and 55,583 in 1971, estimates were that the
population might reach 120,000 in the seventies. The petroleum boom
did create some jobs directly in the refineries themselves but created
more jobs indirectly through the infusion of money that petroleum
implied for the local economy. Somewhere between 10,000 and 15,000
workers were employed by the two refineries, but in 1979 another
2,000 or 3,000 were employed in a construction project for an associated petrochemical facility.[30]

Workers belonging to two COPEI unions and two unions that were

affiliated with the Unión Republicana Democrática (URD)were interviewed. The URD that cooperated with AD and COPEI in setting up a
competitive democracy in Venezuela in 1958 is a minor, pro-system
political party (see chapter 3). The two COPEI unions used for this
study illustrate a pattern of asymmetrical control that has dampened
union militance. In one COPEI union, SINTRAPETROL,[31] there had been
no strike activity since 1970. The other COPEI union, STOPPS,[32] joined
with several other unions in a brief strike in 1972 over alleged mis-
treatment of workers by North American supervisors. But from 1972
to 1981, the union did not engage in another strike. COPEI exercises
tight control over both unions, allowing limited internal democracy.
The same secretary-general of SINTRAPETROL has been elected every
two years since the founding of the union in 1971. An opposition slate
has never been put up to run against the official COPEI slate for seats
on the executive committee. In the case of STOPPS, the previous COPEI
secretary-general had been reelected every two years from 1968 to
1979. The then current COPEI incumbent was elected in 1979. In this
union the only opposition slate emerged during the 1978 national
elections when a rival COPEI slate refused to support the candidacy
of Luis Herrera Campíns.

In the two URD unions, STIP and OSMPM,[33] the same pattern of
asymmetrical control can be observed. In the case of STIP, there has
been a biannual turnover of the secretary-general. However, the new
secretary-general has been affiliated with URD ever since the party
gained control of the union and has not been officially challenged by
another candidate. The official URD slate for the executive committee
also never loses. In the OSMPM union, the same incumbent secretary-
general has been reelected unanimously by the executive committee
three times. Generally, union members are offered only a single URD
slate (*la plancha unitaria*) to ratify for members of the union directorate.

In general, Venezuelan petroleum workers are very well paid by
standards of the Venezuelan work force.[34] Union contracts for 1980
to 1983 provided for a daily wage between approximately U.S. $20
and $30. The benefits and services extended to Venezuelan oil work-
ers, however, do not *appear* to be as generous as those extended to
Mexican *petroleros*. Furthermore, union leaders in Venezuela expressed much dissatisfaction with some services, especially housing,
medical care, and public education.[35] However, even though the samples are not representative of each national petroleum industry, it can
still be noted that Venezuelan *petroleros*, like Mexican petroleum workers, live well compared to other workers.

To summarize this overview of the Venezuelan incorporated

unions studied, varying degrees of external control by political parties were found. As with Mexico, control was most strict in the case of unions located in the strategic petroleum industry. As a general rule, the union leadership in all cases was primarily concerned with immediate benefits and salaries of workers. However, they tended to avoid frequent strike activity, preferring instead cooperation with management. As chapter 8 will show, political activity was a secondary concern to all of the union leaders who were interviewed. Their attention was focused primarily at the plant level, not on national politics.

Two autonomous unions in a nonstrategic industrial setting were selected for this study. One union was the Sindicato de Trabajadores de la Industria de Bebidas (Union of Beverage Industry Workers) located at Licorerias Unidas in La Miel. Of the 233 unionized workers at Licorerias Unidas, 46 were sampled for the current study. While geographic mobility has been a major feature of the life experience of many Venezuelans,[36] some Venezuelan workers have experienced changes of a rather dramatic sort in the very communities where they were born.[37] Such was the case at La Miel, a small town outside the provincial capital of Barquisimeto, where a sugarcane-producing *hacienda* was transformed in 1960 by the construction of a distillery for the production of rum, whiskey, and a local drink called *cocuy*. The regimentation of factory life became a reality for many workers who did not leave rural homes to experience industrial life.

The early secretaries-general of this union were either politically independent or affiliated with COPEI. After 1966, however, the left-wing AD forces, which abandoned the party in the 1968 electoral campaign, came to be ascendant at La Miel. All secretaries-general since 1966 have been affiliated with the leftist Movimiento Electoral del Pueblo (MEP), a nominally socialist group. The union has struck three times since 1970, but each strike was brief.

The union at La Miel is characterized by competitive internal elections,[38] by the apparent ideological sophistication of senior union leaders,[39] by a high sense of solidarity among union members, and by the frequency of membership participation in union activities. Comparatively speaking, however, the workers at La Miel do well. Their wages are higher, on balance, than those of other Venezuelan workers sampled in nonstrategic industries. They are housed reasonably well and enjoy a considerable array of fringe benefits. Few have experienced a desire to be rid of their union (15 percent), and even fewer (5 percent) have considered leaving La Miel. The degree of union "autonomy" attained in La Miel from the democratic state-capitalist regime is considerable but mitigated by the decision to remain within the framework of the AD-dominated Confederation of Venezuelan Workers (CTV). Those who argue that the state ought to be transformed are able to come to power in this local union and to generate a highly participatory organization that produces results. However, that very degree of "success" may, in subtle ways, erode the conviction that it is necessary to transform the state. No evidence was uncovered that leaders at La Miel had engaged in any political activity designed to strengthen MEP or any other socialist party.

The last group of workers in an autonomous union in a nonstrategic industry (n = 26) consisted of workers at a small plastics manufacturing firm with approximately 50 total laborers in which the Communists and other leftists controlled the executive committee. This union was affiliated with the Unitary Confederation of Venezuelan Workers (CUTV), the Marxist labor confederation created in the early sixties. This particular plant was organized in 1976 by the CUTV-affiliated Plastic Workers Union soon after the plant opened production in Phase II of the Barquisimeto Industrial Park. As in the case of the other leftist union in a nonstrategic industry (La Miel), attendance at union meetings was high and was encouraged by union leaders. The leaders of this union employed conventional Marxist terminology with greater coherence than did other union leaders, interpreting the concept of "class struggle" both in immediate and abstract terms. The apparent degree of militance in the union was not matched by behavior, however, for no strikes had been undertaken by the union since its creation. There seemed to be a disjunction in the consciousness of the union leaders who foresaw the transformation of the state but had no clear plan in mind for how their local union could be used as an instrument of class struggle leading toward a transition to socialism.

Two autonomous unions in the petroleum industry in Punto Fijo were used as representative of autonomous unions in a strategic industry. One union, SUOEP,[40] was controlled by a leftist coalition of five MEPistas, one MIRista, and one MASista.[41] Three *adecos* also sat on the executive committee of the union in 1981. The secretary-generalship of the union has been dominated by MEP since 1968 except for a brief interlude in which AD gained control. The coalitional composition of the executive committee demonstrates the high degree of internal union democracy. Unlike the incorporated unions used for this study, the secretary-general position is routinely contested.

The other union, UNMPM,[42] was also dominated by MEP. In this union both AD and MEP were actively organized and offered opposing slates for all union elections. At the time of interviewing union leaders in 1981, five of seven positions on the executive committee were held by MEPistas. The secretary-general at the time was also a MEPista, but AD had held the position in the sixties when it dominated the union. Like SUOEP this union was characterized by a high degree of internal democracy.

The leadership of both autonomous unions employed leftist ideological rhetoric during the course of personal interviews and identified themselves with the leftist struggle for system transformation. Nevertheless, these unions were not highly disposed to strike, as these two unions together had only engaged in three strikes since 1970, none of which lasted more than two days. Perhaps, these unions realize the possible repressive response that prolonged strikes in Venezuela's most strategic industry might provoke. Also, they might not wish to jeopardize the relatively high wages of oil workers that the Venezuelan state has been willing to grant. This avoidance of work-place militancy in both incorporated and autonomous unions in the petroleum industry is interesting, given that leaders were not generally satisfied with the public services and benefits previously obtained. A few leaders also expressed open dissatisfaction with the most recent contract negotiated in 1980.[43]

In summary, autonomous unions in Venezuela are characterized by a high degree of internal democracy. Indeed, without the existence of internal democracy, it is unlikely that leftist parties could have captured control of the executive committees of these unions. Even though the left has gained control of these unions, there does not appear to be any marked increase in labor militance or union-sponsored political activity. The rhetoric of the leadership changes without any significant change in behavior as seen by the low strike frequency in these unions. Leftist union factions, like leftist parties in general, seem to accept the rules of the game that emphasize accommodation of diverse interest and moderation in demand making.[44]

Eighty-five nonunionized workers were interviewed in Barquisimeto. As in Mexico these individuals worked in a variety of small shop settings, ranging from furniture manufacturing to automobile repair work. Like their Mexican counterparts, these workers also experienced an unmitigated "state of nature" in a third-world market economy. They were entirely at the mercy of the market and the goodwill of their employers. As with nonunionized workers in Mexico, this group constitutes a type of control group with which to compare the effects of union membership.

Table 2. Socioeconomic Characteristics of National Samples

	Mexico Mean[a]	Venezuela Mean[a]	Eta Correlations[b]
Years of formal	7.0	6.9	.02
education	(2.1)	(2.4)	
Weekly family	4.3	4.4	.03
income[c]	(1.5)	(1.8)	
Standardized	.10	−.04	.07
SES scale[d]	(.99)	(1.05)	
Respondent ranking of social			.12
class on 1-10 self-anchoring	4.1	3.8	
scale	(1.3)	(1.3)	
N of persons living in house	6.0	6.9	.16
	(2.5)	(3.3)	
Age	31.0	32.1	.06
	(8.3)	(11.2)	

[a]Standard deviations are reported in parentheses.

[b]The reported Eta correlations measure the degree of association between country (Mexico vs. Venezuela) and each characteristic.

[c]The weekly income scale was formed by collapsing reported incomes from both national samples into nine ordinal categories in which the range in U.S. dollars is approximately $23. In terms of early 1980 rates with U.S. dollars, these income ranges were approximately (1) 0-$23; (2) $24-$46; (3) $47-69; (4) $70-$92; (5) $93-$115; (6) $116-$138; (7) $139-$162; (8) $163-$185; (9) $186 and up. Above, the grouped mean is reported.

[d]Factor scale using weekly income, education, and an ordinal measure of job skill.

Individuals interviewed for this study generally belong to the upper strata of the blue-collar work force. While there is significant socioeconomic variation within the two national samples, unionized workers who were interviewed tend to be privileged by third-world standards. These workers generally have far better incomes and access to public services than do urban workers in the tertiary sector of the economy.[45] While these workers are not "penny capitalists" who must daily struggle for survival, neither do they enjoy the standard of living of workers in the industrialized West. They stand on the margins of the consumer society, lacking many of the amenities and comforts associated with a middle-class life-style.

Table 2 shows various mean scores for both national samples. In the aggregate these are young workers (mean = 31 for Mexico; mean = 32.1 for Venezuela) with an elementary school education and a weekly income in 1979 between U.S. $70 and $92.[46] The mean per capita annual income of working-class families sampled in Mexico

Table 3. Availability of Household Goods and Neighborhood
         Services

Percentage having	Mexico	Venezuela
Electricity	99.0	98.8
Piped water	97.8	98.7
Sewerage	95.4	80.5
Paved streets	82.8	91.5
Street lights	98.8	96.3
Neighborhood public schools	94.2	97.1
Medical services	85.0	86.7
Garbage collection	94.6	89.8
Telephone	19.8	9.1
Family car	27.6	—
Refrigerator	88.4	—

falls in the category of U.S. $560 to $735.84. These figures are somewhat higher than the mean category for Venezuelan working-class
families, U.S. $486.95 to $640.[47] Table 2 shows that workers in both
countries tend to identify with the lower-middle class (that is, both
means are slightly below the midpoint on a ten-point self-anchoring
scale of social position). Thus, these workers appear to be aware of
the social distance between themselves and *los humildes* ("the humble
ones"), as well as between themselves and the social strata above
them.

There are marginal differences between the national samples, but
in general the samples are quite similar. Mexican workers have a
slightly higher per capita income, as was noted. There is virtually no
difference in formal educational level (table 2) and very little difference
in reported rankings of social class or in age. A multidimensional
indicator of socioeconomic status varies across nations, but insignifi-
cantly (Eta = .07, see table 2).

Table 3 shows the availability of neighborhood services and a few
household goods to workers in this sample. These workers have access to a wide array of public services and generally do not live in
neighborhoods typified by urban squatter settlements.[48] Greater accessibility to public services is a major characteristic differentiating
the urban industrial work force from the burgeoning tertiary sector.
However, far fewer workers in this sample have access to such consumer goods as a telephone or a family car, goods almost always
found in professional middle-class homes in each country.

Let us now examine patterns of variation across work settings in

Table 4. Socioeconomic Characteristics of Venezuelan Job Settings

		Incorporated Union		Autonomous Union	
Mean	Nonunion	Nonstrategic Industry	Strategic Industry	Nonstrategic Industry	Strategic Industry
Years of formal education	6.5 (2.8)	6.4 (2.5)	7.6 (3.3)	6.0 (2.1)	7.4 (3.3)
Weekly family income[a]	3.6 (1.6)	4.0 (1.2)	5.9 (1.5)	3.3 (1.2)	5.9 (1.5)
Respondent ranking of	3.6 (1.3)	3.3 (1.4)	4.5 (1.2)	3.5 (1.4)	4.3 (1.2)
N of persons living in house	6.5 (2.7)	7.5 (3.5)	(3.4) (3.4)	(3.5) (3.5)	(2.9) (2.9)
Age	28.9 (10.2)	28.5 (8.0)	38.4 (12.3)	29.5 (9.7)	37.3 (11.6)

Note: Standard deviations are reported in parentheses.

[a]The weekly income scale was formed by collapsing reported incomes from both national samples into nine ordinal categories in which the range in U.S. dollars is approximately $23. In terms of early 1980 exchange rates with the U.S. dollar, these income ranges were approximately (1) 0-$23; (2) $24-$46; (3) $47-$69; (4) $70-$92; (5) $93-$115; (6) $116-$138; (7) $139-$162; (8) $163-$185; (9) $186 and up. Above, the grouped mean is reported.

each country. In both national samples, weekly income tends to be highest in the strategic industries (tables 4 and 5). This finding holds up when per capita income is also calculated (table 6). On rankings of perceived social class and years of formal education, there is relatively little variation across subsamples. On the average these workers consider themselves lower-middle class (that is, they rank themselves generally in the 3-4 category on a ten-point self-anchoring scale of social status) and have generally completed between six and seven years of formal education.

While extreme caution must be exercised in generalizing from the data to the national work force, it is interesting to note that variation in per capita income (table 6) is far better predicted by strategic location than by unionization. In both countries workers in strategic industries have per capita incomes significantly higher than do workers in nonstrategic industries (compare columns 3 and 5 with columns 1, 2, and 4). Unionized workers outside of strategic industries either make mar-

Table 5. Socioeconomic Characteristics of Mexican Job Settings

| | Nonunion | | Incorporated Union | | | | Autonomous Union | | | |
| | | | Nonstrategic Industry | | Strategic Industry | | Nonstrategic Industry | | Strategic Industry | |
	X	SD	X	SD	X	SD	X	SD	X	SD
Years of formal education	7.0	2.4	7.5	1.8	7.5	1.9	5.0	2.1	7.5	2.4
Weekly family income[a]	3.6	1.3	4.3	1.1	5.4	1.1	3.3	0.8	5.1	1.8
Respondent ranking of social class on 1-10 self-anchoring scale	4.2	1.4	4.1	0.9	4.2	1.1	3.9	1.2	4.2	1.0
N of persons living in house	5.9	2.7	5.8	1.9	2.2	7.1	3.2	5.4	1.5	
Age	31.5	8.7	33.9	10.4	29.6	6.1	27.2	7.8	32.9	5.8

[a]The weekly income scale was formed by collapsing reported incomes from both national samples into nine ordinal categories in which the range in U.S. dollars is approximately $23. In terms of early 1980 exchange rates with the U.S. $47-$69; (4) $70-$92; (5) $93-$115; (6) $116-#$138; (7) $139-$162; (8) $163-$185; (9) $186 and up. Above, the grouped mean is reported.

X = mean; SD = standard deviation.

ginally more than do nonunionized workers in nonstrategic industries (compare column 2 with column 1 for Mexico) or else make less (compare column 4 with column 1 for Mexico and compare colummns 2 and 4 with column 1 for Venezuela).

It is also interesting to note that union autonomy is associated with higher wage levels in strategic industries (compare column 5 with column 3) but much more so in Venequela than in Mexico.[49] Notice, however, that the reverse pattern is observable among nonstrategic industries for both countries. Incorporated union workers fare better than do autonomous union workers (table 6) in industries that are not crucial to the national economy.[50] This may suggest that in strategic *industries* union autonomy captures the attention of those

Table 6. Mean Range of Annual per Capita Family Income for
Mexican and Venezuelan Subsamples

Mean Range of per Capita Income	Nonunion Workers/ Nonstrategic Industries	Incorporated Union		Autonomous Union	
		Non-strategic	Strategic	Non-strategic	Strategic
Mexico Sample	$569.49 – 748.47	$579.31 – 761.38	$811.63 – 1003.64	$317.75 – 466.48	$826.67 – 1022.22
Venezuela Sample	$516.92 – 679.38	$448.00 – 588.80	$795.43 – 932.57	$313.33 – 460.00	$928.00 – 1088.00

Note: The weekly income scale was formed by collapsing reported incomes from both national samples into nine ordinal categories in which the range in U.S. dollars is approximately $23. In terms of early 1980 exchange rats with the U.S. dollar, these income ranges were approximately (1) 0-$23; (2) $24-$46; (3) $47-$69; (4) $70-$92; (5) $93-$115; (6) $116-$138; (7) $139-/4162; (8) $163-$185; (9) $186 and up. Above, the grouped mean is reported.

public authorities who supervise bargaining between labor and management, thereby yielding favorable results.[51] When the industry is not so important tot he national economy, the way to "get along is to go along"; hence, incorporated unions seem to fare better. While such an interpretaiton of the data is plausible, it is also probable that other factors are involved in determining relative salary levels within comparable industries.

This chapter has sought to provide an overview of the types of workers who were interviewed and their immediate work environment. It is now time to turn more fully to data analysis, but first the history of industrialization in these two countries and of incorporation of the lower classes into the political system will be explored.

Chapter Three

Social Transformation
and Political Incorporation

The purpose of this chapter is to provide the reader a historical overview of twentieth-century transformations in Mexico and Venezuela that have shaped the role of urban labor in the politics of these countries. Rapid import-substitution industrialization necessitated a strong state that could (1) maintain political stability and (2) assume an active role in promoting economic development. These goals could not be achieved unless the work force was kept politically quiescent. To achieve this objective, elites turned to incorporation of the lower classes into the political system rather than to exclusion. Social pacts were designed to incorporate the lower classes without threatening the power and privileges of traditional power contenders (chapter 1).

This chapter first shows why the traditional state in Venezuela and Mexico was incapable of providing political stability, incorporating emerging power contenders, and promoting rapid import-substitution industrialization. Then it reviews how social pacts were negotiated for the construction of more stable political systems adequate to the task of supervising state-sponsored industrialization. Last, an overview of import-substitution industrialization in both Mexico and Venezuela is presented.

The abdication of the Americas by the Spanish in 1820 and the failure of Bolivar's efforts at federation created a void of centralized authority in the emergent nation-states of Latin America. Into this void moved regional strongmen or *caudillos* who sought to gain control over the state by eliminating rival *caudillos*, usually by force. Consequently, *caudillismo* introduced a high level of political instability into the region. Nineteenth-century Venezuela and Mexico were racked by the extreme political instability. On occasion, a *caudillo* would impose a dictatorship that would eliminate potential rivals. Only prolonged dictatorship in postindependence Venezuela and Mexico

This chapter was coauthored with Professor Kenneth M. Coleman of the University of Kentucky.

provided periods of political stability in which economic development could proceed. In effect, political stability depended on effective *exclusion* of rival *caudillos* from the political arena. No formula for institutionalized *inclusion* was ever found. These periods of extended economic development and political stability were generally the exceptions in nineteenth- and early twentieth-century Venezuela and Mexico. Economic transformation was often delayed by pervasive political instability.

Let us now examine more closely the Mexican and Venezuelan experience with *caudillismo*[1] in the nineteenth and in portions of the twentieth century.

The result of *caudillo* politics for Venezuela was a great deal of political instability. It is estimated "that 39 major and 127 minor revolts occurred between 1830 and 1900, lasting a total of 8,847 days."[2] The most serious breakdown of political order occurred during the Federal Wars of 1858-63, a protracted civil war between rival *caudillos* for control of the Venezuelan state.[3] However, there were periods in which a strongman would gain ascendancy and use the coercive or cooptive resources at his disposal to eliminate or control rivals. Strongman rule provided Venezuela with periods of political stability in which economic development did proceed.

Four such strongmen in Venezuela's past should be mentioned: Generals José Antonio Pérez, Antonio Guzmán Blanco, Juan Vicente Gómez, and Marcos Pérez Jiménez. Pérez, Venezuela's first president, dominated Venezuelan political life during the 1830s and 1840s. It was during this period that Venezuela's economy was transformed from "the cacao-oriented colonial economy" into "a coffee-producing international economy."[4] The next period of strongman rule occurred after the Federal Wars with the ascension to power of Guzmán Blanco. John Lombardi characterizes the period of his rule as follows: "Under this remarkable leader, landowners, merchants, intermediaries, and perhaps even a few peasants found peace and prosperity, while foreign commerce found security for investments, reasonable prices for commodities, and attractive profits for manufactured goods. In line with this perspective, Antonio Guzmán Blanco also instituted a wide-ranging program of public works and beautification projects, every one of which promised the center of the North Atlantic world a more efficient Venezuela, providing useful crops and a sophisticated market for manufactured goods."[5]

It was during the brutal dictatorship of Gómez (1908-35) that Venezuela was transformed from a coffee export economy to the contemporary petroleum-based export economy. North American-based oil companies obtained major concessions to Venezuelan oil reserves following the end of World War I, sometimes through graft.[6] Oil soon became the country's most important export and provided the resources for the expansion of a strong, centralized state under Gómez. However, during his time relatively little money went into infrastructural development and education. Most resources were expended on building up the repressive apparatus of the state.[7] Not surprisingly, little import-substitution industrialization was undertaken even though petroleum revenues permitted a dramatic expansion of the internal market for consumer goods. Manufacturing did not begin on a large scale in Venezuela until after World War II.[8]

Another period of protracted political instability followed the death of Gómez in 1935. It was during the post-Gómez years that Venezuela attempted its first experiment with an institutionalized competitive democracy (1945-48). That experiment failed in large measure because far-reaching policy changes were attempted that traditional power contenders refused to accept. The growing importance of labor was reflected in increases in real wages conceded in exchange for a diminution in the frequency of strikes.[9] At the end of the *trienio* (three-year period) in 1948, the Venezuelan state was captured by the last of the military-type *caudillos*, Marcos Pérez Jiménez. Pérez Jiménez ruled much as any typical nineteenth-century *caudillo*, committed in large measure to his own self-aggrandizement. The Pérez Jiménez era did provide a time of sustained economic growth as resources earned by petroleum were plowed back into industrial development by the state.

Industrialization during the Pérez Jiménez era was characterized by (1) its oligopolistic and foreign ownership structure, (2) state ownership of many basic industries, (3) a high import component and high capital intensity, (4) low employment generation, and (5) high income concentration.[10] In short, industrialization during the Pérez Jiménez years (1948-58) took on many of the characteristics found in most other late industrializing countries (see below). As during previous dictatorships, economic expansion was facilitated by extended political stability. Ultimately, however, even private sector industrialists came to oppose the Pérez Jiménez style of governance, and a new agreement had to be negotiated over the functions of the Venezuelan state in promoting development.

Similar to Venezuela's historical experience, the postindependent period in Mexico was characterized by extreme political instability as rival *caudillos* struggled for control of the state. Peter Smith writes of this period in Mexico's history.

Mexico emerged from a decade of physical destruction during the Wars for Independence (1810-21) in a state of disorder and decay. With unemployment high, capital scarce, industry in ruins, and roads in near-total disrepair, the level of economic integration was exceedingly low. Nor was there a strong political center. Between 1821 and 1860 Mexico had no less than 50 separate governments, for an average duration of less than one year. The standard means of gaining office was the military coup, an instrument employed so ably, and mischievously, by Antonio Lopez de Santa Anna, who occupied the presidency on nine separate occasions between 1832 and 1855. Underlying this appearance of anarchy, however, there was a system-*caudillismo*, or the hegemony of transient "bosses" or caudillos whose main purpose was to sack the treasury.[11]

Like in Venezuela before 1958, political stability in prerevolutionary Mexico depended on extended dictatorship. Such a dictatorship was to be provided by Gen. Porfirio Díaz from 1876 to 1911. While repression was widely used, Díaz relied primarily on bargains with regional *caudillos* to respect each other's respective turf. Díaz would not meddle in the affairs of regional and local *caudillos* provided that they accepted his authority on the national level.[12] The consequent political stability provided fertile grounds for economic expansion. As Smith explains:

Development there was. After initial (and unsuccessful) efforts to construct railroads with public funds, Díaz gave the concessions to foreign entrepreneurs in late 1880. Within four years, the amount of track had grown from 750 miles to 3,600 miles; by 1910 Mexico had about 12,000 miles of track, most of which were taken over by the government-run National Railways in 1907. The volume of foreign trade increased nine times between 1877 and 1910. Aside from silver and gold, Mexico started exporting other metals (such as copper and zinc), fiber and pastoral goods, while the United States became the country's leading partner in trade. Industry grew, with notable advances in cotton, iron, cement, and consumer goods. And by 1895, the national government showed a budget surplus, an unthinkable achievement for earlier generations, and the Díaz regime maintained a balanced budget for the remainder of its tenure. As the centennial celebration approached in 1910, Díaz could proudly boast that the positivistic slogan "order and progress" had become reality in Mexico.[13]

The regime of the Porfirato was to come to an end with the outbreak of the Mexican Revolution in 1910. This revolution was to end rule by a supreme *caudillo*. The latter phases of the revolution were marked by struggle among rival revolutionary chiefs for control of the national government. This struggle among revolutionary *caudillos* was in many ways similar to traditional *caudillismo*.

During the immediate postrevolutionary era, power was diffused among a number of regional strongmen. In this respect, the nature of politics during this era changed little from the *caudillismo* of the nineteenth century. A strong, centralized nation-state independent of domination by a succession of regional *caudillos* was not established until the presidency of Lázaro Cárdenas (1934-40).

Certain common features of *caudillo* politics in postindependence Venezuela and Mexico can be noted. First, the legitimacy of a given government rested primarily on force rather than on popular consent. An absence of popular consent posed no problem for system stability as long as the masses were politically excluded and acquiescent, as was the case during much of this era. However, rivalry among regional and local *caudillos* led to a great deal of political instability, mainly on the elite level. Second, political stability depended on rule by a single, powerful *caudillo* capable of coopting or repressing rivals. Third, succession crises were likely to generate periods of extreme political disorder. Fourth, economic transformation during this era was often hampered by political instability, weak institutionalization of political authority, and diversion of potential capital into the *caudillo*'s self-aggrandizement and maintenance of a repressive apparatus. Fifth, any large-scale incorporation of the masses into a framework of traditional *caudillismo* held the potential of further exacerbating political instability; hence, the masses were generally excluded.

The entrance of Latin American states into the era of industrialization in this century was marked by a growing state role in the economy, a role that was incompatible with governance by transient *caudillos*. Hence, as industrialization proceeded, new social pacts were often negotiated for the construction of more stable political systems adequate to the task of supervising state-sponsored industrialization. These pacts and the incorporation of the lower classes into the contemporary Mexican and Venezuelan status are now reviewed.

Late industrialization "requires" a strong public sector role in the development process. A strong state presence is needed to develop the economic infrastructure, to promote capital formation and technology transfers, to structure labor relations, and to manage social tensions and conflicts that develop.[14] State supervision of development efforts and of labor relations also required a modicum of political stability. Traditional *caudillismo*, therefore, needed to be superseded by new formulas for governing. The solution sought in both Mexico and Venezuela was not to discard *caudillismo* per se but rather to transform and institutionalize it through the negotiation of pacts among competing power contenders. As Lorenzo Meyer notes about Mexico, "The main difference between the old system and the new regime, therefore, lies not in the internal struggle of the elite but in the fact that this struggle does not destroy the governing coalition and that the divisions created by infighting do not last."[15] This same difference can be noted between the old system and the post-1958 democratic regime in Venezuela.[16] This difference leads Meyer to conclude that "the Mexican Revolution is not a negation of the past, but rather an impressive step forward in the modernization of the Mexican authoritarian state."[17] Likewise, one can say that the post-1958 Venezuelan experiment with competitive democracy represents a modernization of an earlier experiment with democracy that survived only three years before being overthrown by the military in 1948. In the 1945-48 era, power contenders attempted to destroy each other; after 1958, buttressed by petroleum revenues, elites have succeeded in accommodating each other.[18]

The next point to study is how Venezuelan and Mexican elites used social pacts to form inclusionary political systems that would prove compatible with the goals of rapid import-substitution industrialization and political stability. To accomplish these goals, the founders of present-day Venezuelan and Mexican states *wanted to include emergent power contenders but in ways that would not threaten traditional power contenders and long-term political stability.*

Old-style *caudillo* politics in Venezuela ended in 1958 when the military forced the dictator, Pérez Jiménez, into exile. Unlike the earlier experience with democracy during the *trienio* (1945-48), a conscious attempt was made to accommodate all significant power contenders, particularly established economic elites and the military that had ended Venezuela's earlier experience with competitive democracy.[19] The bourgeoisie "became convinced it would have to give up aspirations for political control in exchange for security." Party elites representing Acción Democrática (AD), the Christian Democratic Party (COPEI), and the Union Republicana Democrática (URD) were willing to accommodate "all social forces with significant economic or political resources. . . . This included industry and commerce as well as the other political parties, organized labor, and the peasantry."[20]

Additionally, the three major parties agreed via the Pact of Punto Fijo to a type of neoconsociational democracy in which electoral results would be respected and power shared by contending parties.[21]

Agreement on fundamental economic policy was achieved largely through "The Statement of Principles and the Minimum Program of Government." Since this pact was signed by the major presidential candidates before the first elections were held, the agreements it included were effectively removed from challenge within the electoral arena. The pact basically ensured that profit making within the private sector would be recognized and promoted by the state. "In return for their acquiescence to guarantees for foreign and local capital, the political parties received assurances that they could distribute greater benefits for labor, the peasantry, and the middle class." Organized labor received assurances of better income distribution, a full employment economy, a new labor code, and social legislation.[22]

A pact between labor and management was signed in April 1958. The Pacto de Avenimiento Obrero-Patronal was signed by both leftist as well as AD/COPEI labor elites. By this pact labor was committed to maintaining democratic stability by agreeing to seek conciliation of conflicts with management. For its part management agreed to avoid layoffs. In effect, organized labor accepted the regime norm of *concertación* or accommodation with management. At the same time, the right to strike was seriously compromised as any strike could be portrayed as a betrayal of Venezuelan democracy.[23]

As Terry Karl notes, "Industrialization was the 'ideological glue' that cemented together the class compromise."[24] Oil revenues would be used not only to facilitate private capital accumulation but also to satisfy the demands of the popular sector. The results were expected to be greater social equity within the context of rapid state-capitalist industrialization. It was hoped that industrialization would provide profits for the rich, jobs for the poor, and consumer goods for everyone.

Attention now turns to Mexico. The Mexican state has been defined as " 'a balancing act' because it is based on a constantly renewed political bargain among several ruling groups and interests representing a broad range of ideological tendencies and social bases. To a greater degree than in most stable and mature modern states, the political bargain is at the forefront of Mexican politics and of the administrative decision-making process. The politics of daily renewal takes precedence over politics-as-usual. Those who do play politics-as-usual must be constantly aware of their interest in holding together the fragile association upon which their power is based."[25] "The constantly renewed political bargain" had its genesis with the adoption of the Constitution of 1917 and the reorganization of the ruling party during the Cárdenas presidency. Both events represented efforts at forming social pacts upon which the legitimacy of the postrevolutionary Mexican state rests. Both the Constitution of 1917 and the formation of the sectoral party sought not only to institutionalize "new rules of the game" but also to establish goals for future economic policy. The state would act simultaneously to meet the economic demands of all sectors of Mexican society—the new commercial agriculturalists, the military, the bourgeoisie, organized labor, peasants, and other marginal groups.

The Constitution of 1917 not only set forth a procedural framework of government but also sought to satisfy the substantive demands of various sectors of Mexican society. It provided, for example, for land reform (Article 27); similarly, the rights of organized labor to collective bargaining were recognized by Article 123. The Constitution of 1917, however, sought to satisfy not only the policy demands of the agrarians and of organized labor but also the demands of the emergent bourgeoisie and urban middle class.[26]

A second decisive event in the formation of a viable social pact in Mexico was the creation of a sectoral political party during the presidency of Lázaro Cárdenas.[27] This party, known as the Party of the Mexican Revolution (PRM), was to incorporate a labor sector, a peasant sector, a popular (middle-class) sector, and the military. The party was later to drop the military sector and change its name to the current Party of the Institutional Revolution (PRI). Thus, these important sectors were integrated into the new revolutionary state. Incorporation represented a bargain or pact in which organized interest groups representing these sectors were willing to give up a degree of autonomy in return for expected benefits and protections. To understand the process of incorporation (that is, the formation of the official ruling party), one must look closely at the politics of the postrevolutionary era in Mexico.

Manuel Camacho has characterized labor relations with the state during the twenties as "semi-pluralist."[28] The dominant labor confederation of the period, the Mexican Regional Labor Confederation (CROM), used its support of the presidential candidacies of Alvaro Obregon (1920-24) and Plutarco Elias Calles (1924-28) to extract various government positions for labor leaders, government support for CROM unionization efforts and strikes, and financial subsidies. The relationship between CROM and the state is best characterized as one of *interdependency*. The dependency of CROM on the state was shown by its rapid decline after 1928 due to the rupture of its close alliances with the national political leadership. With the demise of CROM after 1928, the Mexican labor movement entered a period of extreme fractionalism.[29] This period would last until the Cárdenas presidency.

The Cárdenas presidency witnessed the reconsolidation of organized labor with the creation of the elite-sponsored Confederation of Mexican Workers (CTM) in 1936 and the sectoral reorganization of the ruling party. Both events must be understood in the context of Cárdenas's effort to put together a "progressive alliance" to challenge the control of the Mexican state by the dominant "conservative alliance." The latter alliance included the Calles faction within the state and foreign and national entrepreneurials.[30] This alliance could count on support from other groups like the *hacendados*, old-line labor bosses linked to CROM and elements of the military elite.[31]

The coalition that Cárdenas put together to challenge the conservative alliance was comprised of the progressive faction within the government along with a mobilized working class and peasantry. To mobilize the support of the peasantry, Cárdenas undertook the most massive land redistribution program of any Mexican president since the revolution. To win the support of labor, Cárdenas encouraged unionization and generally supported strikes. With the support of this alliance, Cárdenas was able to enact significant reforms in the face of opposition from the *Callistas* and vested economic interests.[32]

More important, Cárdenas sought to institutionalize the progressive alliance by creating a sectoral ruling party. New government-sponsored confederations created to unify the peasant and labor movements[33] gained control of the peasant and labor sectors of the new PRM. The creation of the new PRM, thus, formally incorporated lower-class groups into the political process. While the labor and peasant movements realized significant economic and political gains during the Cárdenas presidency, they also lost much of their autonomy through incorporation. Both labor and peasants were in a weakened position to challenge the conservative development policies that began under President Avila Camacho (1940-46) and lasted to Díaz Ordaz (1964-70).[34] Labor relations with the state after incorporation are aptly characterized by Camacho as "semi-corporatist."[35]

The consequences of incorporation once the state was again captured by the conservative alliance have been well described by Hamilton.

. . . in contrast to the Cárdenas victory, the victory of Avila Camacho marked not merely a defeat of the progressive alliance but its virtual elimination as an effective force for change. The possibility of an alliance between progressive groups within the state and the working class and peasantry was foreclosed by the cooptation of the former into the dominant alliance and by the loss of autonomy of the latter. The control of the working-class and peasant movements by their leadership and their incorporation into the state-dominated political party was in fact decisive in enabling the state to control class conflict and thus contributed significantly to the strength of the dominant coalition.[36]

The social pacts upon which the contemporary Venezuelan and Mexican states were established implied a different legitimacy formula from those typically found in industrial democracies. The legitimacy of the state rested not simply on the compliance with the "rules of the game" but on the capacity of the state to satisfy simultaneously the demands of multiple power contenders. Thus, the Venezuelan and Mexican states have been committed ideologically both to rapid capital accumulation and to improvement in the welfare and standard of living of the masses. Neither state has possessed the resources to achieve both goals simultaneously; hence, a choice between priorities has been made. In both countries the main priority over the long term has been rapid capital-intensive industrialization at the expense of short-term improvement in mass welfare. As noted, the lower classes have failed to challenge these priorities. Next, I shall examine how the Venezuelan and Mexican states promoted rapid industrialization and why this goal has proved to be incompatible with significant improvement in mass welfare.

The earliest manufactured goods produced in the industrial development of all countries appear to be basically similar, and Venezuela's experience conforms to this general pattern. These goods might be called *traditional consumer goods*; they include a number of manufactured food products, tobacco products, clothing items, household furnishings (from heavy furniture to crockery, cutlery, and draperies), jewelry, clocks, and watches.[37] In Venezuela, as in most of Latin America, such manufactured goods were the dominant features of the manufacturing industry up through the beginning of the forties. In 1936, for example, fully 79 percent of the industrial work force was employed in the production of traditional consumer goods. These goods accounted for at least two thirds of the value added in the manufacturing process. But shop sizes at this time were very small, averaging fewer than ten employees per establishment.[38] These were still relatively labor-intensive industries, with small-scale production for relatively local markets and with very low barriers to entry.

Two other important developments were occurring during this period, however. One was that major socioeconomic changes began to occur, some of which had substantial consequences for the political economy after 1935 when the dictator, Juan Vicente Gómez, died. The second was that the state began to assure that basic infrastructural investments in transport, communications, and utilities were available for nascent industrialists. This was especially true during the *trienio* (1945-48) and after but can be traced to the early post-Gómez regimes as well.

A major change occurring in the world economy as the twentieth century unfolded was the growth of demand for petroleum. Venezuela's petroleum industry experienced major expansions from the twenties onward, under the guidance of foreign petroleum companies (Shell from the Netherlands; Gulf and Standard Oil-New Jersey from the United States). Given the ability of the Venezuelan government to derive revenues from the petroleum industry via royalties on each barrel produced, governmental attention to traditional sources of revenue generation began to decline. Between 1920 and 1930, for example, the percentage of government revenues derived from petroleum production grew from 1.4 percent to 19.39 percent and continued to grow by about 2 percent a year throughout the thirties.[39] As a consequence of the relative ease with which new revenues could be generated, the dictatorship began to ignore traditional sources of revenue, such as those derived from taxing agricultural exports.[40]

An unintended consequence of such a policy orientation was the setting in motion of vast numbers of rural Venezuelans. One analyst has noted the "tremendous geographic mobility that has marked recent Venezuelan history," one feature of which has been "a progressive depopulation of the countryside."[41] Migration and associated changes created an urban labor pool from which Venezuela's own industrializers would draw and which would determine some of the characteristics of that industrialization.

The pre-1950 era was marked by the construction of much basic infrastructure. Construction of the national highway system was first undertaken by Juan Vicente Gómez himself, as much for security reasons as for integrating a national economy. Other activities designed to integrate the national economy via creation of basic infrastructure were undertaken by the succeeding governments of Eleazar López Contreras (1936-40) and Isaias Medina Angarita. During the first experiment with democracy, known as the *trienio* (1945-48), these trends continued with "the creation of the Venezuelan Development Corporation in 1946. . . . Its original interest in agricultural development quickly was broadened to include promotion of steel, electric power, and private industrial investment. The Development Corporation received from 2 to 10 percent of the government budget during this period. Electric power consumption increased 50 percent from 1945 to 1948, as did the import-substituting consumer goods industry."[42] Thus, the end of the forties found that much basic infrastructure had been constructed, the state presence in creating attractive conditions for capitalist growth had been established as a precedent, the ideology of investing petroleum revenues in industrial development had already been generated, and an early spurt of import-substitution industrialization had been attempted in the *trienio*.

The further development of a light consumer-goods industry and of selected intermediate-goods industries, each of which had begun earlier, accelerated in the Venezuela of the fifties. This transformation has been called, alternatively, "horizontal import substitution" or the "easy phase of ISI." An illustrative case of import substitution in this era was the case of Venezuelan cement production, where imports declined from 82 percent of national consumption in 1938 to 28 percent in 1951, to 1 percent in 1956.[43] But similar declines were occurring in other products, such as beer (totally national production by 1956) and biscuits (totally national by 1955). In addition, initial steps were taken in these years toward the next phase of ISI, one in which modern consumer durables (such as automobiles) came to play a crucial role. Some tire production and initial assembly operations began in this era.

The move from the reformism of the *trienio* toward the military conventionalism of the Pérez Jiménez era (1948-58) did not imply an attenuation of the role of the state in guiding the development process but the redirection of that role. Decreasing emphasis on public investment in human capital, on land reform, and on regularizing labor relations were one side of the reorientation; accelerated public-private investment in infrastructure and in the production of intermediate goods, such as iron and steel, were the other.[44]

By the end of the Pérez Jiménez dictatorship in 1958, a number of patterns had emerged. A state role in guiding the industrialization process was firmly consolidated; the state was to participate jointly with the private sector in large projects designed to bring into existence an intermediate-goods sector, principally iron and steel. Other public expenditures on infrastructure were made in such a way that private sector entrepreneurs could profit, such as the expansion of the cement industry during the boom of public works construction. While long-term trends tended to operate against foreign capital in the petroleum industry, foreign investors entered into an incipient triple alliance with the Venezuelan state and the Venezuelan bourgeoisie during the horizontal phase of ISI. That alliance was not to be severed in subsequent stages; rather, it was to be systematized and reoriented.

Vertical import-substitution industrialization can be defined as a "deepening" by which local production of consumer durables increases, as does local manufacture of capital and intermediate goods whose importation has been stimulated by the horizontal stage of import substitution.[45] The automobile industry is a classic case of how vertical ISI operates. The manufacture of automobiles can eventually have backward linkages with other industries in that demand is generated for a host of products, such as steel, rubber, and glass. Since in the earliest stages of auto industries few countries are in a position to fabricate many of the component parts, much has to be imported, at a cost to the balance of payments. This is the "easy" and horizontal stage of ISI; in terms of the auto industry, it is an era of *assembly*, not of the manufacture of automobiles. But ISI is deepened as the industry begins to incorporate more and more components produced locally, which accelerates when a local capital-goods industry begins to develop. Often the deepening occurs as a result of conscious government policy, because governments are seeking to cope with a balance-of-payments problem that horizontal ISI has only exacerbated.

In the Venezuelan case, vertical ISI has involved a number of developments in the post-1958 era of democratic state capitalism. First, a political formula was devised that allowed the containment of conflicts unleashed in the *trienio*. This afforded private investors some degree of confidence in the political environment so that they could be induced to commit capital to the economic environment.[46] Second, continued increases in petroleum revenues were associated with further expansion of the state presence in the industrialization effort. Third, the characteristic vehicle employed for expanding that state presence was the "third sector enterprise," which combined public and private activity in a way that is sometimes difficult to unravel. Gene Bigler notes that third sector agencies,[47] or quasi-governmental bodies (such as regional development corporations), have expanded during this period in waves that were strongly correlated with the availability of petroleum revenues.[48]

The post-1958 political formula that guided Venezuelan industrialization was one in which the state played a major role in creating the institutional network within which capital accumulation could occur in private hands. Certainly, the Venezuelan political authorities have been committed to import-substituting industrial growth and diversification and the maintenance of a private sector. The movement to acquire national control of strategic industries, such as iron/steel and petroleum, did not imply a desire to obliterate the private sector. But state authorities did desire to direct profits generated in such industries toward investment in other sectors of the economy, so as better to integrate economic activity into an ongoing network of exchange in which more Venezuelans could participate.

As Venezuela entered the eighties, vertical import substitution had made considerable progress. Venezuela produced more automobiles per capita than were produced in either Mexico or Brazil, for example.[49] Venezuela's small market (13 plus million in 1978) should have precluded such a rapid growth of the industry. However, strong state regulation of petroleum prices made vehicle operating costs lower in Venezuela, thereby providing an indirect stimulus to market expansion. In other branches as well, substantial expansion of industrial production and employment was occurring. Employment grew rapidly in the early seventies in diverse sectors: traditional consumer-goods production (tobacco, +13 percent a year; textiles and wearing apparel, +10.2 percent a year); quasi-service sector industries (printing/publishing, +10.1 percent a year); intermediate goods (chemical products, +6.2 percent a year; iron and steel, +12.6 percent a year); producers' goods (electrical equipment, +12.3 percent a year; nonelectrical equipment, +31.6 percent a year); and in modern consumer goods (plastics, +33.1 percent a year).[50] This varied growth reflects the deepening of the import-substitution process implied by the label of "vertical" ISI. More and more goods were being produced inside Venezuela.

Not surprisingly, major problems remained. First, Venezuela remained dependent on imported goods[51] and on foreign capital in a number of industrial operations. Second, the capital intensivity of the process of ISI did not come close to providing the number of jobs needed in Venezuela (see table 7).[52] Service sector employment was even more extensive in Venezuela (54 percent in 1979) than in Mexico (37 percent), as would be expected in a more urban environment (83 percent urban versus 67 percent urban in Mexico). Starting later in ISI than did Mexico, Venezuela achieved a rate of industrial employment (27 percent) equivalent to that yielded by the "Mexican miracle" (26 percent). But since much service sector employment tends to be low-wage employment,[53] Venezuela remains troubled with many of

Table 7. Sectoral Distribution of Employment: Venezuela and
Mexico, 1960 and 1979

	Venezuela		Mexico	
	1960 %	1970 %	1960 %	1979 %
Agriculture	35	19	55	37
Industry	22	27	20	26
Services	43	54	25	37

Source: World Bank, *World Development Report, 1981* (Oxford and New York: Oxford
Univ. Press, 1981), 171, 173.

the same problems of mass poverty that beset Mexico. Venezuela,
like Mexico, finds that late state-capitalist industrialization does not
guarantee that poverty will disappear. Even the occurrence of a mid-
seventies petroleum "bonanza" did not suffice to generate the industrial jobs that would need to be created in order to achieve a
markedly higher level of national welfare under a state-capitalist regime. In the eighties these problems have been further exacerbated
by the debt crisis and falling petroleum prices on the world market.[54]

The persistence of income inequality in Venezuela reflects the
peculiar features of state-capitalist industrialization in the late twentieth century. Even an activist state, blessed with a policy consensus
around mildly reformist goals and endowed with petroleum revenues, cannot turn industrialization into the motor of immediate abun-
dance. In comparative terms much has been accomplished in the
Venezuela development effort, but much remains to be done. Venezuela's accomplishments are relative and do not imply a substantial
qualitative difference from the rest of Latin America. Venezuelan industrial development seems equally incapable of providing an escape
from fundamental developmental dilemmas as is the formula devised
by other late industrializers of Latin America.

Because of the existence of a sizable market attractive to domestic
entrepreneurs, public policy favorable to industrialization during the
dictatorship of Porfirio Díaz, and proximity to sources of capital in
the United States, Mexican industrialization efforts began a bit earlier
than those in Venezuela,[55] getting under way in the late 1800s. The
Mexican Revolution of 1910-17 and the ensuing climate of political
uncertainty in the twenties, however, slowed down the pace of industrialization. The percentage of the economically active population
employed in industry was 17.2 percent at the outbreak of the revolution but declined during the revolution and remained virtually con-

stant over the next two decades, reaching 16 percent in 1940.[56] Similarly, manufacturing output constituted 14 percent of Gross National Product in 1910 but only 11 percent in 1925, returning to 14.3 percent in 1935 and 16.7 percent in 1940.[57] By 1940, then, Mexico had done little more than catch up with its prerevolutionary industrial standing.

During the Cárdenas presidency (1934-40), the basis for a state partnership with the private sector was laid. Relationships between the private sector and the reformist state authorities were troubled, but ultimately the operative norms for the Mexican variant of state capitalism were established. Those norms involved a substantial state presence in the economy. The nationalization of the petroleum industry in 1938 no doubt troubled private investors in other sectors but may have served indirectly to unify the nation. Some authors have argued that this act had the consequence of increasing Mexican self-confidence to the point that private Mexican capital was thereafter more likely to stay in Mexico.[58] Be that the causal mechanism or not, after the Cárdenas presidency, the role of the Mexican state as producer (of electricity, iron and steel, railroad cars, sugar, etc.), as cofinancier[59] of private development efforts, and as regulator increased steadily, as did profits for private sector entrepreneurs. Mexican state authorities taxed those profits at a very low rate[60] but devised ways to guarantee that a substantial percentage of these profits were available for investment in productive activity via manipulation of bank reserve requirements. The Mexican variant of state capitalism, then, involved "early emergence" of an activist state operating on behalf of the private sector.

The activism of the Mexican state became even more apparent in the era from 1940 to 1954 when the bases for subsequent industrial growth were laid. During World War II and later, the state played a major role in preserving the opportunity for private sector industrialists to acquire the profits to which they became accustomed in the war years. One route was via control over the labor movement, through the imposition of acquiescent labor leaders for those who proved more combative; a second route was through permitting the continuation of a substantial discrepancy between urban and rural wages, thereby attracting workers to the city in excess of the jobs available in industry. The excess urban labor supply kept wages low and undermined the bargaining power of the organized labor movement. A third way in which the state put itself at the disposal of the industrialists of the forties was via low taxation and concentration of public spending on economic-development activities. This pattern was established in the forties and continued through 1970, when first halting attempts to reorient the allocation of costs and benefits were made by the Echeverría administration.[61] Yet for many years distributional issues remained a low priority. Roger Hansen notes that "no other Latin American political system has provided more rewards for its new industrial and commercial agricultural elites" while in no other Latin American polity "has less been done directly by the government for the bottom quarter of society."[62]

On many occasions cooperative arrangements that involved the Mexican state, private domestic capital, and foreign investors were set up. It was, without doubt, an "alliance for profits," as the expanded role of the state was not redistributive. It was in this era between 1940 and 1954 that the Mexican state began forcefully to "take on the role of making capitalism work for Mexico . . . (by imposing) major restrictions on the demands of the lower classes and (by) the . . . entry of the state into areas of the economy where the private sector was unwilling or unable to enter, or had entered and failed."[63]

One scholar argues that during this era the "public sector bore the unproductive side of industrialization, receiving only 10 percent of GNP for its 50 percent share in total investment."[64] Some of the public investment consisted of "substantial transfers from the federal government to decentralized agencies, transfers that were primarily designed to allow them to maintain low prices of essential goods and services." The effort to get the industrialization process on track again led to substantial growth in the import of capital goods, which in combination with the subsidies just mentioned meant that domestic budgets were unbalanced, as were international trade accounts. The domestic deficits were financed by inflationary monetary policies,[65] which ultimately led to an overvalued peso. Ultimately, two devaluations from 4.05 to 8.65 (1948) and from 8.65 to 12.5 pesos to the dollar (1954) were necessary to allow Mexico to cope with its external disequilibria. By the end of the 1940-54 era, however, considerable progress had been made in extending the import-substitution process, for now only 6 percent of nondurable consumer goods were imported, 39 percent of intermediate goods, and 68 percent of capital and durable consumer goods.[66]

From 1955 on through the Díaz Ordaz presidency (1964-70), Mexican industry grew apace in an environment that was conducive to private sector confidence in a "favorable investment climate."[67] One element of that climate was the maintenance of price stability, with inflation dropping to 2 to 3 percent a year between 1960 and 1970.[68] Another was the continued use of public policy to ensure that profits were attainable in Mexican industries. This was done via a variety of policy instruments, such as tax holidays, outright subsidies, licensing, and manipulations of tariffs. By 1970, for example, almost 80 percent of goods imported to Mexico required a license. If a proposed item for import would compete with a domestically produced good, the Mexican state would often prohibit importation or impose a high tariff. Tariff protection, especially when applied to capital-intensive industries, was almost purely for the purpose of maintaining high rates of profit.[69] Investors responded actively to these opportunities, leading to what some enthusiastic boosters called "the Mexican miracle." Clark Reynolds, for example, has estimated that the growth of Mexican industry exceeded the "expected level" for an "average developing country" in twelve out of fifteen basic manufacturing industries between 1950 and 1960.[70] Continuing expansion occurred in the sixties. Industries founded in earlier decades continued to increase production, as in the auto industry, a modern consumer durable industry with backward linkages to intermediate goods. In 1955 the Mexican industry produced only 17,225 vehicles, but by 1970 the total annual production was up to 133,218 vehicles. Here the Mexican state fostered backward linkages by negotiating (in 1962) for eventual movement toward a standard of 60 percent of the value of the components being produced in Mexico. Just as in automobiles, import substitution got under way seriously in other consumer durable/capital goods industries during this era, with domestic production increasing from 30 percent to 49 percent of national consumption. Similarly, isi deepened in the intermediate-goods industries, where domestic production now reached 78 percent of national consumption, up from 61 percent in 1955.

Four features of this movement toward vertical isi deserve brief comment. First, foreign investment increased considerably in Mexico, although most often in combination with domestic public and private capital. Mexican state-capitalist industrialization was distinguished by the degree to which foreign capital was invited into the country but forced into partnership with domestic private capital.[71] Unintentionally, this collaboration may ultimately have exacerbated the tendencies for capital to flow outside the country when either foreign investors or major domestic capitalists found themselves displeased with public policy. A pattern of interaction may have been established that regenerated tendencies for Mexican capital to become "psychologically denationalized."

Second, while many new jobs were created in industry, they were insufficient to absorb the labor being driven out of the countryside by the export-oriented agriculture that public policy supported in order to pay the costs of continuing to import much capital equipment. Those urbanites who found employment in industry often found relatively remunerative employment. For example, a 1966 labor cost survey of twelve member countries of the Latin American Free Trade Association reported that Mexican workers received real wages that were 96 percent higher than those of the average worker in all twelve countries.[72] Unionized industrial workers were particularly likely to be well protected in Mexico, having access not only to higher wages but also to collective goods, such as health care via the social security system. Urban unionized workers have been estimated as being among the top 40 percent of the income distribution during this period.[73]

However, the third characteristic was the dependence of the new industries on a very narrow market of the richest segments of Mexican society. David Felix has calculated that in 1968 57 percent of household software, 53 percent of household durables, 60 percent of recreational equipment, and 95 percent of passenger vehicles and accessories were purchased by the richest 20 percent of Mexican households.[74] Once that market was saturated, the prospects of further industrial expansion were limited, given the existing degree of income concentration. Implicit in the "Mexican miracle" of 1955-70, then, were some disturbing indications that the pace of industrialization and of rapid economic growth (which averaged over 3.5 percent per capita a year in the sixties) was about to come to an end.

Fourth, Mexico became increasingly dependent on loans from abroad to finance the public sector deficit generated in the attempt to stimulate industrialization, while maintaining a stable exchange rate and political order. The foreign public debt tripled between 1961 and 1970, implying that "debt service would reach the level of 22.5 percent of current account earnings."[75] Eventually, this debt would drive Mexico into the hands of the public international lending agencies and would have implications for labor policy during the eighties.

An economic slowdown occurred in 1972, when the aggregate growth rate dropped to 3.5 percent annually, from the range of 6.5 percent in the late sixties. This slowdown was, in fact, planned by the Echeverría team, who wished to bring the rising government deficit under control by lowering public spending in 1971. But another goal of the Echeverría administration was to attain more balanced growth with some degree of income redistribution. These goals proved difficult to reconcile. The slowdown of 1972 was greater than expected and led to a consequent Keynesian overreaction in 1972, when government spending and public indebtedness began to balloon in an attempt to reactivate the economy.[76] Substantively, public investment was reoriented toward human capital expenditures; health and welfare expanded rapidly in this era, but some low-priority projects were also undertaken as well because they could be done quickly. The post-1972 spending boom created the need for new revenues, which the Echeverría administration first hoped to raise via a tax reform. Resistance from the private sector apparently led the president to back off, after which point both inflation (circa 20 percent to 30 percent a year in the late seventies) and continued recurrence on foreign loans (foreign debt quadrupled between 1970 and 1976) soared upward. Continuing private sector distrust over Echeverría's reformist economic policy led to massive capital flight in 1976, culminating in two devaluations of the peso (to a rate of 22.5 to the dollar).

During the succeeding López Portillo presidency (1976-82), some initial success was had in calming the fears of domestic and foreign capital, primarily by playing up Mexican petroleum reserves. However, a downturn in the petroleum market in early 1982 revealed Mexico's continuing vulnerability caused by its public foreign debt. Capital flight again resumed, and repeated devaluations of the peso were stimulated throughout 1982, leading ultimately to the nationalization of the banking industry by José López Portillo, who began his administration as the darling of the private sector and terminated it as the *bête noir* thereof.

Nonetheless, import-substitution industrialization continued during this period. Passenger car and truck production zoomed ahead until the mid-seventies, when a temporary downturn occurred. Intermediate-goods industries were also expanding during the seventies. Iron production was up 52 percent between 1970 and 1976; steel production up 35 percent; chemicals up 42 percent; fertilizers up 61 percent; artificial fibers up 142 percent; and petrochemicals up 93 percent.[77] But of the traditional consumer-goods industries, only textiles continued to grow rapidly in the seventies (up 139 percent by 1976). In most areas where industrial expansion was occurring in the seventies, state investment played a key role (for example, iron and steel, petrochemicals, and fertilizers), often in very large plants.[78]

Much discussion has occurred about the exhaustion of the horizontal stage of import-substitution industrialization and about the political consequences that appear to flow from the need to deepen this process.[79] The disputed issues do not have to be resolved here, but one should note that a political pact between the Mexican private sector and state authorities lasted for about thirty-two years before serious disagreements began to surface over Echeverría's 1972 tax proposals and over the reformist direction of public policy. A fraying of the alliance between the state and private capital *did* occur as Mexico attempted to complete the process of import-substitution industrialization. Given that a Mexican president and the economists advising him felt that the task could be accomplished only if a wider market were created via income redistribution, the private sector came to question whether the state truly existed to serve their needs. Private investment declined, and public investment increased to maintain the rhythm of growth. The Mexican economy became more statist. Distrust increased, and political conflict sharpened between the state and private capital after 1972, even though public policy was not sufficiently reformist to generate enthusiastic support from the working classes.[80] Mexico's petroleum boom did not provide the means to soften such conflict because to exploit it required contracting further foreign debt.[81] Hence, Mexican state capitalism was deeply troubled as it confronted the tasks of late industrialization in the post-1970 period. The ability of the state to manage conflict was increasingly subject to question.

The effects of economic development on mass welfare and living standards in Venezuela and Mexico have been amply documented elsewhere. Suffice it to note here that income distribution in both countries has tended to become less equitable, that wage levels of both organized and unorganized workers have tended to deteriorate in real terms during inflationary periods, and that the wretched living conditions of urban marginals and peasants may have improved in some cases, but extensive poverty remains.[82] These conditions are related to choices made by public officials about how to spend government revenues. Social welfare expenditures declined from 47 percent of total central government expenses in Mexico in 1972 to 39 percent in 1981. In Venezuela the corresponding decline was from 38 percent in 1972 to 32 percent in 1981.[83] The next chapter will discuss the structural constraints in both the Venezuelan and Mexican polities that may have precluded organized labor and peasants from mobilizing opposition to the dominant pattern of economic development.

Chapter Four

Mechanisms of Political Control

Chapter 1 noted that corporatist interest intermediation, restricted partisan competition, weak representative institutions, elite consensus, and the use of repression might facilitate political control. This chapter, will examine more closely these facets of control in the Mexican and Venezuelan political systems.

Corporatist interest intermediation in Mexico is asserted primarily through the sectoral organization of the ruling party. In the case of organized labor, most large labor federations in Mexico are incorporated into the labor sector of the ruling Partido Revolucionario Institutional (PRI) and into the overarching Congreso del Trabajo (CT). Both the labor sector of the PRI and the CT are dominated by the Confederation of Mexican Workers (CTM). This confederation, created by the Cárdenas administration in 1936 to unify the labor movement, exercises hegemony over Mexican organized labor by virtue of its symbiotic relationship with the state.[1] Headed for the past several decades by the indomitable Fidel Velasquez, "the official labor movement can be mobilized quickly on a national scale, for everything from mass demonstrations in support of government policies to campaign rallies and voter registration drives."[2]

The Congreso del Trabajo, created by the Díaz Ordaz administration in February 1966, is an umbrella organization that in 1978 "grouped 33 major confederations and industrial and national industrial unions that represented a total of 7,801 unions and 2,238,287 workers."[3] The CTM is able to dominate the national assembly of the CT by virtue of representing a substantial majority of unions in the CT (63.9 percent of the total unions). Seats are allocated to confederations on the basis of number of unions, not on the total number of union members. It is worth noting that the CTM is not the largest confederation in terms of actual members but only in terms of number of affiliated unions.[4]

The relationship between the CTM and the Mexican state is not one of unilateral state control. It is rather a case of both sides perceiving their optimal strategy as one of "going along, in order to get along." While the CTM has often engaged in rhetorical radicalism, especially in response to the growth of independent unionism in the seventies, and in response to recent economic crises,[5] it tends, ultimately, to close ranks in support of PRI economic policies even when workers' interests seem to be sacrificed by the party. The rules of the Mexican political game are generally respected. These norms preclude open criticism of the president, limit mobilization, and call for the closing of ranks around presidential policy decisions.[6]

In turn, the Mexican state has been willing to go along with many of labor's demands. The regime is particularly disposed to satisfy the demands of the CTM hierarchy in exchange for demonstrations of support and for the imposition of control during crises. The support of the CTM for the government during the railroad workers' insurgency in 1958 and 1959 led to a substantial increase of seats in the federal Chamber of Deputies going to the labor sector. One analyst believes the welfare programs of the Echeverría government (1970-76) were in part a payoff for CTM support during the student rebellion in 1968.[7]

The "get along, go along" perspective of labor elites in the incorporated labor movement is buttressed by cooptation and subsidy. Cooptation may take forms ranging from external assistance to union leadership in putting down dissident movements to rewards of legislative seats. As Mexican legislatures, from the national to the local level, are almost totally dominated by the executive, legislative seats provide little opportunity for input into policy-making. Rather, legislative seats "supply substantial income, prestige, perquisites, and the opportunity to engage in other lucrative endeavors."[8] The same cooptative purpose is also served by positions in the official party or bureaucracy.

Attempted cooptation extends to rank-and-file union members as well. A unionized job itself represents a kind of patronage, since wages and benefits obtained are generally far better than what unorganized labor receives. Additionally, organized workers receive "state-subsidized credit, housing, health care, basic commodities, technical training and assistance, and participation in enterprise profits."[9] Coverage and the range of benefits has expanded rapidly since 1970.[10] As only a relatively small portion of the Mexican work force is unionized,[11] unionized workers constitute in one sense a labor aristocracy. Whether their relative privilege produces conservative attitudes is a separate issue to be analyzed in later chapters.

Another mechanism of control is economic subsidy. The CTM has had a historic problem with collecting dues from its affiliates. Consequently, it had to depend on direct state subsidies in order to balance its books. Subsidies are also channeled to state and regional CTM federations as well as to other national confederations affiliated with the labor sector of the party. Subsidies, therefore, have the effect of furthering the dependence of incorporated unions on the Mexican state.[12]

Finally, the state can use repression, should other mechanisms of control fail. Contemporary Mexican labor history is replete with examples of repression of dissident labor movements. Two of the best-known examples are the forceful suppression of a movement of dissidents in the railroad workers' union in 1959 and the suppression of a dissident faction of the Electrical Workers' union during the Echeverría administration.[13]

A main repressive mechanism at the rank-and-file level is the exclusion clause provision (*clausula de exclusión*) generally found in collective contracts. These provisions set up a closed union shop compelling workers to become union members. In addition, employers are required to dismiss any worker who loses his union membership. This clause provides union bosses a tool to stamp out insurgency and to maintain control.[14] Union bosses can simply take steps to expel recalcitrant workers from the union and, thus, from their jobs in order to bring them into line.

How management and the union leadership exert dual control over Mexican workers has been explained well by Larissa Lomnitz.

In the larger private corporations, the management will fire undesirable workers or even close down a plant in the knowledge that any subsequent claims will be settled to their satisfaction at a suitable level. In general, individual workers have no redress and tend to shy from any action which has not been approved by the union leadership. The union in effect controls all jobs in the plant. Loyal members are awarded better jobs, less dangerous assignments, more pleasant tasks, and better shifts. Such practices encourage the passitivity and depoliticization of labor. In the long run, a worker needs the support of his section boss to get access even to the fringe benefits he is entitled to.[15]

Ian Roxborough takes a somewhat different but compatible position. He argues that while "union militancy and rank-and-file insurgency . . . are an integral part of the dynamic of the (Mexican) industrial system . . . (nonetheless) Mexican automobile workers engage in predominantly 'economistic' struggles. They do not agitate for specifically political demands."[16] Perhaps part of the reason for the latter is the existence of the *clausula de exclusión*, also noted by Roxborough.[17]

As in Mexico linkages between dominant parties and the labor movement have fostered a vertical pattern of control in Venezuela. One of the two dominant parties in Venezuela, Acción Democrática (AD), has been able to dominate the major labor federations and the overarching Confederación de Trabajadores Venezolanos (CTV). Domination has come about through subsidy, cooptation, and less frequent, but still consequential, use of repression. Fusion of union and party leadership roles is a central mechanism of control. As one scholar has noted: "This pattern of fused union-party careers is virtually universal. There is no strictly 'labor career' pattern."[18]

In Venezuela union leadership is determined by competitive elections in which all political parties represented in the union are free to present a *plancha*, or slate of candidates. Seats on the union directorate are divided, after elections, on the basis of proportional representation. Each political party has a "multi-level labor bureau to which its union faction is responsible."[19] Party labor bureaus can presumably impose guidelines on the formation of coalition slates and in some cases can impose their own nominees in local union elections. "In order to achieve its electoral objectives in local unions, a national labor bureau works through its factional heads in the federation—or, more infrequently, the bureau hierarchy at the regional or local level."[20] Federation leaders in turn work actively in local union elections to ensure the election of their preferred slate.

The fusion of union/party leadership roles represents a pattern of cooptation by political parties. Consequently, as several observers of the Venezuelan scene have noted, union leaders have been willing to shape union demands so as not to disrupt elite goals of rapid import-substitution industrialization.[21] Cooptation extends to rank-and-file workers as well. Only a minority of Venezuelan workers are unionized.[22] These workers, like their counterparts in Mexico, tend to be employed in the capital-intensive sector of the economy that can best absorb demands for higher wages and benefits. Consequently, the wages and benefits of unionized workers in Venezuela tend to be much better than those of unorganized workers.[23]

Although cooptation, subsidy, and repression are used to maintain AD/COPEI domination of the Venezuelan labor movement, one should not overlook the reciprocal nature of the party-labor union relationship. As in Mexico both parties (labor union leaders and political parties) perceive instrumental value in labor union ties to political parties.[24] Parties need the electoral support of unions; unions need ties with party patrons in order to promote the political interests of organized labor. Daniel Levine recognizes both the asymmetry of the relationship as well as the instrumental basis for interest group ties with hegemonic parties.

Party ties became a central kind of social affiliation, knitting together and often overriding more limited group and sectoral loyalties. Thus, for example, peasant, trade union, and student activists were simultaneously group leaders and party militants. As such, they could be called upon by party leaders to modify strategies, tactics, or goals in order to accommodate the long-range political interests of the party. In this way, party organization *per se* became strong and complex because it incorporated and reinforced other kinds of loyalties and affiliations. In addition to cutting across group ties, AD pene-trated the society vertically as well, creating organizational ties from the na-tional level through regions to blocks and precincts in cities, towns, and countryside alike. This set of party-based structures took root in the 1940s and, after surviving a decade of brutal military repression after the 1948 coup, became firmly established in the democratic period as the major channel of political action. To be effective in Venezuelan politics, groups and interests have been largely required to work through the matrix of party organization. This structural trait, added to the heterogeneous composition of Venezuelan parties, gave leadership a great deal of leverage *vis-à-vis* any single group. Moreover, in the case of AD, the combination of public office with party office gave leadership many key resources in its struggle to control intra-party dis-sent. Thus, in many ways the particularly powerful organization of Vene-zuela's political parties, and the degree to which they continued to channel popular support, strengthened the hand of leaders in the search for stability.[25]

As in Mexico the most powerful labor confederation was created by a hegemonic party, AD. This party established the CTV in 1947. The formation of the CTV came during Venezuela's first experience with competitive democracy, an era known as the *trienio* (1945-48).[26] The CTV was revived after the downfall of the dictatorship and restoration of competitive democracy in 1958. Acción Democrática either alone or in coalition with COPEI[27] has been able to dominate the fifteen-member executive council of the CTV ever since the Betancourt ad-ministration.[28] How control over the CTV was initially exerted in the post-1958 era and the consequences of AD control over the labor move-ment has been well described by Terry Karl.

Before the insurrection (of the left in the early 1960s), AD youth and the Communist Party exerted important influence in the union structure. The unions had been militant under this leadership, raising economic demands and demonstrating the willingness to strike. The only redistribution of income which took place during the democracy occurred under the pressure of strong leadership within the mass organizations. The expulsion of AD's youth wing in 1960 removed aggressive leadership in the unions. In November 1961, militants of the Communist Party and the URD were also purged under the auspices of the government, which moved quickly to consolidate its hold over the unions. The government awarded financial subsidies to the CTV, discriminating against non-AD organizations established later. Eventually, the Confederation received over 50% of its funds from the government. CTV leaders had access to officials at the Ministry of Labor and their strikes were supported by the government. In exchange for a degree of docility, several of their demands were met. The unions, while securing benefits for the organized workers, were transformed into institutions that could guarantee social peace, by controlling strikes, an arrangement made possible through the defeat of radical forces.[29]

In summary, several similarities between the Venezuelan and Mexican systems of control can be noted. In both countries incorporated union leaders extract benefits in exchange for labor peace and acquiescence to official policies. In both countries cooptation and subsidy are used to keep the incorporated union leadership as well as rank and file in line. Rank-and-file union members in both countries constitute a labor aristocracy whose collective bargaining power ensures them a much larger share of the economic pie than unorganized workers receive. In both countries officials have resorted to repression when other mechanisms of control fail.[30]

There are significant cross-system differences, however, in the capacity of corporatist organizations to contain insurgency. Meaningful partisan competition can emerge within Venezuelan unions; therefore, the union hierarchy can less easily ignore or manipulate rank-and-file workers. AD/COPEI control over unions is more easily challenged than is PRI control over Mexican unions due to institutionalized partisan competition within union organizations. Consequently, incorporated union leaders in Venezuela are under more pressure to respond to rank-and-file demands if they wish to continue AD/COPEI domination of organized labor.

Both countries have experienced labor insurgency, as dissatisfaction with the performance of government in dealing with economic crises during the seventies and eighties has increased. In Mexico some unions have disaffiliated from the CTM or other government-controlled federations and realigned with newly formed independent confederations, such as the Independent Labor Organization (UOI) and the Authentic Labor Front (FAT).

However, the defection of labor unions from the PRI-controlled federations has not been followed by realignment with left-wing parties. The autonomous unions have tended to be formally apolitical, concentrating their efforts on improved collective bargaining. There are several reasons for the apolitical nature of independent unionism in Mexico. First, political alignment with opposition parties runs the risk of stimulating government repression, were the hegemony of the PRI to be threatened. Second, alignment with Mexico's weak and divided left promises few rewards in terms of access to patronage.[31] Third, the total number of independent unions is still rather small, not large enough to form a significant electoral bloc, thereby removing motivation to engage in explicit partisan activity. Fourth, leaders in autonomous unions fear, with some reason, that explicit commitment to the political left would undermine the unity of union members and thereby weaken the bargaining power of their unions.[32] For these reasons autonomous unions are not likely in Mexico to become formally aligned with left-wing parties as found in many western European contexts.

By contrast, leftist parties in Venezuela should be able to forge alliances with dissident labor movements more easily than in Mexico. As noted, leftist parties can gain seats on union directorates through proportional representation and, if strong enough, can gain control of union directorates.[33] However, recent dissident movements in Venezuela in the eighties, such as the case of textile workers in Caracas and steel workers in Ciudad Guyana, manifested a deep suspicion of the traditional left because of its accommodation with the established order and have sought to organize independent of the traditional left.[34] Moreover, as will be shown, the political left in Venezuela suffers from fragmentation and disunity and other weaknesses that hinder it from taking advantage of growing political dissatisfaction.[35] We shall now turn to problems faced by opposition parties in Mexico's semiauthoritarian polity and Venezuela's aggregative two-party system.

In both Venezuela and Mexico, partisan competition is restricted, although to different degrees. In Venezuela there is meaningful partisan competition between two hegemonic centrist parties, the Christian Democratic Party (COPEI) and the Democratic Action Party (AD). The incumbent party has been voted out of office in the last four national elections of 1968, 1973, 1978, and 1983. Additionally, competitive partisan elections are often employed to select the leadership of private associations.

Meaningful competition in Venezuela, however, does not extend to parties of the left. This point is illustrated by the 1983 national elections. In this election in which AD regained the presidency and overwhelming control of the legislature, AD and COPEI presidential candidates received 91.3 percent of the total valid vote, and their legislative candidates received 78.6 percent of the votes.[36]

What factors account for the relative weakness of the left in Venezuela? Certainly, factionalism has weakened the left. But even were the left permanently united, it would constitute a distinct minority. The systemic mobilization of bias favoring the two dominant parties must be taken into account. The allocation of public goods and services is controlled by the party in control of the presidency. Both AD and COPEI have more patronage to distribute than do minor parties of the left. The latter must rely, therefore, primarily on ideological appeals to mobilize supporters.

The hegemonic position of the two major parties also ensures that financial contributions are likely to flow to them. As David Myers points out about the 1978 presidential campaign: "This level of expenditure (for the 1978 campaign) necessitated support from powerful interests, who expected some return in the form of favorable government policies. Since parties with little chance of winning are not likely to receive contributions from those interests, it has become increasingly difficult for any group other than the two dominant political parties to obtain sufficient funds to mount a competitive election campaign."[37] Their superior financial position gives AD and COPEI the opportunity to utilize the media more fully than do minor parties even though there is legal provision for "equal time."[38]

Another factor that has weakened the left is its links to armed insurrection in the early sixties against the budding democracy. Surveys have uncovered a high level of mass support for democratic institutions in Venezuela.[39] The left may have difficulty in dissociating itself in the minds of some voters from its violent past, even though leftist parties having renounced violence are recognized now as legitimate power contenders in the electoral arena.[40]

While AD and COPEI enjoy mobilizational advantages over parties of the left, there are still incentives for leftist parties to attempt to mobilize supporters. While leftist control of a government in Caracas is unlikely in the foreseeable future, the left can gain legislative seats and representation on union directorates through proportional representation. In the short run, this opens the possibility of leftist parties becoming an important swing bloc in these bodies.

The Mexican party system presents a different picture. While there is party turnover in Venezuela, there is none in Mexico except for a few legislative seats and positions at the municipal level. The ruling PRI has never lost a gubernatorial or presidential election. Nor has it lost control of the national or state legislatures since its inception in 1928. The explanation for sixty years of PRI hegemony is quite similar to the biparty hegemony of COPEI and AD in Venezuela. Control over patronage and financial resources gives the PRI an overwhelming advantage over opposition parties. Indeed, the hegemony of the PRI in Mexico is so extreme that opposition parties are sometimes financed by the government in order to maintain the facade of a truly competitive democracy.[41]

Even more than in Venezuela, leftist parties in Mexico remain very weak. As in Venezuela the left suffers from extreme factionalism.[42] Furthermore, the PRI coopts the symbols and rhetoric of the left.[43] Unlike in Venezuela the political left can win seats via proportional representation only in the Chamber of Deputies. Restricted proportional representation for the Chamber of Deputies has existed in Mexico since the early sixties, most recently having been expanded in 1977. Given that the Chamber of Deputies is a politically unimportant institution, it is not likely that this "opportunity" would stimulate intense mobilizing efforts by leftist parties.[44] Indeed, the left is so weak in Mexico that the strongest electoral challenge to the PRI has come from the center-right National Action Party (PAN).[45]

In sum, leftist and other parties that favor alternative strategies of economic development are placed at a distinct competitive disadvantage in both the Venezuelan and Mexican political systems. This has both collective and individual consequences. Collectively, this disadvantage should weaken the capacity of leftist parties and interest groups affiliated with them to mobilize working-class opposition to dominant parties. In addition, the institutional weakness of the left might well explain the lack of political activism on the part of those working-class individuals who are discontented with the course of state-capitalist development. Such individuals may be inhibited from political activity, not by their own cognitive or attitudinal deficiencies, but rather by the absence of realistic opportunities for parties that favor alternative allocative patterns to gain power.

Political control can also be asserted by removing political institutions from popular influence. Hence, one must ask if the institutions most deeply involved in making vital public policy decisions are subject to popular influence via mass mobilization. Working-class inclusion can be restricted to political institutions that play an insignificant role in public policy making.[46] Elites, thereby, can more easily ignore popular sector demands in formulating development policies if they wish. Opportunities for working-class access to vital policy-making centers are restricted in both Mexico and Venezuela but more so in Mexico than in Venezuela.

The three-sector structure of the PRI provides for formal representation of organized Mexican workers in the party. Formal representation in the party, however, does not provide rank-and-file workers any significant input into party decisions. The CTM hierarchy, especially Fidel Velasquez, has a voice in party decisions, but rank-and-file workers rarely do. Furthermore, the party itself has little or no influence over the formulation of public policy. Described as "one of the world's most accomplished vote-getting machines," the PRI's principal function is to ensure that large PRI majorities are produced in all elections, only secondarily to provide a mechanism for interest articulation.[47]

Likewise, legislative bodies in Mexico have little or no influence on policy-making. Legislative seats from the municipal to the national level are distributed through patron-client networks. As noted previously, some of these seats are distributed to union leaders as a cooptative device. In return for the rewards that go with the seat, PRI legislators are expected to support presidential policy. Given the overwhelming PRI majorities in all legislative bodies, bills backed by the chief executive are not defeated.[48]

Policy-making in Mexico is virtually the exclusive prerogative of the president who is limited to a single six-year term. While there is maneuvering and bargaining among various factions within the government, ranks close once a presidential decision is made.[49] This falling in line can be explained by the rather extraordinary power that the Mexican president has. As Wayne Cornelius and Ann Craig note:

All but a few public officeholders in Mexico serve at the pleasure of the president. State governors, leaders of Congress and the PRI, some high-ranking military officers, heads of state-owned industrial enterprises, and hundreds of other officeholders down to middle-level administrative positions are hand picked by each incoming president. For lesser offices, the president can veto any nomination recommended by his subordinates and substitute his own choice. Officeholders whose actions have proven embarrassing, disruptive, or otherwise troublesome to the president or his inner circle of advisers can be arbitrarily unseated. Even popularly elected state governors who fall badly out of favor with an incumbent president are faced with almost immediate dismissal, which is accomplished simply by ordering the federal Congress to declare the offending state government "dissolved."[50]

A strong presidency or chief executive is not incompatible with popular accountability, as liberal academicians in the United States have argued ever since the New Deal. However, in Mexico there is little accountability. The "no-reelection rule" means that the performance of the incumbent is not assessed by the electorate. Public influence over the electoral process is very circumscribed by limited partisan competition (the PRI candidates always win) and by exclusion of the electorate from the nomination process. The PRI presidential candidate is selected by a process shrouded in mystery. The major actor is the outgoing president, but just how the selection is made is not fully understood.[51] The important point to be emphasized is that the process is a closed one, excluding most Mexicans from any input into the selection of their next president.

We are not suggesting that policymakers in Mexico remove themselves completely from input from the so-called popular sector. To the contrary, political elites in Mexico are particularly sensitive to maintaining system stability by upholding the social pacts upon which the system rests. Ever since President Cárdenas began the practice of the *giras de trabajo* (working trips among the masses), Mexican presidents and *politicos* in general worked hard at cultivating an image of responsiveness and of concern for the social welfare goals of the Mexican Revolution.[52]

Nonetheless, Mexican political elites have considerable flexibility either to respond to or to ignore popular demands. As Evelyn Stevens puts it, "The regime's success in limiting, discouraging, and manipulating demand input is the system's most distinguishing characteristic."[53] Political elites will often choose to ignore popular sector demands when seeking to implement austerity/monetary stabilization policies or when seeking to regain the confidence of domestic and international capitalists. Such seems to have occurred under the de la Madrid administration as it sought to restore the Mexican economy from the 1982 economic collapse.[54] At other times, however, elites will adopt more populist policies in response to political crises or as a means to restore confidence and system support. Echeverría's and Lopez Portillo's economic reform policies, for example, must be seen in the context of rebuilding system support following the trauma of the 1968 Tlateloco massacre and the near economic collapse of 1975.[55] This flexibility either to ignore or to respond to popular demands is rooted in the virtual removal of the presidency from popular control.

Clearly, some political elites in Mexico are situated in positions more removed from interaction with the masses than are others. As a general rule, so-called *politicos* interact more with the masses than do *tecnicos*. The former serve in positions that require them to cultivate large mass constituencies. These include PRI officials, state or local chief executives, and legislators. *Tecnicos*, by contrast, generally occupy highly technical positions in the bureaucracy where they have not had the opportunity to develop large mass followings.

In recent years high-ranking positions in the Mexican government have been increasingly filled by *tecnicos*. Each of Mexico's last three presidents (Luis Echeverría, José Lopez Portillo, and Miguel de la Madrid) came initially from bureaucratic rather than political backgrounds.[56] Given the increasing complexity of industrial development in Mexico, the trend toward technocratic domination of policy-making is not surprising. However, this trend, some argue, will tend to isolate policymakers even further from public opinion. In addition, technocratic decisionmaking obscures hidden policy biases that shift the burden of austerity implied by economic stabilization programs to the poor and working class.[57]

Like the Mexican political system, the Venezuelan polity can aptly be characterized as "presidentialist." A president who cannot be reelected for ten years dominates the policy-making process, although not to the degree of presidential dominance seen in Mexico. Unlike in Mexico the president can sometimes be constrained by opposition parties, by a rival faction in his own party, or by the legislative branch. Still, the power of the Venezuelan president is considerable. Like in Mexico major economic policy decisions have increasingly been made by technocrats and corporatist planning boards that bypass mass-based institutions like parties and legislatures. Furthermore, the Venezuelan president, like his Mexican counterpart, has extensive appointment powers, including state governors and other top-level positions in state enterprise. The major difference in Venezuelan presidentialism comes in the nomination and election process, which is considerably more open and competitive than in Mexico.

Unlike in Mexico nominations for national office are decided through institutionalized processes, not through secretive, closed consultation among elites. Presidential nominees of both AD and COPEI are decided through conventional party conflict resolution mechanisms—national conventions or primaries. In the past both parties have used national conventions to select their presidential nominee. In recent elections (and in 1967), AD has experimented with a national primary.

Conflict generally revolves around various personalist factions within the party. In the 1978 presidential election, for example, the battle for the AD nomination was fought between the Betancourt faction[58] backing Luis Pinerua Ordaz and the Andrés Pérez faction backing Jaime Lusinchi.[59] While Lusinchi failed in 1978 to capture the nomination, he won the presidency in 1983. He has since split with his mentor, Andrés Pérez, and tried unsuccessfully to promote another candidate for the 1988 presidential election in order to block Andrés Pérez's nomination.[60] Opportunities are thus available for mobilized groups to influence the nomination process as well as the general election within parameters set by Venezuela's two-party system.

Political parties also determine nominees for the Venezuelan Congress. "Every party's national executive committee (or its functional equivalent) reserves to itself the prerogative of making the final decision concerning the persons to be listed as legislative candidates and the position of each on the list."[61] Following Venezuela's system of proportional representation, the number of seats that a party wins within an electoral district is determined by its share of the total vote.

Centralized control by party elites over the nomination process for Congress gives the Venezuelan president control over his party in the legislature, assuming that the president does not lose control over the national executive committee. If his party is dominant in the legislature, the president has a free hand to get his legislative program passed. Such was the situation of Carlos Andrés Pérez when a large AD majority was also elected to the Senate and Chamber of Deputies in 1973. If, however, the opposition party controls Congress, the president must often negotiate and bargain with Congress as the COPEI president, Rafael Caldera (1968-73), was forced to do with an AD majority in Congress.[62]

In sum, the political process is considerably more open in Venezuela than in Mexico, providing more opportunities for mobilized groups to exert influence. There are, however, constraints on mass influence over policy-making. When commanding legislative majorities, Venezuelan presidents can dominate the legislative branch just as completely as the Mexican president. Like the PRI in Mexico, dominant parties in Venezuela are mechanisms to mobilize mass electoral support.[63] The nature of the linkage between masses and elites, as in Mexico, tends to be downward through patron-client networks. Due to a highly centralized authority structure in the dominant parties, few opportunities exist for opposition groups to mobilize within the dominant parties. Rather, the trend has been for dissident factions to split from the dominant parties and join the ranks of other impotent minority parties.[64]

As in Mexico technocrats have come to exercise an ever-increasing role in policy-making. This trend was exacerbated during the Andrés Pérez administration (1973-78). Confronted with an inordinately large amount of petroleum dollars, Pérez was persuaded that state administration needed to be rationalized by removing partisan politics. In lieu of existing administrative agencies dominated by the parties, newly created tripartite boards and planning commissions would employ more technical criteria in formulating policy. In effect, political institutions, like parties and legislatures, were to be bypassed. Karl shows how the various tripartite boards that Pérez set up to nationalize administration favored a conservative, probusiness strategy of development.[65] Karl's argument does not have to be examined in detail except to note that the "technification" of policy-making in Venezuela and the concomitant demise of traditional party politics limits opportunities for workers and other popular sector groups to exercise political influence over policy-making.

Elite consensus is another mechanism of political control in Venezuela and Mexico. While it would be difficult to quantify the degree of elite consensus in either Venezuela or Mexico, most students of politics in either country would agree that there is a high level of consensus among political elites. The rules of the political game are almost universally accepted, and there is basic agreement on the desirability of a state-capitalist strategy of development, that is, the use of the state to enhance the role of a private sector, taking over activities necessary to the private sector but that are unattractive to it. Leftist elites reject this model of development and in some cases, particularly in Mexico, also reject the political rules of the game. But leftist elites generally exercise little political power and generally opt for cooptation via the electoral system rather than risk repression by engaging in revolutionary activity.

There is a certain irony here. As Levine notes, "Historically, AD came on the national scene as spokesman for a broad coalition of the marginal and dispossessed of Venezuelan society—above all, lower classes from peripheral regions."[66] The same observation applies to the PRI in Mexico, which traces its roots to the Mexican Revolution. Yet these ruling parties have generally retained the tacit support of the bourgeoisie and upper class by recognizing and upholding social pacts with privileged groups (chapter 3).

Conflict and dissension do develop at the elite level between reformers and conservatives.[67] However, conflict is contained and resolved within existing institutions, thereby also containing mass mobilization within the contours of the established political system. Elites are *not* tempted to mobilize the poor "to do in" their antagonists among other elite factions. What factors account for this high degree of elite consensus?

A major factor promoting elite consensus in both countries is the historical memory of elites. Mexican elites are painfully aware of the costs of the Mexican Revolution in which more than a million lives were lost. A decade of war did not end until competing revolutionary leaders agreed to a pact in which "they pledged themselves to mutual toleration and a division of the spoils that reflected the existing balance of power among them."[68] A major factor sustaining the commitment of contemporary elites to renewing the pact is fear of repeating the trauma and violence of the revolution were the system to break down again.

The memory of Venezuelan elites is not of the costs of violent revolution but rather of the costs of a dictatorship that developed when Venezuela's first experience with competitive democracy failed. Venezuela's experiment with democracy during the *trienio* (1945-48) collapsed largely because of elite polarization and fragmentation. The social pact upon which competitive democracy was reinstituted in Venezuela in 1958 signified an effort to reach an elite accommodation (see chapter 3). Levine notes:

With the overthrow of military rule, steps were taken to correct the errors of the past. The most striking feature of Venezuelan politics after 1958 is the conscious, explicit decision of political elites to reduce interparty tension and violence, accentuate common interests and procedures, and remove, insofar as possible, issues of survival and legitimacy from the political scene. This orientation took concrete form in an agreement signed between AD, COPEI, and URD in October 1958—the Pact of Punto Fijo. As Romulo Betancourt noted, this pact reflected a belief that extreme partisanship and intense conflict during the *trienio* had opened the doors to military intervention."[69]

Another factor that has contributed to elite consensus in both countries is a deideologizing of politics. Among major power contenders, there is ideological agreement on the basic model of state-capitalist development. Political conflict does not reflect fundamental ideological issues.[70] Such issues are resolved through the negotiation and renegotiation of social pacts. Rather, conflict is centered on issues of allocation of resources and their distribution within the established sociopolitical framework. The political weakness of the left in both Mexico and Venezuela is a function of and contributes to fundamental ideological consensus on the elite level.

The management of conflict in both systems is contingent on the distribution of benefits to major power contenders. The capacity to satisfy distributive demands is dependent on stable economic growth.

A shrinking or devalued economic pie would mean fewer resources to distribute. Both Venezuela and Mexico have faced severe economic crises in recent years. By shrinking the pie, these crises may well strain an important mechanism for sustaining elite consensus.[71]

A final factor contributing to elite consensus in both countries is the centralization of authority. Hierarchy reinforced by patron-client networks enables top-level elites to impose discipline on subordinates. As noted, power is more concentrated in the Mexican political system with the rather extraordinary power of the president. However, even in Venezuela power is concentrated in the dominant parties and in the presidency. The concentration of power makes elite dissensus less likely than if power were more widely diffused.

The last control mechanism, the use of political repression in both the Venezuelan and Mexican political systems, has already been touched on. In order to understand the effectiveness of cooptation, we need to consider the other side of the coin, threatened or actual repression. To refuse cooptation is to risk repression.[72] In both polities it is important to emphasize the last-resort character of political repression. This is not to imply that repression is unimportant in either polity, only that repression is generally used only when other control mechanisms have failed.

As with elite consensus, it is also difficult to quantify the level of repression in either system. Scholars have generally made subjective judgments consistent with their preconceptions about either polity.[73] Still, scholars most surely would agree that both polities have relied far less on repression than have the present and past bureaucratic-authoritarian regimes in the southern cone.[74] Part of the attractiveness of inclusionary systems to elites must rest on the availability of other mechanisms, besides repression, for controlling political mobilization.

The critical questions to ask are (1) whether legal or extralegal means of repression are used and (2) for what purposes is repression used. In respect to the first question, there are no hard facts to judge which polity utilizes extralegal repression more fully. Impressionistic evidence suggests that such extralegal repression as the use of thugs to disrupt opposition activities, arbitrary firings, or disappearances and assassinations are far more common in Mexico than in Venezuela. However, such activities are not unknown in Venezuela as shown by some of the arbitrary actions taken to establish AD control over the labor movement in the sixties,[75] by the harassment of the People's Electoral Movement during the 1968 electoral campaign,[76] or by the attempt to purge leftist leaders from the SIDOR steel mill in Ciudad Guyana in 1982.[77]

In both Venezuela and Mexico, political repression has been used for purposes other than ensuring that mass political activity remains nonviolent. It has also been used to ensure that strategic economic activity is not disrupted, to suppress groups that challenge the prevailing social pacts and alliances that cement the established state, and to maintain the hegemony of dominant parties in labor and peasant mass organizations. Each of the purposes for which repression is used will be studied.

In both polities political elites do not look kindly toward the disruption of production in strategic industries. Labor unions in these industries are generally able to extract attractive benefits and wages for workers. These workers tend to be among the best paid in the work force. In return, workers are expected to keep production going. The oil workers' union in Mexico perhaps provides an extreme but yet an instructive case. The union has acquired a vast array of community services and personal benefits for workers. Close ties between the union leadership and PRI officials enable the union to deliver the goods. However, the union leadership is expected to and does stamp out dissidence and militancy by both legal and extralegal means, including assassinations and arbitrary dismissals.[78] Both factors, cooptation and repression, explain why Section 24 of the STPRM (the Oil Workers' Union), which was studied in Salamanca, has never gone out on strike.

In Venezuelan strategic industries, one is not as likely to find repression exercised through the internal governing structure of unions, as these structures tend to be more open and democratic than in Mexico. However, the government can and does act to suppress strikes in strategic industries. Strikes are suppressed in two ways: (1) by the Organic Law of Security and Defense that "allows the president to declare security zones in which the armed forces can impose 'exceptional means' of preserving order"[79] and (2) by the Labor Ministry declaring a strike illegal, thereby allowing the government to use the police and military to break up the strike.[80] Both powers have been used to break up strikes principally in strategic industries.[81]

The rules of the game in both polities provide limited space for opposition political parties to challenge the existing allocation of political and economic resources; however, that space is restricted to the electoral arena dominated by the hegemonic parties. In Venezuela's case labor unions and peasant associations can freely affiliate with socialist parties opposed to the dominant socioeconomic pacts. By contrast, autonomous-interest associations in Mexico generally choose to remain apolitical. However, political parties and labor unions in both countries may not mobilize a broad-based movement to challenge existing distributional patterns outside of the electoral arena without risking repression.

The leftist insurrection in the sixties in Venezuela would have provoked repression from virtually any state. What is significant is that repression was lifted for those parties willing to limit political mobilization to the electoral arena.[82] At this point, it would be pure speculation to guess how political elites would react to a *broad-based* sociopolitical movement of workers and peasants that sought to challenge peacefully existing distributional systems by calling for a *re*distribution of political and economic resources. The guess is that such mobilization would be tolerated only if it were confined to the electoral arena. However, the example of Chile under Allende suggests the possibility of a military coup and repression if power were ever gained through the electoral process.[83]

The experience of a dissident faction of the electrical workers' union during the seventies illustrates well conditions that lead to political repression in Mexico. A union known as the SUTERM union was formed in 1972 by the Echeverría administration to consolidate a militant independent union with a CTM union. Unity was short-lived as the independent faction pushed for greater militance and internal democracy. In March 1975 the independent faction was expelled from SUTERM. Organized afterward as the Democratic Tendency, the militant electricians organized a meeting of 20,000 workers in Guadalajara on April 5, 1975. A Declaration of Guadalajara was issued. It called not simply for greater benefits and privileges for electricians within the existing distributional system but for radical reform that would lead to a fundamental reallocation of wealth and political power. While it contained bread-and-butter economic demands, it also called for specific steps to democratize *all* unions, for collectivization of agriculture, for expropriation of foreign firms, and for increased worker participation in public planning.[84]

Later that same year, a large demonstration was organized in Mexico City. One account describes the event as follows: "On the afternoon of November 15, 250,000 supporters of the democratic movement filled the streets of Mexico City: Members of the SME [Union of Mexican Electricians], railroad workers, telephone workers, university employees, representatives of independent unions and caucuses, militants from the left political parties, residents from the colonies of Netzahualcoyotl, Ixtacalco, Ecatepec and others, members of the *Central Campesina Independiente* (the Independent Peasant Central), and representatives of independent campesino organizations from 12 states. It was the largest and most important demonstration since 1968."[85]

The next year the Democratic Tendency was suppressed by both the extralegal and legal means available to the Mexican state.[86] This case study illustrates well conditions that are likely to lead to political repression in Mexico: (1) the electrical workers did not confine their demands to bread-and-butter demands that the regime could satisfy but called for radical change; (2) the dissident movement refused to be coopted by the benefits offered through consolidation with a CTM union; (3) the dissident movement of electricians sought to expand into a broad-based movement unifying disparate elements of the lower class and the progressive element of the middle class; and (4) the movement operated outside the electoral arena using mass demonstrations and other unconventional means to articulate demands.

Susan and John Purcell have defined well the parameters of "acceptable" mobilization. "Mexican populism has always been highly successful at activating particular categories of people in the name of specific bread-and-butter demands while dampening, through cooptation and repression, further demands as well as the rapid spread of those demands to other groups. Tiny segments of social classes are mobilized in the name of social justice, but class-based mobilization is firmly and successfully discouraged."[87] The Democratic Tendency encountered repression once these limits were broached just as other past dissident movements have.[88]

Thus far, the use of repression by Mexican and Venezuelan political elites to protect strategic industries and to contain challenges to the dominant social pacts has been discussed. Repression has also been used to maintain control by the hegemonic parties over the official labor movement. The use of repression by Acción Democrática to put down a leftist challenge to its hegemony in the Confederation of Venezuelan Workers (CTV) in the early sixties[89] and to crush a leftist insurgency in Ciudad Guyana has already been noted.

A similar example is provided in Mexico by the suppression of the Coalition of Worker and Peasant Organizations during the Aleman presidency (1946-52). This organization mobilized dissident unions and presented "a serious challenge to the CTM's claim to be the country's principal labor organization." This challenge was inspired by the CTM's policy of avoiding strikes and wage demands that would disrupt the "Pacto Obrero-Industrial" to guarantee labor-management peace. The Aleman administration eliminated the coalition by using trumped-up charges of corruption and by forcefully imposing a more conservative leadership in unions that had supported the coalition.[90]

In summary, this chapter suggests that the Mexican and Venezuelan political systems are inclusionary but are polities that leave the working class and the poor relatively powerless to effect meaningful change in the development strategy preferred by elites. Elites choose development strategies that the poor "accept." Political elites may well adopt preemptive reform measures, fearing rebellion from below. When the political situation calls for it, political elites in both Mexico and Venezuela will pursue economic reforms. But it should be emphasized that reform measures are better understood as an elite choice, not as a response to pressures generated by widespread mass mobilization. How specific control mechanisms affect working-class mobilization will be examined in chapters 6 to 8. First, chapter 5 will examine patterns of working-class political mobilization.

Chapter Five

Patterns of Political Mobilization

Chapter 1 examined alternative patterns of political mobilization. *Autonomous* and *controlled* political mobilization along with *demobilization* were discussed. As noted, each of these patterns of mobilization is characterized by subordinate groups manifesting a particular syndrome of political attitudes and participatory behaviors.

Autonomous political mobilization occurs when subordinate groups (1) perceive their collective interests in conflict with those of other groups and/or with the state and (2) engage in collective political action to defend those interests. Individuals who are so mobilized become aware of their collective interests and tend to be psychologically involved in politics. Furthermore, they tend to be political activists whose involvement in politics extends beyond periodic voting. Furthermore, the autonomously mobilized individuals are likely to support political parties that most closely identify with the collective interests of the class or groups with which they identify. In the case of workers in capitalist systems, they are likely to support socialist or reform parties that are committed to the promotion of working-class interests (see chapter 1).

By contrast, controlled political mobilization implies limited capacity of a subordinate group to pursue collective interests. As a consequence of control, individuals within the group are not likely (1) to acquire motivations to engage in collective political action or (2) to engage in political activity beyond periodic voting or (3) to vote for militant, antisystem political parties. In the case of a working-class population in a contemporary state-capitalist regime, one would expect to find (1) strong support for hegemonic parties and weak support for leftist parties, (2) low levels of psychological involvement in politics and of *concientización*, (3) minimal political activity except for regular voting in periodic elections.

In this chapter the analytic task is to explore whether Venezuelan and Mexican workers who were interviewed for this study exhibit characteristics of controlled or of autonomous political mobilization

Table 8. Electoral Choice of Venezuelan Workers

	1973 Presidential Election %	1978 Presidential Election %	1979 Municipal Election %
AD	29.2	17.5	14.5
COPEI	30.8	42.7	40.2
MAS	16.1	15.5	15.9
MIR	3.9	7.0	9.8
MEP	9.2	7.3	8.7
PCV	1.3	1.0	1.4
LS	a	a	1.8
Null ballot	4.9	6.3	3.3
Other parties	4.6	2.9	4.3
Total leftist vote[b]	30.5	30.8	35.8

[a]Liga Socialista voters for 1973 and 1978 were coded in "other parties" category.
[b]Compilation of percentages for MAS, MIR, MEP, and PCV. LS percentage in 1979 was not counted in order to keep figures compatable.

and to what extent. The aggregate levels of electoral support for hegemonic parties and for leftist parties will be explored first. Comparable data from individual workers in pre-1973 Chile and in Western European countries will also be used. Then, the aggregate levels of psychological involvement in politics and *concientización* for both samples of workers and the aggregate levels of political activity will be examined.

Tables 8 and 9 show the percentage of the vote obtained by each party among reported voters for three elections. Care should be taken in interpreting these results, given the nonrandom sampling procedures used. Nevertheless, the results show that hegemonic parties in both countries captured a sizable portion of the vote. The PRI obtained a significantly higher percentage of the vote for each election than did AD and COPEI in Venezuela. This difference holds up even if one excludes the 1976 presidential election in which the PRI was the only party listed on the ballot.[1]

It is significant to note a slight decrease in AD/COPEI strength in the 1979 elections and a much larger decrease in PRI support in the same year. One cannot determine if this decline in electoral support is related to declining satisfaction with government performance. Such a hypothesis might seem reasonable, especially in Venezuela

Table 9. Electoral Choice of Mexican Workers

	1970 Presidential Election %	1976 Presidential Election %	1979 Legislative Election %
PRI	78.8	90.0	65.0
PAN	14.6	——	20.4
PARM	1.0	——	1.0
PPS	1.1	——	2.0
PDM	0.0	——	2.8
PMT	b	——	b
PST	b	——	1.5
PCM	b	4.6	5.1
Null ballot	4.7	5.3	2.0
Total leftist vote	1.1	4.6	8.6

[a]In 1976 the PRI was the only party listed on the presidential ballot. Hence, a sizable number (n = 67) who reported voting for the PAN were excluded. This point as well as the inclusion of the PCM vote is explained further in chapter 9, note 10.

[b]Not officially listed on ballot.

where the petroleum boom of the seventies had already expired. However, other factors may have played a determining role. The 1979 elections in both countries did not involve a presidential election. Hence, there was no coattail effect. The message of opposition parties might be more easily transmitted in nonpresidential elections when attention is not focused on the top of the ticket. In Mexico's case, PRI strength might also have been eroded by the effects of the 1977 political reform that provided greater incentives and opportunities to opposition parties to wage an effective campaign.[2]

Tables 8 and 9 show that leftist electoral support is low in both samples but much lower in Mexico than in Venezuela. Perhaps, the presence of a centrist opposition alternative in Mexico, the National Action Party (PAN), accounts for some of the difference. However, even if one adds the PAN percentage for 1970 and 1979 to the percentage for leftist parties,[3] the combined opposition vote remains lower than the leftist percentages for Venezuela. Of course, we would not presume that PANistas would convert to leftist partisans if the PAN were dissolved.The point is to emphasize that electoral opposition to hegemonic parties is greater in Venezuela than in Mexico.

To summarize, the propensity to vote for the left appears to be low both among Venezuelan and Mexican workers. Nevertheless, the

Table 10. Electoral Support for the Left by French and Italian
           Industrial Workers

Party	French workers 1969	Italian workers 1964
Communist/Socialist	57.2%	68.0%
Christian Democratic	16.9	28.0
Right-wing parties	25.9	4.0
Total %	100.0%	100.0%
N	717	392

Note: Based on surveys reported in Brian H. Smith and José Luis Rodriguez, "Comparative Working-Class Political Behavior: Chile, France, and Italy," *American Behavioral Scientist* 18, no. 1 (Sept. 1974): 63, 64, tables 2 and 3.

data reveal substantial differences between the Mexican and Venezuelan workers. Fewer Mexican workers vote for leftist parties than do Venezuelans. This difference suggests more effective political control over working-class mobilization in Mexico than in Venezuela.

To place these results in a comparative perspective, let us examine the extent to which industrial workers in other regimes support the left. The available survey data show that industrial workers (males) in Chile were far more likely to have preferred the socialist Allende than either the Christian Democratic or Conservative party candidate in the 1970 election. Fully 44 percent of respondents supported the socialist Allende, while the next highest candidate, Allessandri, was supported by only 25 percent of the respondents. In the 1958 and 1964 presidential elections, electoral support of industrial workers for Allende was less but still noticeably higher than the leftist support given by Mexican and Venezuelan workers.[4]

Leftist voting by industrial workers in France and Italy provides an even more striking contrast with the cases of Venezuelan and Mexican workers. Table 10 reports political preferences of industrial workers in France and Italy in 1969 and 1964 respectively. In both of these countries, Communist and Socialist parties are the overwhelming preference of industrial workers. Brian Smith and José Luis Rodriguez present data to show that this same pattern is almost universally found in Western European democracies.[5]

These comparative results suggest then that worker support for the left is effectively discouraged in the Mexican and Venezuelan political systems. Why leftist parties fail to harvest greater electoral support from industrial workers will be examined in chapter 8. The next point to consider is the extent to which these Mexican and Venezuelan workers acquired motivations to engage in collective political action, focusing on psychological involvement in politics and then *concientización*.

Psychological involvement in politics implies long-term attentiveness to the world of politics. It has been defined by Sidney Verba, Norman Nie, and Jae-on Kim as an issue-neutral motivation to participation, entailing long-term attention to politics independent of issue or ideological concerns.[6] Certainly, elites who wish to control mass mobilization are well served by a low level of psychological involvement in politics. The political activity of inattentive citizens is more easily manipulated and controlled than that of an attentive public.

Two dimensions of psychological involvement in politics can be examined: a cognitive and a predispositional component. The cognitive component refers to knowledge or awareness of the sociopolitical system. Without such knowledge it is difficult to see how individuals could develop long-term attention to politics. The other component is predispositional—the level of interest in politics. Both components will be examined, focusing first on the levels of political interest exhibited by Mexican and Venezuelan workers.

Studies of participation in the industrial democracies have demonstrated a relatively low level of citizen interest in politics.[7] While there is evidence of increased interest among younger generations, interest still remains quite low in absolute terms.[8] The implications of these findings for democratic theory have been fully explicated in the ongoing debate between theorists of elite democracy and its critics.[9]

One would expect workers in both polities to exhibit minimal political interest but levels of interest to be higher in democratic Venezuela than in authoritarian Mexico. The data analysis shows that levels of political interest are low among workers in both countries. As shown in table 11, a substantial majority of workers in both countries exhibit little or no interest in discussing or following political events. In fact, levels of political interest are substantially less in both countries than levels reported for the U.S. populace. It is instructive to compare these findings with those reported for a U.S. working-class sample interviewed in 1976 (figure 1). U.S. workers appear to be far more attentive to politics than either Venezuelan or Mexican workers interviewed for this study.[10] Thus, the data provide evidence of very limited political interest in the case of Venezuelan and Mexican workers.

Table 11. Political Interest among Mexican and Venezuelan
Workers

	Mexico		Venezuela	
	Regularly/ Frequently %	Almost Never/ Once in a While %	Regularly/ Frequently %	Almost Never/ Once in a While %
Discuss politics at home	20.6	79.4	16.6	82.4
Discuss politics at work	20.0	80.0	9.9	90.1
Read political news	34.8	65.2	34.0	66.0
Watch news on TV/radio	37.4	62.6	33.8	66.2

Contrary to expectations, the study found Mexicans to be slightly more interested in politics than Venezuelan workers (table 11). The differences are small except for one item. That item refers to the discussion of politics at work. Only 9.9 percent of the Venezuelans engage in such activity. Perhaps, the partisan and ideological diversity of the Venezuelan work force leads to avoidance of discussion of politics on the job. By contrast, no such avoidance behavior appears to be operative on the job in Mexico's one party dominant polity.

To assess political knowledge, respondents were asked an array of questions ranging from the name of the immediate past president to more esoteric subjects, such as identifying the major national export or estimating the size of the national population. Six items were used for both countries and a six-point index was constructed. The mean score for the Venezuelan national sample was 5.2 items correct (standard deviation = .74); for the Mexican sample, the mean number identified correctly was 5.1 (standard deviation = .5l). Certainly, these results show an awareness of the sociopolitical environment in which workers operate.

These data are consistent with additional data to be presented in later chapters that show these workers to be politically sophisticated. These workers are not cognitively incapable of attention to politics. Still, few workers are disposed to follow current events or to discuss

Figure 1. Interest in Politics, by Occupational Level and Employment Status among Workers in the United States

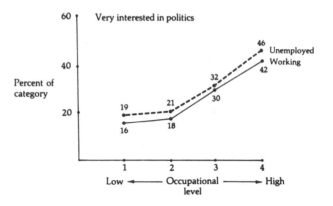

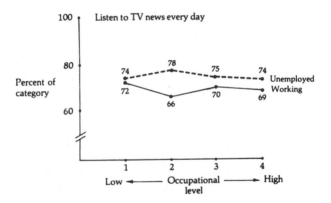

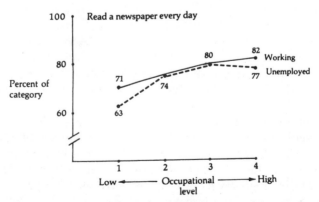

Reprinted from Kay Lehman Schlozman and Sidney Verba, *Injury to Insult: Unemployment, Class, and Political Response* (Cambridge: Harvard Univ. Press, 1979, 243, by permission of Harvard University Press.

politics. Politics is perceived as remote from their daily lives. Thus, their psychological involvement is limited to awareness of the political environment but with little corresponding interest. Low levels of interest in politics are consistent with the ideal type of controlled political mobilization as outlined in chapter 1.

Let us turn to an issue-based motivation, *concientización*. Workers are not likely to mobilize in defense of working-class interests unless they are aware of distinct interests that need to be articulated through the political process. If workers believe that their interests are protected by higher social classes or by the state, then they have little reason to mobilize politically. Therefore, working-class mobilization might be controlled by inculcating beliefs in a benevolent state or bourgeoisie. Conversely, autonomous mobilization by the working class requires an awareness of antagonistic class interests. The next point to consider is how Venezuelan and Mexican workers who were interviewed perceive the bourgeoisie and the state.

First we examine the workers' attitudes toward management. Table 12 reports the percentage of workers in each work setting who expressed accommodative attitudes toward management. The most striking finding is the relatively low percentage of workers *in both countries and in every type of work setting* that expressed favorable attitudes toward management. On almost all indicators, fewer than a majority of workers in each setting expressed an accommodative attitude toward management. The only noticeable exceptions are the substantial number of nonunionized workers and workers in scattered union settings who linked worker welfare with company profits and who expressed satisfaction with company salaries (table 13). But the general trend is toward dissatisfaction.

Similarly, neither Mexican nor Venezuelan workers believe that working-class interests are well served by political elites. In both countries most workers believe that their political leadership pays little attention to workers. Fully 71.8 percent of the Mexicans indicated that their government paid little or no attention to workers. The percentage of Venezuelan workers who expressed this opinion is 82.8 percent. Later on, the data will show that these workers are also dissatisfied with recent government performance.

In sum, these workers tend to perceive antagonistic interests with the bourgeoisie and with the state, indicating relatively high levels of *concientización*. However, as has been seen, high levels of *concientización* do not coexist with high levels of support for the left or of political interest. Nor are high levels of political activism found among these workers, as will be shown next.

Table 12. Indicators of Accommodative Attitudes toward Management

Percentage favorable to management	Mexico					Venezuela				
	Nonunionized/Nonstrategic Industries	Unionized				Nonunionized/Nonstrategic Industries	Unionized			
		Nonstrategic Industries		Strategic Industries			Nonstrategic Industries		Strategic Industries	
		Incorp.ᵃ	Auto.	Incorp.	Auto.		Incorp.	Auto.	Incorp.	Auto.
General fairness of workers' salaries	49.0%	35.0%	47.0%	37.0%	25.0%	25.9%	36.0%	31.0%	52.5%	47.5%
N =	(100)	(100)	(100)	(100)	(100)	(85)	(100)	(100)	(99)	(99)
Employer concern for workers	41.0%	17.0%	36.0%	38.0%	24.0%	9.2%	7.0%	17.3%	25.3%	31.4%
N =	(100)	(100)	(100)	(100)	(100)	(85)	(100)	(98)	(99)	(99)
Fairness of management salaries	16.0%	9.0%	17.0%	22.0%	14.0%	3.6%	13.0%	24.5%	31.6%	23.5%
N =	(100)	(100)	(100)	(100)	(100)	(84)	(100)	(94)	(98)	(98)
Satisfaction with company salaries	54.0%	35.4%	67.0%	54.0%	38.0%	43.5%	54.0%	48.0%	30.8%	31.4%
N =	(100)	(99)	(100)	(100)	(100)	(85)	(100)	(98)	(99)	(99)
Linkage of worker welfare to company profits	59.0%	49.0%	74.0%	18.0%	31.6%	33.8%	30.9%	45.6%	43.2%	43.6%
N =	(100)	(98)	(100)	(100).	(95)	(74)	(97)	(90)	(95)	(94)

ᵃIncorp. = Incorprated union; Auto. = Autonomous union

Previous research has demonstrated in a variety of political contexts that political participation is multidimensional. There are a variety of ways by which citizens may be politically active. Activism in a particular mode does not necessarily imply activism in other modes. What is rather remarkable is that functionally equivalent modes of conventional political activity have been empirically uncovered in a variety of political systems.[11] However, there is evidence that the political environment can alter modal structures most commonly encountered.

In a seven-nation study, Verba, Nie, and Kim found functionally equivalent modes of participation in all countries except Yugoslavia. Using the statistical technique of factor analysis, they identified four equivalent modes in all the competitive polities: voting, campaign activism, communal activism, and particularized contacting of public officials.[12]

Empirical studies of political participation in Latin America have generally confirmed the cross-national functional equivalence of the conventional modes reported in the Verba and associates' studies.[13] Still there is ample evidence that *the political environment can affect the availability of these modes.* Not surprisingly, studies in nonelectoral polities do not find a voting or campaign activism dimension. Electoral modes are simply nonexistent. However, studies conducted while Ecuador and Peru were ruled by military dictatorships show that citizens in these countries did use nonelectoral modes, such as communal activity and particularized contacting.[14] These cases illustrate that even in exclusionary regimes political activity involving little or no collective mobilization might be tolerated.

Citizens tend to be more active in some modes of participation than in others. Those modes that impose fewer costs in terms of time, energy, and money tend to attract more participants than do the more "costly" modes. Thus, empirical studies have consistently found voting to be a more popular mode than more demanding activities, such as campaign work, community problem solving, or protest. While there is considerable cross-national variation in voting turnout, voting tends universally to be the activity in which citizens most frequently engage. Verba, Nie, and Kim found that in their six democratic nations virtually all of their indicators of voting participation yielded percentages above 50 percent (the highest being 96 percent in Austrian national elections), while indicators of other modes were substantially lower in all nations.[15]

Empirical studies from Latin America have generally found conventional participation to be in the same range as reported in the early industrializing nations. As found elsewhere, voting is the most common activity. More demanding activities attract fewer participants. One of the more intriguing findings from Latin America is that in some contexts levels of particularized contacting and communal activism are often higher than the levels generally found in the industrial nations of the first world.[16] Conditions of poverty and resource scarcity in Latin America explain the difference. These conditions force the poor to seek greater government assistance and to seek their own collective solutions when government assistance is not forthcoming.[17]

Studies conducted in advanced industrial nations show that few citizens engage in unconventional political activities outside the institutionalized electoral system.[18] This is not to say that outbreaks of protest activities and even of extreme forms of unconventional participation do not periodically occur. Clearly, such phenomena do occur and occur more frequently in some political contexts than in others.[19] The same pattern seems to hold in Latin America. Despite Latin America's reputation for political violence, empirical studies have uncovered little evidence of widespread unconventional political participation in the region even among deprived lower-class populations. Wayne Cornelius, for example, found that only 2 percent of his sample of urban squatters in Mexico City had ever participated in a protest meeting or demonstration.[20] Low citizen involvement does not mean that periodic outbreaks of protest will not occur among aggrieved groups at various times;[21] but except in revolutionary situations, wide-scale involvement in protest activities is generally muted.

As Verba, Nie, and Kim correctly note, caution must be exercised in making cross-national comparisons of levels of participation. Lack of equivalence in survey items and in response formats creates problems. Similar activities may vary considerably in difficulty for participants. For example, the act of voting might be considerably more difficult in some locales than in others due to variations in registration procedures and accessibility of the polls. In using survey data on voting, the analyst must also be cautious about possible overreporting by nonvoters.[22] Care must also be taken in interpreting cross-national differences in frequency of participation in other modes. Are differences due to different sampling techniques, to compositional differences in the makeup of the samples, or to regime effects?

As reported in Appendix C, both Venezuelan and Mexican workers utilize multiple modes of political participation. Here the interest is in examining the extent to which workers utilize various modes of political activity. One presumes that under conditions of controlled mobilization, workers would engage in periodic voting and relatively

Table 13. Reported Voting in Recent Elections

		Voted (%)	Did not vote (%)
1970 Presidential race:	Mexico	80.3	19.7
1973 Presidential race:	Venezuela	93.5	6.5
1976 Presidential race:	Mexico	82.6	17.4
1978 Presidential race:	Venezuela	95.2	4.8
1979 Legislative race:	Mexico	84.0	16.0
1979 Municipal race:	Venezuela	62.2	37.4

Note: Individuals ineligible because of age were excluded.

little else. In particular, one would expect to find low levels of political involvement in demanding modes of political participation, such as political protest or campaign activity that requires a high level of political mobilization. To complete the picture, I shall also examine worker involvement in contacting public officials and communal activity. The latter are political activities that elites might tolerate and even encourage because they do involve limited demands on scarce resources by small groups rather than demands for fundamental changes in resource allocation.

First, levels of voting are examined. Consistent with all past studies, voting is the political activity in which these Venezuelan and Mexican workers most frequently engage. Even if inflated by over-reporting, a substantial majority appears to be fairly regular voters (see table 13).

In presidential elections Venezuelan workers are more likely to participate than Mexican workers. Indeed, the percentages for Venezuelan workers rank higher than all countries that were examined by Verba, Nie, and Kim, except Austria.[23] The explanation cannot be entirely attributed to more rigorous enforcement of compulsory voting laws in Venezuela than in Mexico. In both countries enforcement is lax. Still, these laws no doubt increase voting turnout beyond what it would normally be.[24]

But there are other explanatory factors as well. Meaningful competition between Venezuela's two major parties provides greater incentive for voting than Mexico's one-party system. Proportional representation in national, state, and municipal legislative bodies provides minor parties with an incentive to turn out voters. With the exception since 1978 of elections for municipal councils, legislative elections occur simultaneously with presidential elections.[25] In the two presidential elections reported in table 13, there was no comparable system of proportional representation in Mexico to stimulate greater partisan mobilization by minor parties.[26] Finally, otherwise cynical Venezuelans express pride in their electoral system. This pride might generate further motivation for voting. No such motivation is found among Mexicans about their electoral system.[27]

A different picture develops for the 1979 elections—legislative races in Mexico, municipal races in Venezuela. As shown in table 13, participation was significantly less among Venezuelan workers. Some unique circumstances might explain these results. In 1978 the Organic Law of the Municipalities was passed. This law introduced several reforms to open up the political process at the local level. In order to provide for greater visibility, municipal elections were to be held at different times from national and state elections. For the first time since the overthrow of the Pérez Jiménez dictatorship in 1958, Venezuelans could select their local representatives without the distraction of national elections.[28] The effect of separating local elections from national and state elections, however, may have been to remove an important stimulus to voting for local offices. The data show a sharp drop-off in voting in the 1979 elections.

In general, both Venezuelan and Mexican workers tend to be regular voters. If there is controlled mobilization, one would not expect political participation to extend to more demanding modes that would indicate more intense political mobilization. To assess participation in demanding forms of participation, I shall examine levels of campaign activism and protest.

Three items, as reported in Appendix C, loaded on the campaign-activism factor for both national samples. These items are frequency of attending campaign rallies, of discussion of politics in one's organizations, and of working for candidates. The data in table 14 show that few workers in either polity participate in campaign activities with any regularity.[29] This finding is consistent with the study's analysis of political interest. Campaign activity is demanding of one's time and energy; hence, it is not likely to appeal to the politically disinterested. These findings are consistent with Verba, Nie, and Kim's findings that also show relatively few campaign participants in the countries used in their sample.[30]

The data show only one striking difference between the two samples. Mexicans are significantly more likely to participate in campaign rallies. Perhaps, this difference is related to the increasing use of Madison Avenue–style campaigning in Venezuela. Robert O'Connor

Table 14. Campaign Activism among Mexican and Venezuelan Workers

	Mexico		Venezuela	
	Regularly/ Frequently	Once in a While/ Never	Regularly/ Frequently	Once in a While/ Never
Participate in campaign rallies	17.2%	82.6%	7.7%	92.3%
N	(86)	(413)	(40)	(475)
Participate in election campaigns	9.6%	90.4%	6.9%	93.1%
N	(48)	(452)	(36)	(481)
Discuss politics in organizations	11.0%	89.0%	12.0%	88.0%
N	(55)	(445)	(62)	(452)

provides some interesting insight into the character of the 1978 presidential campaign.

During the 1978 election campaign the sophistication and variety of televised political communication were truly remarkable. Anyone watching Venevision, one of the two national commercial networks, on November 26, 1978—a typical evening late in the campaign—was exposed to forty-one political advertisements between 8:00 P.M. and 11:15 P.M. Each of the eleven advertising breaks or "sets" also included an announcement from the Supreme Electoral Council with instructions on the mechanics of voting. The forty-one political advertisements, each lasting between fifteen seconds and five minutes, and the eleven Supreme Electoral Council messages were interspersed among the many advertisements for commercial products. In addition, the news and interview shows with political guests conveyed political messages. Even the casual viewer of Venezuelan television during the campaign could not have avoided encountering hundreds of political messages.[31]

The effect of increased use of television might be decreased face-to-face campaigning in Venezuela if the experience of other countries is a guide. Even if rallies remain as common since the advent of television, participation may have dropped off if potential participants opt for television coverage in lieu of actual participation. By contrast, face-to-face campaigning is still utilized extensively in Mexico even by the PRI presidential candidate as a way to mobilize system support.

These arguments should not be pushed too far, however, as face-to-face campaigning is still extensively used in Venezuela, as in Mexico, and Mexican candidates also use the mass media.[32]

Levels of political protest are next examined. There is a variety of forms that unconventional participation might take outside the institutionalized electoral system. Edward Muller, for example, includes in his measure of aggressive political participation illegal strikes, refusal to pay taxes, seizure of buildings, willingness to fight police and demonstrators, and use of violence against the government.[33] Because of the sensitivities of the marketing research firms that were contracted for these surveys, the more extreme forms of unconventional participation, such as those used by Muller, were not attempted. Only involvement in legal protest demonstrations was utilized.

The number of workers who report participation in a legal demonstration is very small for both national samples. Only 2.6 percent of Mexican workers and 6.5 percent of Venezuelan workers indicated that they had participated in a legal demonstration. It seems highly unlikely that the percentages would be higher for more "aggressive" or violent forms of participation. It is safe to assume that occurrence of all forms of unconventional participation is very low among the workers interviewed in 1979 and 1980. Furthermore, the number of strikes carried out by the unions in which these workers were affiliated is very low (chapter 2).

Next, the levels of communal activism and particularized contacting will be studied. The investigation of communal activism was limited to only one type of community problem-solving activity: membership in formal community organizations. Community problem solving can take place informally as well. In general, the data in table 15 show that few workers in either country are members of these organizations, at least the ones examined. The data show far less community-oriented participation than often reported for lower-class populations in Latin America. For example, one study of six squatter settlements in Lima found that 73 percent of the residents "had cooperated with other residents in some community improvement activity."[34]

Workers in this sample might have been less active in this mode because of greater economic security and access to government and union benefits than those enjoyed by more marginal peasant and urban squatter populations. These workers can generally secure, through their own personal resources or by access to government or union services, the goods and services that marginal groups must

Table 15. Communal Activism among Mexican and Venezuelan
          Workers

	Mexico		Venezuela	
	Yes	No	Yes	No
Membership in parents' association	12.4%	87.6%	8.7%	91.3%
N	(62)	(438)	(45)	(473)
Membership in cooperative	2.8%	97.2%	21.8%	78.2%
N	(14)	(486)	(113)	(406)
Membership in neighborhood association	8.6%	91.4%	5.0%	95.0%
N	(43)	(457)	(26)	(492)

frequently secure by cooperative activity. Still, one cannot rule out
the alternative explanation that low participation is simply an artifact
of measuring activism only by formal community activity.

  With one exception Mexicans and Venezuelans appear to be
equally inactive in community organizations. The one exception is the
greater activity of Venezuelans in cooperatives. Venezuelan activity
in this mode perhaps reflects the strength of *cooperativismo* in the
metropolitan Barquisimeto area where many of these unions are located. In Barquisimeto one finds numerous small business, consumer,
credit, and transportation cooperatives.[35]

  The levels of particularized contacting are examined last. Cor-
nelius reports a variation between 6 and 42 percent in the number of
lower-class respondents contacting government in samples from
Mexico, Peru, Brazil, and Chile.[36] In this sample of industrial workers,
only 3 percent of the Mexican sample had contacted public officials.
This figure is considerably less than the 25.8 percent reported by
Cornelius or the 8.3 percent reported for Mexican urban areas in the
Sidney Verba–Gabriel Almond five-nation study.[37] Noticeably more
Venezuelans reported contacting public authorities (11 percent). This
figure falls within the range reported by Cornelius but toward the
lower end of the continuum. This study also found that very few of
these workers utilized services furnished by political parties to low-
income neighborhoods. Only 2.9 percent of the Venezuelans and 0.8
percent of the Mexicans had ever utilized these party favors.

  How might the relative absence of particularized contacting in our sample be explained? Again, the explanation lies with the relatively privileged position of industrial workers when compared to workers mired in the tertiary sector of third-world economies. While these industrial workers enjoy substantially lower incomes than do their counterparts in industrial countries, their income levels usually far exceed those of peasants and urban service sector workers in urban areas. Additionally, they receive a larger share of basic public services.[38] Therefore, industrial workers have less need to petition government. To illustrate this point, workers in this sample can be compared to urban migrants interviewed by Cornelius in Mexico City. A total of 25.8 percent of his sample reported contacting government officials. Not surprisingly, most of these contacts made by urban squatters involved either security of land tenure or water supply. For workers in this sample, these were simply not problems.[39]

One can think of autonomous political mobilization in terms of (1) psychological capacity and (2) collective political action. It is clear that Venezuelan and Mexican workers interviewed for this study exhibit the capacity for autonomous mobilization. They tend to be aware of the political environment and of antagonistic class interests. However, they tend to eschew collective political action and are politically inactive except for periodic voting. Furthermore, electoral support is extended to hegemonic parties rather than to leftist parties that have historically attracted working-class support in Western Europe. In short, Venezuelan and Mexican workers do not challenge hegemonic parties even though they believe that their interests have not been well served by the status quo. The next two chapters will try to provide a better understanding of why this situation exists.

In closing, let us note one other point. The data indicate patterns of controlled mobilization for both Venezuelan and Mexican workers at the behavioral level. Nevertheless, the study found that Venezuelan workers are marginally more likely to engage in elite-challenging behavior than are Mexican workers. This is true for both protest and leftist voting. Here is the first indication that the type of regime affects working-class political mobilization. Elite-challenging participation is more likely to occur in Venezuela's competitive polity than in Mexico's authoritarian, semicompetitive polity.

Chapter Six

Political Control and Participatory Motivations

Two types of political mobilization can occur: external and cognitive.[1] External mobilization results when individuals otherwise lacking motivations to political participation in politics are drawn into participation by interest groups or political parties with which they are aligned.[2] Cognitive mobilization, on the other hand, occurs when individuals participate in politics based on their own long-term motivations.[3] Cognitive mobilization involves two stages: (1) the acquisition of long-term motivations and (2) the conversion of these motivations into specific political action. Typically, cognitive mobilization is self-initiated, while external mobilization is normally guided participation. This chapter focuses on stage 1 of cognitive mobilization, the acquisition of participatory motivations.

Motivations to participate in politics can be issue-based or issue-neutral.[4] Issue-based motivations derive from salient policy issues that capture the public's attention or from more abstract ideologies that stimulate them to political action. This chapter considers worker acquisition of an issue-based motivation, labeled *concientización* or critical consciousness. This motivation ought to be a prerequisite for workers to mobilize autonomously in pursuit of their collective interests. *Concientización* has been defined as "a multifaceted orientation to the social order, rooted in an interpretation of the obvious social differences that exist in capitalist societies. Some workers may see the existing order as an organic, cooperative whole in which various social classes have their roles to fulfill, but in which all classes contribute to the functioning of the greater social whole. By contrast, other workers may see the existing order as a system of domination in which certain social interests prevail in imposing costs on other social groups. Individuals who perceive a system of domination are exhibiting what is herein called critical consciousness."[5]

Motivations to participate can also be issue-neutral. Issue-neutral orientations are generally considered prerequisites for self-initiated participation in democratic polities and are seen as necessary for "participant citizenship."[6] They include such orientations as political efficacy, civic duty, awareness of the relevance of government, and psychological involvement in politics. This chapter focuses on the latter variable also necessary if individuals are to engage in self-directed political activity. Autonomous working-class mobilization is only possible if rank-and-file workers are attentive to the political environment and have some conception of their class interests.

Chapter 5 established that Mexican and Venezuelan workers tend to be fully aware of antagonistic class interests but not particularly involved in politics. This chapter examines whether exposure to alternative mechanisms or agents of control reduces critical consciousness of the established sociopolitical order and attention to politics. Variables considered related to political control are analyzed. These include (1) membership in an incorporated union, (2) loyalty to a hegemonic party, and (3) satisfaction with government performance. Additionally, the extent to which opposition groups are able to foment these motivations among rank-and-file supporters is analyzed. As will be discussed, political control over mobilization involves not only effective cooptation by hegemonic organizations but also enervation of the opposition groups' mobilizational capabilities.

Last, relationships between relevant personal characteristics (socioeconomic status and age) and psychological involvement in politics are explored to determine whether personal resources lead Venezuelan and Mexican workers toward attention to politics. Incapacity to convert personal resources into increased psychological involvement in politics would constitute further evidence of effective political control over working-class potential for cognitive mobilization. Before turning to data analysis, two theoretical issues will be discussed: (1) how various control mechanisms might affect the capacity of workers to acquire participatory motivations and (2) how the capacity of workers to convert personal resources into psychological involvement in politics might be conditioned by the political environment.

Obreros concientizados by definition perceive potential conflict between their interests and those of higher classes and of political elites. To prevent the emergence of such workers, hegemonic parties and incorporated unions may try to preempt negative images by identifying closely with the lower classes. Hegemonic organizations, as found in Venezuela and Mexico, identify with reform or revolutionary traditions and promise to continue such traditions. The underlying message to the lower classes is that the existing state-capitalist state serves the interests of all social classes comprising the national community. This message is reinforced by distribution of national benefits and services to clientele groups. Of course, dominant parties, particularly their labor sector, and incorporated unions occasionally criticize privileged groups and advocate reform.[7] However, the rhetoric and proposed reforms are generally designed to strengthen social pacts with labor and, thereby, to preempt radical movements.[8] By identifying with lower-class interests, hegemonic organizations can help, nevertheless, to forestall workers from becoming critical of the existing order.

In like manner, hegemonic parties and incorporated unions might discourage workers from psychological involvement in politics. If workers believe their interests are well protected by hegemonic organizations, they might believe that there is little benefit to be gained from political involvement. In addition, hierarchical and centralized patterns of authority in these organizations might create difficulties in gaining access to important officials (see chapter 4) and, thereby, discourage active political interest.

Finally, psychological motivations for cognitive mobilization could be weakened by satisfaction with the performance of incumbent government. Satisfied workers would have reason to believe that their interests are well served by the existing state-capitalist order and that there is little need to devote attention to the world of politics, with trusted leaders and institutions already serving their interests. In sum, performance satisfaction might prevent the emergence of a critically conscious, politically attentive working class.

Control mechanisms examined so far discourage workers from developing long-term motivations associated with political participation. Another facet of political control also deserves examination. Political control over mobilization can also be asserted by weakening opposition groups as agents of cognitive mobilization (Chapter 1). Lacking patronage resources, they must frequently try to promote self-generated political activity by instilling in their members consciousness of group interests and attention to the political universe.

Several factors might explain why opposition groups fail as agents of cognitive mobilization. These groups may lack resources for extensive political resocialization of rank-and-file members. Additionally, access to the mass media and educational institutions might be monopolized by hegemonic institutions. Finally, opposition groups could be weakened by an ineffective or coopted leadership more interested in self-gain than in professed political objectives.[9]

Evelyne Stephens and John Stephens have shown that leftist organizations do occasionally serve as vehicles for cognitive mobilization of the working class in third-world capitalist regimes. They make clear how this phenomenon occurred in the case of Michael Manley's People's National party in Jamaica. They assert:

During the 1970s, Jamaica achieved considerable prominence on the international level through forceful advocacy of the New International Economic Order and because of externally visible repercussions from internal social and economic changes. Both internationally and nationally, the importance of ideological programmatic, as opposed to the previous nonprogrammatic, clientelist politics increased. The move toward ideological politics and the related development of a mass party formed an integral part of the People's National Party's (PNP) democratic socialist development project. Making a deliberate attempt to generate consensus among the party leadership on the new development model and to educate the rank and file about contemplated changes was a necessary feature, insofar as the political strategy for the pursuit of this path required the buildup of a programmatic mass party and the replacement of patronage-based political loyalties with ideologically-based loyalties.[10]

This chapter investigates the extent to which leftist parties and autonomous unions in Mexico and Venezuela foment *concientización* and psychological involvement in politics. A comparison of the Venezuelan and Mexican cases is particularly interesting because of the contrasting electoral settings, with Venezuela providing a more competitive electoral system. Thus, one can study the impact of the larger electoral setting on the capacity of opposition groups to enhance cognitive mobilization among the working class.

Another facet of political control is manifested in the capacity of citizens to convert personal resources into psychological involvement in politics. In the abstract there are a number of reasons why personal characteristics, in particular age and socioeconomic status, might lead to greater psychological involvement in politics. Possession of socioeconomic resources, including education, can easily be imagined to stimulate interest in politics as well as the belief that one can be effective politically. Economic security, working in an intellectually stimulating occupation, or possessing analytical skills imparted by education should facilitate psychological attraction to and involvement in the political process. The data from the Verba, Nie, and Kim seven-nation survey support this interpretation. In all seven countries, those who have most socioeconomic resources consistently exhibit high psychological involvement in politics.[11] Similarly, age might enhance attention to politics; greater maturity may increase one's attention to and psychological involvement in politics.

But does conversion of personal resources into psychological involvement in politics occur irrespective of the wider political context? It is plausible that potentially capable citizens might see little reason to be attentive to politics if opportunities to influence policies and decisions are minimal. If the political context affects motivations in this manner, more conversion of personal resources into psychological involvement in politics should occur among Venezuelan than among Mexican workers. This hypothesis provides a partial test of whether or not the conversion of personal resources into political attention is influenced by the wider political context.

The data analysis will involve an examination of (1) how the type of union membership influences the participatory motivations of Venezuelan and Mexican workers in this sample, (2) how partisanship is related to participatory motivations, (3) how evaluations of incumbent performance are related to these motivations, and (4) the extent to which Mexican and Venezuelan workers convert personal resources into increased psychological involvement in politics.

Are workers belonging to incorporated unions less likely to acquire motivations to participate than are nonunionized workers and workers belonging to autonomous unions? Conversely, does membership in an autonomous union help workers to develop participatory motivations? The first point to consider is the extent to which the acquisition of *concientización* by industrial workers in this sample was contingent on the type of union to which they belonged.

In table 16 standardized regression coefficients (betas) that measure the impact of type of union membership on *concientización* are reported.[12] It is readily apparent that neither membership in an incorporated nor in an autonomous union is related significantly to levels of *concientización*. Whether workers in this sample are critical of the existing sociopolitical order has little to do with the type of union (incorporated versus autonomous) with which they are affiliated.

These conclusions are supported by the multiple classification analyses reported in figure 2. Here, the type of union is disaggregated according to location in either a strategic or a nonstrategic industry (see chapter 1). In this analysis the sample of nonunionized workers can be considered a control group with which to compare samples of unionized workers. A quasi-experimental design is also approximated by adjusting the deviations from the grand mean of the dependent variable for socioeconomic status and age. Thereby, possible sources of confounding variation can be controlled in analyzing the effects of

Figure 2. Union Membership and Level of *Concientización*

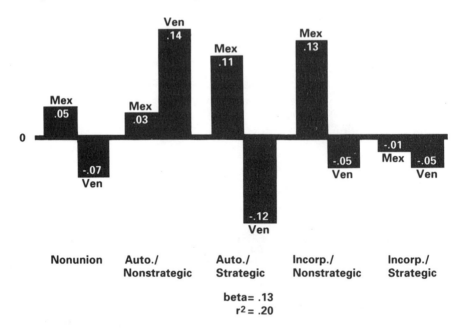

beta= .13
r^2 = .20

Note: Multiple Classification Analysis, controlling for socioeconomic status, age, and partisanship.

union membership on *concientización*. The results of the multiple classification analysis also demonstrate that unions with ties to hegemonic parties do not inhibit rank-and-file workers from becoming critical of the existing socioeconomic order. Workers are likely to exhibit similar levels of *concientización* regardless of the type of work setting in which they are located. This is shown by the weak beta of .13 as well as by the patterns of deviations reported in figure 2.

Next, this study considers how union incorporation affects the propensity of workers to become attentive to national politics. The results in table 16 show that the type of union with which Venezuelan and Mexican workers are affiliated has little effect on attention to politics. There are modest relationships in the expected direction for Mexican workers, with workers in incorporated unions being less attentive to politics and workers in autonomous unions more attentive to politics. However, these relationships are too modest to conclude

Table 16. Labor Unions and the Acquisition of Motivations to
Participate: Regression Analyses

	Beta Coefficient	
	Psychological Involvement in Politics	*Concientización*
Mexico		
Membership in		
incorporated union	−.11	−.03
autonomous union	.08	−.03
r² change	.03[a]	.00
Venezuela		
Membership in		
incorporated union	.03	.04
autonomous union	−.03	.06
r² change	.00	.00

Note: Socioeconomic status, age, partisanship, and performance evaluation are controlled. In analyzing determinants of psychological involvement in politics, *concientización* is controlled.

[a]Significant at the .01 level.

that union incorporation accounts well for low levels of attention to national politics on the part of Mexican workers.

The Multiple Classification Analyses (MCA) reported in figure 3 provide a more complete picture of how Mexican and Venezuelan unions affect the attentiveness of workers to the world of politics. The MCA analysis for Venezuelan workers (figure 4) helps to account for the previous findings of weak relationships between membership in an incorporated or an autonomous union and psychological involvement in politics. The determining factor in whether or not Venezuelan workers become attentive to politics is not whether they belong to an incorporated or an autonomous union but whether or not they belong to a union located in a strategic industry (figure 3). Unionized workers in Venezuela's oil fields are likely to become more psychologically involved in politics than are unionized workers in nonstrategic industries. This relationship holds up for oil workers in both autonomous and incorporated unions.

These findings suggest that the type and size of the enterprise in which Venezuelan workers are employed determines in part whether they become attentive to politics. Workers in larger, more capital-intensive industries may be more aware of their collective capability

Figure 3. Union Membership and Psychological Involvement in
          Politics

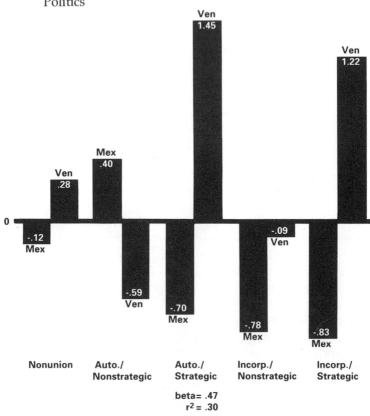

Note: Multiple Classification Analysis, controlling for socioeconomic status, age, and
partisanship.

to capture the attention of state authorities. Thus, they have more
incentive to pay attention to national politics than do workers in nonstrategic industries. In the case of Venezuelan oil workers, one should
also recognize that these workers are employed in a nationalized industry. Public sector employment may well have heightened their
attention to national politics.

This same relationship between employment in a strategic industry and psychological involvement in politics does *not* hold up for
Mexican workers.[13] Workers in strategic Mexican industries exhibited
low levels of psychological involvement in politics (figure 3). The
Mexican findings suggest that workers in strategic industries do not

inevitably believe that they can gain the attention of state authorities. If the political system is relatively closed, as in Mexico, workers in strategic industries may believe that the state cannot be compelled to act on their behalf.

What is striking about the Mexican data (figure 3) is that the level of psychological involvement in politics in three out of four union subsamples is lower than for the nonunionized subsample. The tentative conclusion to be drawn is that Mexican unions, whether incorporated or autonomous, tend to discourage workers from attention to the world of politics. As such, both incorporated and autonomous unions appear to blunt cognitive mobilization by industrial workers. Unions in Mexico may serve a control function similar to that observed for grass-roots organizations in other authoritarian regimes. They divert attention from the national scene by focusing attention at the local level.[14]

In sum, data analysis provides very little, if any, support for the proposition that corporatist-interest intermediation inhibits workers from acquiring participatory motivations. Likewise, union autonomy does not facilitate acquisition of such motivations. Union linkages to hegemonic parties in Venezuela and Mexico, therefore, cannot adequately account for the relative absence of cognitive mobilization by the industrial workers interviewed for this study.

The findings do suggest, nevertheless, that unions in Venezuela and Mexico are significant agents for political socialization. Mexican unions, with one exception, tend to inhibit worker attention to politics. On the other hand, unionized workers in the Venezuelan oil fields are likely to be politically attentive. The tradition of political activism in the Venezuelan oil fields[15] might account in part for this finding. However, there is no evidence that unions in this industry promote a critically conscious work force. The same is true for all unions examined for the study, suggesting that Venezuelan and Mexican unions are unlikely to promote any type of radical political action.

The next point to examine is how partisanship affects the acquisition of participatory motivations. First, one must assess how partisanship is related to levels of *concientización* exhibited by Venezuelan and Mexican workers. Table 17 shows beta coefficients for hegemonic and leftist partisanship. For both samples partisanship exerts a stronger influence on *concientización* than does type of union membership (compare table 16 with table 17). It is particularly striking to note that hegemonic partisanship is related differently to *concientización* in Venezuela than in Mexico. Partisans of Mexico's PRI are significantly less critical of the existing order than are other Mexican workers (beta = −.18, table 17). By contrast, partisans of AD and COPEI in Venezuela tend to be slightly more critically conscious than other workers (beta = +.05, table 17). How might these differences be explained? It may be that Venezuelan workers are more exposed to a wider variety of critical perspectives in election campaigns than are Mexican workers. The Venezuelan electoral context provides for more open discussion of issues and criticism of the incumbent performance than does Mexico's semicompetitive electoral system. Thus, it is more difficult for hegemonic parties in Venezuela to generate contentment with the status quo among industrial workers.

Table 17 shows that *concientización* is significantly higher among leftist workers than among other workers. This finding is to be expected, but it underscores the importance of leftist partisanship for the formation of a critically conscious industrial work force. Again, it is clear that leftist partisanship is a far more important determinant of *concientización* than is affiliation with an autonomous union.

In the Multiple Classification Analysis reported in figure 4, the deviations of various subsamples of Venezuelan and Mexican partisans from the mean on the *concientización* scale are reported. Here, deviations have not been adjusted for the performance evaluation variable as was done in the regression analysis.[16] Consequently, the differences between partisan subsamples are greater than they appear in the regression analysis (table 17).

Contrasts between Venezuelan and Mexican workers become more apparent in the MCA analysis. The PRI appears to be more effective than AD and COPEI in Venezuela in preventing working-class supporters from becoming critical of the existing order. Furthermore, leftist workers in Venezuela are more critical than are leftist workers in Mexico. Thus, the data indicate that the larger electoral context affects the capability of political parties to suppress or promote working-class *concientización*. Limited competition increases the likelihood that hegemonic parties will suppress *concientización* among working-class supporters and that leftist parties will be less successful in developing *obreros concientizados*.

Let us now turn to an analysis of the relationship between partisanship and psychological involvement in politics. The data analysis in table 17 shows that partisans of both hegemonic parties and of the left in Venezuela are more likely to be attentive to politics than are nonpartisans. These results are consistent with findings from other competitive electoral systems that show nonpartisans to be disinterested in politics.[17] Interestingly, no such relationship is found among Mexican workers in this sample. To the contrary, PRI supporters tend

Table 17. Partisanship and the Acquisition of Motivations to Participate: Regression Analyses

	Beta Coefficient	
	Psychological Involvement in Politics	*Concientización*
Mexico		
Partisanship:		
Hegemonic party	− .06	− .18[a]
Leftist party	.04	.13[a]
r² change	.01	.06[a]
Venezuela		
Partisanship:		
Hegemonic party	.12[a]	.05
Leftist party	.17[a]	.19[a]
r² change	.03[a]	.03[a]

Note: Type of union membership, age, SES, and performance evaluation variables are controlled. In analyzing psychological involvement in politics, *concientización* is controlled.

[a]Significant at the .01 level.

to be slightly less psychologically engaged in politics than other workers (beta = − .06, table 17). In contrast to the Venezuelan results, leftist partisanship produces virtually no increase in political attentiveness among Mexican workers (beta = + .04, table 17). These results suggest that the absence of meaningful partisan competition in Mexico produces a type of disengaged partisanship particularly among supporters of the ruling PRI.

The effects of restricted partisan competition are even more apparent in the Multiple Classification Analysis (figure 5). As before, deviations of partisan groups have not been adjusted for performance satisfaction and *concientización* as in the regression analysis. Neither the opposition parties of the right nor those of the left in Mexico are as capable as the Venezuelan left in sustaining political attentiveness among rank-and-file partisans.[18] Furthermore, the PRI is more likely to restrain attention to politics among its working-class supporters than is AD or COPEI in Venezuela. Clearly, the degree of partisan competition is an important determinant of working-class attentiveness to the political environment. Restricted partisan competition decreases the likelihood that partisanship will generate a politically aware work force.

Satisfaction with the performance of incumbent governments is

Figure 4. Political Party Affiliations as Determinants of *Concientización*

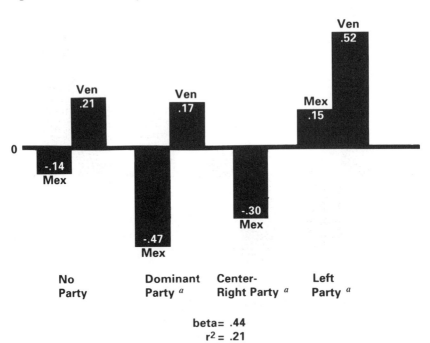

No Party

Dominant Party [a]

Center-Right Party [a]

Left Party [a]

beta= .44
r^2 = .21

Note: Multiple Classification analysis, controlling for age and socioeconomic status.

[a]Dominant Parties: Venezuela, AD and COPEI; Mexico, PRI. Center-Right Parties: Mexico, PAN, PARM, and PDM. Leftist Parties: Venezuela, MAS, MEP, MIR, and PCV; Mexico, PCM, PPS, PST, and PMT.

yet another mechanism that might impede workers from acquiring participatory motivations needed for autonomous mobilization. The analytic task is twofold. First, how are evaluations of incumbent performance related to participatory motivations—namely, psychological involvement in politics and *concientización*. Second, levels of satisfaction with performance must be examined. Obviously, satisfaction with performance does not contribute to control if workers are, in fact, dissatisfied with government performance.

The reader interested in knowing more about technical details about operationalization of performance evaluation is referred to the Appendix. Suffice it to note here that workers were asked to evaluate the performance of the then current national administration and the

Figure 5. Political Party Affiliations as Determinants of Psychological
     Involvement in Politics

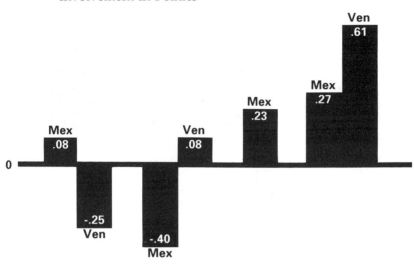

beta= .20
r² = .14

Note: Multiple Classification analysis, controlling for age and socioeconomic status.
     ᵃSee note to figure 4.

previous administration in several policy areas.[19] Factor analysis revealed that Mexican workers structured their evaluations around the
following policy areas: urban services, public education, and economic redistribution. On the other hand, Venezuelan workers structured their evaluations around the presidential administrations of
Carlos Andrés Pérez (1973-78) and Luis Herrera Campins (1978-83).

Table 18 shows that for both samples evaluations of government
performance are more closely related to *concientización* than to psychological involvement in politics. In contrast to relatively strong relationships between *concientización* and performance evaluation, the
relationships between performance evaluation and psychological involvement in politics is quite weak for both samples. However, there
is an indirect relationship between performance satisfaction and psychological involvement in the case of Mexican workers. Performance

Table 18. Performance Evaluation and Motivations to Participate:
Regression Analyses

	Beta Coefficient	
	Psychological Involvement in Politics	Concientización
Mexico		
Evaluation of urban services	−.11[a]	−.23[a]
Evaluation of education	.12[a]	−.12[a]
Evaluation of economic redistribution	.02	.09[a]
Venezuela		
Evaluation of Andrés Pérez	−.01	−.11
Evaluation of Herrera Campins	.06	−.17[a]
r^2 change	.00	.05[a]

Note: Partisanship, type of union membership, SES, and age are controlled.
[a]Significant at the .01 level.

satisfaction tends to lower *concientización*. In turn, low *concientización* leads to lower attention to politics on the part of Mexican workers (table 18).

In sum, if Venezuelan and Mexican workers are satisfied with incumbent performance, they are less likely to become critical of the existing sociopolitical order. Satisfied Mexican workers are also less likely to be attentive to politics so long as they have not developed a critical consciousness. The question then becomes how satisfied were Mexican and Venezuelan workers with government performance at the time of the interviewing in 1979 and 1980.

Workers were asked to evaluate the performance of the incumbent and previous president in the areas of law enforcement, public housing, jobs creation, public transportation, and public education (table 19). Summative indices of performance evaluation for both current and previous presidents were constructed. Each index ranged from 0 to 20, the most favorable evaluation of performance. A mean score below 10, the absolute midpoint on the scale, indicated a negative assessment of performance. Workers in both countries in every type of industry and in every type of union evaluated the performance of both the previous and the then current president negatively. Every mean score reported in table 19 is below the midpoint on the index.

As I have shown elsewhere, that discontent with performance was manifested among both economically privileged and nonprivileged workers alike.[20]

Clearly, political elites in both countries did not impede cognitive mobilization by keeping workers content with government performance. A great deal of discontent was evident among this sector of the working class. Indeed, the relatively high-level *concientización* observed among these workers is, in part, related to discontent with regime performance. As shown elsewhere, preemptive reforms attempted by the Echeverría and López Portillo governments in Mexico failed in their intended effect of regenerating popular support for government policies.[21] The data suggest that the attempted reforms of the Andrés Pérez administration in Venezuela during the seventies also failed in this respect.

The last issue to be addressed is how the larger regime context affects the capacity of workers to convert personal resources into psychological involvement in politics. The research of Verba and others has shown that citizen attention to politics is not shaped entirely by the political environment. To the contrary, socioeconomic status and age have been found to be powerful determinants of psychological involvement in politics. The implications of this research are clear. Demographic changes and improvements in living standards among the lower class could result in a significant increase in the aggregate level of attentiveness to politics. An older, more affluent work force should be more politically attentive. Interestingly, the trend throughout the sixties and seventies in Latin America was toward greater literacy and higher real wages, at least for industrial workers. Accordingly, the work force may have become more politicized, thereby creating problems for the maintenance of political control. While lacking the data to test this proposition, the more restricted hypothesis—that conversion of personal resources into psychological involvement in politics is contingent on the nature of the underlying regime—can be tested.

Table 20 shows that attentiveness to politics among Venezuelan workers is highly contingent on age and socioeconomic status. The level of psychological involvement in politics exhibited by Mexican workers is not contingent on their age or socioeconomic status level. In the case of Mexican workers, primarily the critically conscious are likely to become psychologically involved in politics. In other words, only the more militant Mexican workers pay much attention to politics.

Table 19. Worker Evaluations of the Performance of Recent Presidents

Evaluation of performance	Mexico					Venezuela				
	Nonunionized/ Nonstrategic Industries	Unionized				Nonunionized/ Nonstrategic Industries	Unionized			
		Nonstrategic Industries		Strategic Industries			Nonstrategic Industries		Strategic Industries	
		Incorp.[a]	Auto.	Incorp.	Auto.		Incorp.	Auto.	Incorp.	Auto.
Incumbent president[b]										
mean	7.93	8.03	7.35	7.68	7.26	3.95	4.83	4.49	6.47	4.93
standard deviation	(4.88)	(4.58)	(2.63)	(4.68)	(4.38)	(3.21)	(3.76)	(4.10)	(3.98)	(3.91)
N	(99)	(100)	(100)	(100)	(95)	(83)	(99)	(99)	(94)	(94)
Previous president[b]										
mean	5.76	5.07	5.01	5.13	5.14	4.82	4.99	5.00	7.98	6.71
standard deviation	(5.53)	(4.66)	(2.33)	(3.94)	(4.34)	(4.12)	(3.87)	(4.01)	(5.24)	(5.39)
N	(99)	(100)	(99)	(100)	(97)	(85)	(100)	(100)	(95)	(97)

[a]Incorp. = Incorporated union; Auto. = Autonomous union
[b]Range (0-20)

Table 20. Personal Resources vs. Other Determinants of
Psychological Involvement in Politics: Regression Analyses

	Beta Coefficients	
	Mexico	Venezuela
Issue-based motivations		
1. *Cocientización*	.23[a]	.08
2. Evaluation:		
Urban service (M)		
Andrés Pérez (V)	−.11[a]	−.01
Economic redistribution (M)		
/Herrera Campins (V)	−.02	.05
Education (M)	.12[a]	—
r^2 change	.06[a]	.01
Organization-based motivations		
1. Partisanship		
PRI/AD/COPEI	−.06	.12[a]
Left	.04	.17[a]
2. Union membership		
Incorporated	−.11	.03
Autonomous	.08	−.03
r^2 change	.03[a]	.03[a]
Resource-based motivations		
1. SES	.02	.48[a]
2. Age	−.06	.12[a]
r^2 change	.00	.22
Total r^2	.10	.32

[a]Significant at the .01 level.

The Venezuelan results are consistent with what Verba, Nie, and Kim found in other competitive political systems. The Mexican results are not. Why not in Mexico?

The Mexican political system is obfuscatory and somewhat confusing to all in Mexico, no matter how much income or time they have available or regardless of the analytical skills that might have been developed by formal education. Given the secrecy of the Mexican political system, making sense of what happens is often impossible, even for the educated.[22] Therefore, what would be a politically relevant resource in some contexts is rendered useless in the secretive atmosphere of authoritarian Mexico, where authoritative political information is in short supply and (misleading) rumors are ever present.[23]

In terms of other personal resources, age is weakly but significantly related to psychological involvement in politics in Venezuela (beta = +.12) but not in Mexico. The Venezuelan data resemble data elsewhere in that cognitive involvement in politics seems to grow in response to life-cycle phenomena, with psychological attentiveness to the political process increasing as a function of age until the retirement years. In Mexico that phenomenon cannot take effect because the political system becomes no more comprehensible with the passage of time or with personal maturity.[24]

These findings suggest that political elites in authoritarian polities might be better able to manage the political consequences of rapid socioeconomic transformations than can elites in more democratic polities. However, it should be kept in mind that depoliticization of the lower classes in Mexico's authoritarian polity depends on keeping the masses content with the status quo. By the late seventies, Mexican elites faced new difficulties in generating political support, and these problems have likely magnified in the eighties with Mexico's most severe economic crisis of this century.[25] Furthermore, Mexico's authoritarian polity contains fewer institutionalized electoral channels to absorb political discontent than more competitive polities such as the Venezuelan.

These results show that the political environment shapes in important ways how a working-class population acquires motivations to participate in politics. The political environment can either facilitate the acquisition of motivations to participate or discourage citizens from participation in politics. To the extent that the latter occurs, cognitive mobilization is less likely to occur. Political mobilization is likely to be externally guided and, thereby, controlled by hegemonic organizations.

What is surprising about these results is that corporatist interest intermediation is *not* the key feature of the political environment that inhibits workers from acquiring participatory motivations. Corporatist union structures do not account for weak participatory motivations found among Venezuelan and Mexican workers. Unions matter but not in ways suggested by the literature on corporatism in Latin America. For example, evidence was found that unions in strategic industries in Venezuela foster greater psychological involvement in politics. On the other hand, both incorporated and autonomous unions in Mexico seem to deflect workers' attention from national politics. In no case do the data show that unions in either country promote a politically conscious, militant work force.

The degree of partisan competition shapes working-class participatory motivations far more than do corporatist links between unions and hegemonic parties. Partisans of ruling parties are more likely to pay little attention to politics if they are located in the semicompetitive polity of Mexico rather than in Venezuela's competitive polity. Similarly, "hegemonic partisans" are less likely to be *obreros concientizados* if located in the Mexican political system. In like manner, leftist workers exhibit less psychological involvement in politics and *concientización* if located in the semicompetitive polity of Mexico rather than in the competitive polity of Venezuela.

These results cannot be explained adequately by differences in cognitive sophistication and performance satisfaction between Mexican and Venezuelan workers. Workers in both countries are profoundly skeptical about recent government performance and tend to be politically sophisticated. Furthermore, partisan loyalties do shape participatory motivations in the same manner regardless of the level of political sophistication and of performance satisfaction.[26] The more likely explanation is that meaningful partisan competition sharpens workers' attention to class interests in politics and to the political environment. Thus, cognitive mobilization of the working class becomes more possible in a competitive regime context. Conversely, restricted partisan competition decreases the likelihood of working-class cognitive mobilization as it becomes more difficult for workers to sustain interest in politics and to cognize their interests in the political process.

Chapter 7 considers how the control variables examined in this chapter affect actual political behavior, focusing on voter turnout. Worker involvement in demand-protest activities is not examined because of the infrequency of this type of behavior among industrial workers interviewed for this study.

Political Control and Electoral Mobilization

Chapter 5 presented evidence of controlled political mobilization among Venezuelan and Mexican workers interviewed for this study. These workers tend to engage in little political activity beyond periodic voting. In fact, nonelectoral demand-protest activity is so low as to almost be a constant; therefore, it is not feasible to analyze empirically why these formal sector workers do not protest via nonelectoral means. However, one can analyze why these workers choose to vote in elections and why they tend to support hegemonic parties rather than leftist parties. These main questions are addressed in this and the following chapters. In this chapter the focus is on how workers are mobilized to vote.

As discussed earlier, individuals come to participate in politics as a consequence of either external or cognitive mobilization. Similarly, voters are mobilized either by internalized motivations and resources or through ties to external organizations. The capacity of a regime to control and manipulate voting turnout is clearly related to the way voters are mobilized. External mobilization of voters facilitates control. Conversely, cognitive mobilization of voters lessens the capacity of the regime to manipulate voting turnout. If voting is largely guided by parties and interest groups, hegemonic parties should benefit because they, along with incorporated interest groups, should be able to turn out more voters than opposition parties and interest groups. Furthermore, external mobilization of voters protects ruling parties from a large "floating vote" that could threaten their hegemony. Conversely, cognitive mobilization makes possible an increase in "floating voters" that could strengthen opposition parties.

Previous studies of working-class politics in Mexico and Venezuela have emphasized the capacity of hegemonic parties and incorporated unions to turn out voters. Presumably, workers are often enticed to the polls via exchange relations established by clientelist networks.[1] Sometimes implicit is the notion that the lower classes lack the incentive and sophistication for active participation without these exchange networks. Similarly, the research of Verba, Nie, and Kim suggests that the working class generally lacks the motivation and capacity for active voting unless externally mobilized.[2] Thus, previous research leads one to expect that workers vote in Mexico and Venezuela primarily as a result of external mobilization rather than as a consequence of their motivations or personal resources.

The extent to which organizations mobilize individual workers to vote indicates the degree of externally guided political activation. This, in turn, facilitates controlled political mobilization. Conversely, the extent to which individuals are mobilized as a consequence of acquiring motivations and resources indicates the degree of cognitive or self-directed mobilization. The degree to which electoral mobilization is guided or self-directed will be examined empirically. Then the external mobilizing capability of hegemonic and opposition organizations will be compared.

Mexican workers will be considered first. Are individual Mexican laborers mobilized to vote primarily through organizational affiliations or through personal resources and motivations? The answer to this question is made possible by the use of a scale to measure strength of institutional affiliation. This scale is similar to the one used by Verba, Nie, and Kim in their classic seven-nation study (see Appendix B). Regressing this scale and various measures of resources and motivations on a scale of voting participation produces the results reported in tables 21 and 22. Additionally, regression coefficients for each type of labor union (autonomous versus incorporated) and each type of partisanship (hegemonic or leftist party) are presented.[3]

The data show clearly that workers in the Mexican sample vote primarily as a consequence of external mobilization, not as a consequence of previously acquired participatory motivations or personal resources (table 21). The strongest determinant of voting participation for Mexican workers is strength of institutional affiliation (beta = + .18)[4] and, in particular, affiliation with the PRI (beta = + .22). There is virtually no evidence that workers who have acquired motivations to participate or who possess facilitating resources are any more prone to vote than workers lacking in motivations or resources. To the contrary, there is some evidence that Mexican workers who have acquired participatory motivations or personal resources are *less* likely to vote than other workers. For example, issue-based motivations tend to slightly decrease voting by workers in Mexico. In fact, some discontented workers engage in what might be called "protest abstention." Table 21 shows that critically conscious workers (beta = − .09) and those dissatisfied with urban services (beta = − .14) are less likely to participate in elections. Some discontented workers apparently see more utility in abstention than in voting for opposition parties in Mexico's one-party dominant system.[5] Likewise, there is little evidence that workers attentive to politics participate any more actively in Mexican elections than the less attentive (beta = −.01).

Nor does the availability of personal resources necessarily make voting more likely in Mexico. Age is weakly related to voting frequency (beta = +.10). But notice that socioeconomic status is negatively associated with voting (beta = −.14). In sum, *Mexican workers are more likely to vote as a consequence of external mobilization* rather than as a result of either cognitive mobilization or personal resources. Clearly, these results indicate that the mobilization of individual voters in Mexico is external, subject to control, and not a result of individual motivations.

How about Venezuelan workers? Are they mobilized to vote primarily through organizational affiliation or through personally acquired resources and motivations? The data in table 22 show that external mobilization in Venezuela is not the dominant factor as in Mexico. External mobilization of voters does occur in Venezuela (beta = +.12 for strength of institutional identification).[6] However, voting is also a consequence of resources and cognitive mobilization. Age, for example, is a much stronger determinant of voting than is institutional affiliation (beta = +.31 for age; beta = +.12 for strength of institutional affiliation). Likewise, psychological involvement is a statistically significant predictor (beta = +.13) of voting participation.

Significantly, critically conscious Venezuelan workers and those dissatisfied with Andrés Pérez's performance are more likely to vote than are the satisfied. The relationships are very weak but are in the opposite direction from those operating among Mexican workers. In fact, issue-based motivations generate little voting among either Mexican or Venezuelan workers. But the modest effects observable are in opposite directions in the two countries.

In sum, the data provide evidence of greater external mobilization of individual voters in Mexico than in Venezuela. Workers vote in Mexico primarily because of ties to the PRI, not because of resources or cognitive mobilization. Mexican workers who have acquired resources and motivations needed for self-directed participation tend to withdraw from electoral participation. By contrast, evidence of more self-directed participation in elections is found among workers in the more competitive electoral system of Venezuela. These findings imply, then, that the larger electoral context influences the extent to

Table 21. Alternative Processes of Mobilization for Voting: Mexico

	Beta Coefficient
Resources	
Age	$.10^a$
SES	$-.14^a$
Cognitive mobilization	
Discontent with	
urban services	$-.14^a$
public education	$-.03$
economic performance	$-.06$
psychological involvement in politics	$-.01$
Critical consciousness	$-.09^a$
External mobilization[6]	
Strength of institutional affiliation	$.18^a$
Party Id:	
PRI	$.22^a$
Left	$.11^a$
Membership in	
incorporated union	$-.15^a$
autonomous union	$.02$
Multiple r	$.37$
r^2	$.14$

[a]Significant at .05 level

[b]Beta coefficients shown for disaggregated measure also. These were not used in estimating other beta coefficients reported here. The Multiple R is calculated from the equation using strength of institutional affiliation.

which working-class voting participation can be guided by ruling parties rather than by being self-directed. Guidance of voting participation becomes more problematic when genuine competition exists and the incumbent party can be voted out of office. Under these conditions politically motivated workers, as in Venezuela, might see more reason to vote.

Table 21 shows that the PRI can turn out Mexican voters more effectively (beta = + .22) than can leftist parties (beta = + .11). The virtual absence of self-directed voting combined with the strength of the PRI in turning out working-class voters must surely contribute to PRI's electoral hegemony. By contrast, dominant parties in Venezuela, AD and COPEI, do not turn out their working-class supporters more effectively than leftist parties (table 22). The beta for dominant parties is merely + .05 in Venezuela, while that for leftist parties is + .12,

Table 22. Alternative Processes of Mobilization for Voting:
         Venezuela

	Beta Coefficient
Resources	
Age	.31[a]
SES	−.05
Cognitive mobilization	
Discontent with performance of Andrés Pérez[b]	.09
Psychological involvement in politics	.13[c]
Critical consciousness	.05
Exteneral mobilization[a]	
Strength of institutional affiliation	.12[c]
Party Id	
AD/COPEI	.05
Left	.12[c]
Membership in	
incorporated union	.18[c]
autonomous union	.13[c]
Multiple r	.40
r^2	.16

[a]Beta coefficients shown for disaggregated measure also. These were not used in estimating other beta coefficients reported here. The Multiple r is calculated from the equation using strength of institutional affiliation.

[b]Evaluation of Herrera Campins not used because most elections used in the voting scale occurred before his presidency.

[c]Significant at .05 level.

suggesting clear limits on the capacity of ruling parties in Venezuela to manipulate voting turnout.

The Multiple Classification Analysis reported in figure 6 further reveals how different political parties mobilize working-class voters in Venezuela and Mexico. First, it should be observed that the left in Venezuela's competitive polity is more effective than the left in Mexico's semicompetitive polity in turning out voters. However, note that the center-right parties in Mexico, particularly the PAN, are considerably more effective in mobilizing voters than the left. This apparent anomaly is almost entirely due to the strong voting turnout of PANista voters in León. Most likely, the autonomous union in the León factory maintains some type of informal ties with the PAN.[7] As noted in chapter 2, the FAT union retains ties to the international Central Latinoamericana de Trabajadores (CLAT), which, like the PAN, is committed to the Christian Democratic ideology.[8] When the León shoe workers

Figure 6. Political Parties and External Mobilization of Voters

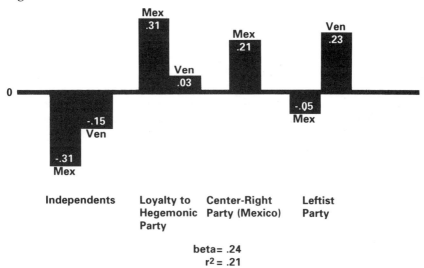

beta= .24
r² = .21

Note: Multiple Classification Analysis, controlling for age and socioeconomic status.

are excluded, PAN exhibits a significantly lower capacity to turn out voters. With the exception of PANistas in León, these results suggest more limited capacity of opposition parties to mobilize their long-term supporters in Mexico than in Venezuela.

The data (figure 6) also indicate that partisanship is a more important prerequisite for voting in Mexico than in Venezuela. Nonpartisans are less likely to vote in Mexico's semicompetitive system than in Venezuela's competitive electoral system. This finding is consistent with the previously reported finding of greater cognitive mobilization of voters in Venezuela than in Mexico. Venezuelan workers need not be mobilized by parties as in Mexico. Individually acquired motivations and resources are sufficient conditions for active voting in Venezuela.

Next, let us examine unions as agents for external mobilization of voters. The data provide little evidence that incorporated unions mobilize voters more effectively than autonomous unions in either country (tables 21 and 22). Still, there are significant differences across regimes. Both incorporated and autonomous unions in Venezuela engage in external voter mobilization. Relationships are still relatively modest (betas of +.18 and +.13, respectively), and incorporated unions enjoy only a marginal advantage in mobilizing capability over autonomous unions. In Mexico's case incorporated unions actually

Figure 7. Union Membership and External Mobilization of Voters

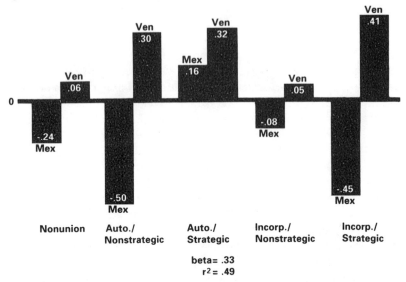

Note: Multiple Classification analysis, controlling for socioeconomic status, age, and partisanship.

demobilize potential voters (beta = $-.15$), while membership in autonomous unions has no effect on voting turnout (beta = $+.02$). These results indicate that Mexican unions, whether autonomous or incorporated, are ineffective in mobilizing voters.

Multiple Classification Analysis of the impact of union membership on voting participation makes it clear (figure 7) that Venezuelan unions, regardless of their incorporation status, are more likely to mobilize voters externally than are Mexican unions. None of the Mexican unions, by contrast, appear to be very effective in turning out voters. In two cases the effect of union membership is to decrease the likelihood of voting in Mexican elections (figure 7).

This analysis suggests a possibe complex interaction between degree of union incorporation and type of industry in the case of Mexican workers. Autonomous unions are most likely to mobilize voters within strategic industries. Conversely, incorporated unions mobilize voters most successfully in nonstrategic industries (figure 7). Only in the case of workers in an autonomous union of a strategic industry, however, is the mean substantially above the mean for nonunionized workers. Therefore, there is little evidence that unions, except in limited situations, effectively turn out voters for Mexican elections. These findings are clearly inconsistent with the conventional wisdom that incorporated unions in Mexico help to perpetuate the electoral hegemony of the PRI.

The larger electoral context appears to be a more important determinant of union capacity to mobilize voters than are ties to hegemonic parties. In neither country do incorporated unions exercise a significantly greater capacity to mobilize voters than do autonomous unions. Whether unions engage at all in external mobilization for voting seems to depend primarily on the context of electoral competition. Where that context provides for partisan turnover on a regular basis, as in Venezuela, both incorporated and autonomous unions are likely to turn out their members on election day. By contrast, all unions appear to have greater difficulty in mobilizing voters when electoral contests are overwhelmingly dominated by one party, as in Mexico. Political parties seem to activate voters in Mexico far more than unions do.

Overall, these results suggest that limited partisan competition facilitates the capacity of a hegemonic party to influence voting turnout to its advantage. In Mexico's semicompetitive polity, virtually no evidence of cognitive mobilization of voters was found. The strongest determinant of voting was found to be PRI partisanship. By contrast, external voter mobilization by hegemonic parties in Venezuela appeared weaker. Evidence of cognitive mobilization of Venezuelan voters was found.

An alternative hypothesis to explain these cross-national differences is that Mexican workers are mired in an authoritarian, working-class culture. In other words, the explanation for the differences found may be cultural rather than structural. However, two problems arise with the cultural explanation. First, as noted in chapter 5, workers in both Venezuela and Mexico exhibited relatively high levels of political sophistication. Other studies have demonstrated that Mexican political culture is far more democratic than is the political system.[9] Second, the data show that Mexican workers who have acquired political motivations and resources tend to be active in nonelectoral activities.

Participation in community organizations (communal activism) is such a nonelectoral activity. While the relationships are generally weak ($r^2 = +.07$), there are some interesting contrasts with voting. The data in table 23 show that some weak external mobilization of communal activists (beta = $+.11$) exists among workers in Mexico and that mobilization is done primarily by the PRI and incorporated unions (betas of $+.07$, respectively). But it should also be noted that

Table 23. Alternative Processes of Mobilization for Communal
         Activism: Mexico

	Beta Coefficient
Resources	
Age	.08[a]
SES	.07[a]
Cognitive mobilization	
Discontent with	
urban services	.01
public education	.01
economic performance	.08[a]
psychological involvement in politics	.17[a]
Critical consciousness	.02
External mobilization[b]	
Strength of institutional affiliation	.11[a]
Party Id	
PRI	.07[a]
Left	.00
Membership in	
incorporated union	.07
autonomous union	
Multiple r	.26
r^2	.07

[a]Significant at .05 level.
[b]Beta coefficients shown for disaggregated measure also. These were not used in
estimating other beta coefficients reported here. The Multiple r is calculated from the
equation using strength of institutional affiliation.

there is also some statistically significant cognitive mobilization to
communal activity as well. Note that workers who are psychologically
involved in politics or discontent with government economic performance tend to become communal activists (betas of +.17 and +.08,
respectively). Neither of these variables was significantly related to
voting. Psychologically involved and discontented Mexican workers
might well perceive greater utility in communal activities than in voting. The former represents a self-help approach to problem solving,
whereas the latter represents an attempt at directive political participation in a system resistant to direction from below.

In general, cross-national differences in electoral mobilization
might better be explained by differences in political structures rather
than in political culture. How then does one account for the greater

mobilizing capability of the Mexican PRI when compared to Venezuela's AD and COPEI?

One possible explanation is that the PRI possesses greater patronage resources with which to mobilize voters than either AD or COPEI. However, the data present problems for this interpretation. Chapter 5 made it clear that industrial workers interviewed for this study almost universally do not depend on the party for access to public services and benefits.[10] The next chapter will show that incorporated unions exercise relatively little influence over the electoral choice of workers, even though these organizations are directly involved in the delivery of public goods. Thus, it seems that hegemonic parties do not depend on the delivery of benefits and services by incorporated unions to turn out voters.

The capacity of the PRI to mobilize voters might depend more on containing the potential for cognitive mobilization among its partisans. Suppression of cognitive mobilization, in turn, is related to limited partisan competition and turnover. Cognitive mobilization of voters occurs to the extent that realistic opportunities exist to remove the incumbent party from power. If such opportunities do not exist, as in Mexico, the cognitively mobilized citizenry may see little to be gained by voting. Mexican voters are more likely to be relatively apolitical partisans of the ruling party. They can be counted on to cast only a perfunctory vote for the PRI.[11] On the other hand, the cognitively mobilized worker in a competitive polity, such as in Venezuela, may see some utility in voting so long as the incumbent party can be removed from power. Such voters decrease the number that can be externally mobilized by parties. Hence, external mobilization of voters seems to occur less in Venezuela's competitive electoral system than in Mexico's semicompetitive system.

In light of the cross-national differences in relationships between partisanship and voting, the relationships between union membership and voting for the Venezuelan and Mexican samples are curious. Unions, not parties, mobilize voters in Venezuela; parties, not unions, mobilize voters in Mexico. How does one explain this seeming anomaly? As indicated earlier, the explanation cannot be that parties are agents of patronage in Mexico, while unions are sources of patronage in Venezuela. The more likely explanation is related to penetration of partisan politics into internal union politics in Venezuela but not in Mexico. Internal partisan politics in Venezuelan unions might cause workers to be more sensitive to partisan politics outside the union and thus more likely voters than nonunionized workers.

Additionally, unionized workers in Venezuela might be more exposed to electoral campaigns than nonunionized workers because partisan-structured unions are a natural target for campaigning. Conversely, the lack of conflictual partisan politics within Mexican unions may weaken their external mobilizing capacity.

This chapter has presented further evidence that control over working-class political mobilization in Venezuela and Mexico may depend more on restricted partisan competition than on clientelist structures operating through corporatist interest associations. Restricted partisan competition as found in Mexico weakens the mobilizing capability of unions; consequently, only the ruling PRI can effectively turn out voters. No such advantage accrues to hegemonic parties in Venezuela's competitive electoral system. As we have seen, restricted competition also helps to explain why cognitively mobilized workers in Mexico, unlike those in Venezuela, do not become active voters. The capability of the PRI to mobilize industrial workers does not seem to hinge on clientelist networks but on perpetuating a type of dis-engaged partisanship explored more fully in the next chapter. Specifically, chapter 8 will examine why interviewed workers tend to deliver their vote to hegemonic parties.

Chapter Eight

Political Control
and Electoral Choice

The fundamental issue to be addressed in this chapter is why industrial workers in this sample tend to vote for hegemonic parties committed to the prevailing state-capitalist model of development rather
than for leftist parties committed to socialist strategies of development. The purpose of this study is to identify control mechanisms
within the inclusionary political systems of Mexico and Venezuela
that enable centrist ruling parties to maintain their hegemony and to
suppress system-challenging mobilization among lower-class populations. This chapter explores how (1) corporatist interest intermediation, (2) restricted partisan competition, and (3) satisfaction with
government performance contribute to working-class support for hegemonic parties rather than for leftist parties. To do so, I shall examine
how (1) partisanship, (2) evaluations of incumbent performance, and
(3) labor union membership are related to voting behavior.

Before examining relationships between partisan loyalty and electoral choice, the nature of partisanship exhibited by workers in this
sample is first examined. The early research of the University of Michigan team of social scientists assumed that partisanship is a long-term
attachment (or loyalty) to a party formed during early childhood. As
such, it guides individual voting behavior unless short-term forces
related to issues or to candidate image lead to defections from underlying partisan loyalties.[1] This view of partisanship, however, has
come under considerable criticism in recent studies. It has been shown
that partisan loyalties of voters may be less stable and shaped more
by short-term forces than previously thought.[2] Additionally, partisan
loyalties may simply reflect more fundamental social and religious
cleavages in society.[3] These revisionist studies have not established
that partisanship is an empirically and theoretically meaningless concept but rather that the nature of partisanship can be variable. Thus,
it is important to understand what party loyalty means to voters if

one is to interpret intelligently the relationship between partisanship and electoral choice.

Three types of partisanship can be identified: (1) an *early socialization-based* partisanship, (2) an *issue-based* partisanship, and (3) a *patronage-based* partisanship.[4] The first type is that developed in the early University of Michigan studies. The second type, an issue-based partisanship, is contingent on consistency between an individual's issue and candidate preferences and partisan preference. A patronage-based partisanship is contingent on access to party patronage resources. Such partisanship ought to be found in the context of party machines and typically among lower-class populations that depend on such machines.

Unfortunately, data are lacking to assess fully the nature of the partisan loyalty exhibited by workers in this sample. However, the data provide some limited insight into the nature of partisanship of workers in this sample.

First, recall that these workers received virtually no personal benefits or public services directly from the party. While a patronage-based partisanship might be pervasive among informal sector workers in both countries,[5] it may be less common among formal sector workers who do not depend on the party for the delivery of personal goods and services. Still, it might be premature to dismiss patronage-based partisanship as altogether irrelevant in the case of Mexican workers. Table 24 shows that the delivery of urban services is more closely linked to PRI partisanship than are evaluations of public education and of economic performance. Perhaps, these differences reflect the type of issues over which Mexican workers believe that they can exercise influence. Mexican workers may believe that macroeconomic policy decisions are beyond their influence as these decisions are generally formulated by top-level technocrats with minimal citizen input.[6] On the other hand, the delivery of urban services may be associated with *politicos* who broker services in exchange for electoral support for the PRI. Thus, loyalty to the PRI on the part of these workers may be partly contingent on the delivery of *urban* services. However, this loyalty does not likely depend on the delivery of *personal* services as may be the case with the more economically vulnerable members of the lower class.

To what extent are the partisan loyalties of workers shaped by their retrospective evaluations of government performance? The latter variable represents a type of "short-term" force that, if partisanship is formed by early socialization, should have little influence on partisanship. Table 24 shows how various performance-evaluation scales

Table 24. Partisan Structuring of Performance Evaluations

	Mexico		
Partisan Loyalty	Urban Services	Public Education	Economic Performance
PRI	.18[a]	.10[a]	.02
PAN	.01	−.12[a]	−.03
Left	−.17[a]	−.16[a]	−.18[a]

	Venezuela	
Partisan loyalty	André Pérez Government	Herrera Campins Government
AD	.45[a]	.00
COPEI	−.07	.23[a]
Left	−.19[a]	−.18[a]

Note: Pearson correlations. Operationalization of evaluation scales are found in Appendix B.

[a]Significant at the .01 level.

are related to partisan loyalty among Venezuelan and Mexican workers.

Two findings are particularly noteworthy. First, leftist partisans in both the Mexican and Venezuelan samples are more dissatisfied with government performance than are other workers (table 24). This finding suggests a significant issue-based component to leftist partisanship in both the authoritarian and democratic polity. Second, it is clear that hegemonic partisanship is more likely to structure evaluations of performance among workers in the democratic polity of Venezuela than in Mexico. This difference can be explained by the fact that partisan loyalty ought to be a more important cue for evaluating policy performance in genuinely competitive electoral systems. In sum, an *issue-based* partisanship might be more commonly found among workers where there is meaningful partisan competition. By contrast, a *socialization-based* partisanship might be more typical of workers in semicompetitive electoral systems. While this interpretation seems plausible, it is not possible to test these hypotheses fully with these data.

One other point about hegemonic partisanship in the case of Venezuelan workers needs to be noted. Interestingly, partisans of hegemonic parties in Venezuela do not tend to evaluate the performance of the incumbent opposition party negatively. AD partisans in this sample did not evaluate the performance of COPEI president, Luis

Herrera Campins, any more negatively than did other workers (beta = .00, table 24). Perhaps, a different picture would have emerged after the 1982 economic crisis, but the data are lacking to assess this possibility. In like manner, COPEI partisans were only slightly more likely to evaluate negatively the performance of the Andrés Pérez administration than were other workers (beta = −.07, table 24). The tendency of voters in two-party systems to view parties in nonbipolar terms has been noted in other national contexts.[7] The lack of bipolar perceptions of Venezuela's two major parties should facilitate more shifting of party loyalties than would be the case if the two major parties were viewed as polar opposites.

Last, I reiterate the earlier point about the disengaged nature of hegemonic partisanship in the case of Mexican workers. Hegemonic partisans who vote in Mexico's semicompetitive polity exhibit little interest in politics (chapters 6 and 7). By contrast, hegemonic partisans in Venezuela tend to be interested in politics, though not to the degree exhibited by leftist partisans (chapters 6 and 7).

Purposes of political control are clearly served better by the type of partisanship exhibited by Mexican workers. Loyalty to the PRI leads to perfunctory voting with minimal psychological involvement in politics or attention to government performance. By contrast, hegemonic partisans in Venezuela are likely to be attentive to politics and to form their partisan loyalties consistent with their assessments of performance. Hence, hegemonic partisans in Venezuela have greater potential to become autonomous participants in the political process than do their counterparts in Mexico.

The next point to examine is how partisan loyalty is related to electoral choice. Obviously, partisan loyalty does not guide voting behavior unless such loyalties have been formed. Thus, the distribution of party loyalties is examined in order to ascertain the number of partisans and nonpartisans. The data show a large number of nonpartisan workers in both the Venezuelan and Mexican samples (table 25). Indeed, nonpartisans are the single largest category for both samples. It becomes important, therefore, to examine not only how partisanship shapes voting behavior but also the voting patterns of nonpartisans.

Tables 26 and 27 analyze the effects of partisanship on recent electoral choice[8] and show how two different types of partisans and nonpartisans voted in recent elections. Of particular interest are any observable tendencies of party loyalists to cross over and to vote for opposition parties. Overall, there is relatively little deviation, showing that party loyalty is a strong determinant of voting behavior. Not

Table 25. Distribution of Party Loyalties: Mexican and Venezuelan
Workers

Mexico		Venezuela	
Party	Frequency Distribution %	Party	Frequency Distribution %
Hegemonic party[a]		Hegemonic party[a]	
PRI	34.8	AD	10.8
		COPEI	22.0
Rightist opposition[a]			
PAN	11.0		
PARM	0.8		
PDM	1.6		
Leftist opposition[a]		Leftist opposition:[a]	
PPS	1.8	MAS	9.2
PMT	2.2	MIR	5.5
PST	1.4	MEP	5.9
PCM	4.6	PCV	1.0
		LS	0.4
		Other parties	1.2
No party loyalty	41.4	No party loyalty	44.0
Total	100.0		100.0

[a]The complete names of these parties are found in tables 30 and 31.

surprisingly, partisanship was found to be the strongest determinant
of electoral choice for both Mexican and Venezuelan workers in the
regression analyses.[9]

Observed patterns of deviations from party loyalties that do occur
can be explained by the nature of partisan competition in these two
political systems. First, note that there is virtually no deviation from
party loyalties in the case of supporters of hegemonic parties. This
pattern can be observed among both the Mexican and Venezuelan
samples (tables 26 and 27). By contrast, deviations from party loyalties
are more apt to occur among supporters of minor opposition parties.
Interestingly, there is a perfect correlation between overall electoral
strength of the party and amount of deviant voting in the case of
Mexican workers. It is particularly important to note that deviations
from opposition party loyalties occur more among Mexican workers
than among Venezuelan workers and that the PRI is more likely to
benefit than are COPEI or AD in Venezuela.

In sum, minor opposition parties in Mexico's semicompetitive

Table 26. Partisan Loyalty and Electoral Choice in the 1979 Mexican
Legislative Races

			Party Loyalty		
	PRI	PAN	Leftist Parties	Minor Rightist Parties[a]	Nonpartisan
Electoral choice:					
PRI	96.3%	13.7%	17.1%	18.1%	61.2%
PAN	2.4	84.3	4.9	9.1	24.8
Leftist party	1.2	1.9	75.6	0.0	10.9
Minor rightist party	0.0	0.0	2.4	72.7	3.1
Total deviation[b]	3.6%	15.6%	24.4%	27.2%	
NT	164	51	41	11	129

[a]Minor rightist parties include PARM and PDM. Leftist parties include PPS, PMT, PST, and PCM.
[b]The percentage of party loyalists who voted for another party.

electoral system seem to be less able to retain the support of their
long-term supporters than are their counterparts in Venezuela's competitive electoral system. Furthermore, opposition partisans who do
deviate are more likely to switch to a hegemonic party if they are
situated in Mexico rather than in Venezuela. These findings suggest
that opposition parties confront difficulty in preventing defections
where party competition is restricted. This weakness on the part of
opposition parties in Mexico clearly contributes to the continuing electoral strength of the PRI among industrial workers in this sample.

Nonpartisan workers are studied next. Keep in mind that these
voters comprise a very large bloc of voters in both samples (N = 128
for Venezuela, N = 129 for Mexico; see tables 26 and 27). The results
show that a large percentage of the nonpartisan vote goes to hegemonic parties in both cases. *The capacity of hegemonic parties to capture
this vote is certainly a major factor in explaining their electoral strength among
industrial workers.* It is probable that the dominant position of these
parties accounts for their success in attracting electoral support from
nonpartisans. Given the unlikelihood of minor opposition parties winning power, nonpartisans may see their options as either nonvoting
or voting for hegemonic parties. In fact, a large number of nonpartisans in both countries do not vote, as was shown in the previous

Table 27. Partisan Loyalty and Electoral Choice in the 1978
          Venezuelan Presidential Election

| | Party Loyalty | | | |
	AD	COPEI	Leftist Parties[a]	No Party
Electoral choice:				
AD	94.1%	1.0%	1.0%	17.2%
COPEI	3.9	99.0	9.8	50.0
Leftist party	1.9	0.0	2.0	26.6
Others	0.0	0.0	2.0	6.3
Total deviation[b]	5.8%	1.0%	12.8%	
N	51	98	102	128

[a]Leftist parties include MAS, MIR, MEP, PCV, and LS.
[b]The percentage of party loyalists who voted for another party.

chapter. Nonpartisans who do vote tend to vote for hegemonic parties.

One should also note that the Venezuelan left is able to capture a significantly larger share of the nonpartisan vote than is the Mexican left. This finding helps to explain why a larger percentage of Venezuelan workers in this sample support the left than do Mexican workers (chapter 5). Greater opportunities for the Venezuelan left than for the Mexican left to gain a share of power via proportional representation might partially explain this difference. Another factor is the absence of a strong opposition on the right in Venezuela. The presence of the PAN in Mexico clearly helps to deflect some opposition voting away from the left.

Overall, the influence of partisanship on voting behavior seems to be very much conditioned by the larger electoral system. In electoral systems with more restricted partisan competition as in Mexico, one is likely to find (1) fewer defections from the ruling party, (2) a type of disengaged partisanship on the part of supporters of the ruling party, (3) the ruling party capturing a large share of the nonpartisan vote, and (4) more defections by loyalists of opposition parties to the ruling party.

There is an expanding literature that examines how perceptions of economic conditions and of government management of the economy influences voting behavior.[10] In these studies the effects of perceived macroeconomic conditions, of perceived personal economic conditions, and of evaluations of government management of the economy on voting behavior have been investigated.[11] In general, these studies have shown that evaluations of incumbent management of the economy are a major determinant of whether voters support the incumbent party.[12] Perceptions of personal economic and of general macroeconomic conditions, however, have been found to have little direct effect on voting behavior.

This chapter investigates the effects of retrospective evaluation of incumbent performance on the electoral choices of Mexican and Venezuelan workers. In addition, the effects of workers' assessments of personal economic conditions on voting behavior are examined. Performance-evaluation scales were devised by using factor analysis for each national sample. The factor analysis shows that Mexican workers did not differentiate the performance of presidents Luis Echeverría and José López Portillo. Rather, respondents differentiated three policy areas: economic performance, public education, and urban services (see Appendix B). By contrast, Venezuelan workers differentiated the performance of AD president, Carlos Andrés Pérez, and COPEI president, Luis Herrera Campins.

The Mexican sample was analyzed to see how workers' evaluations of urban services, of public education, and of economic performance affected their electoral choice in the 1979 legislative races. The 1976 presidential election was not used because of the possibility of greater recall error and also because of PANS failure to nominate a presidential candidate.[13] In the case of Venezuelan workers, the effects of evaluations of Andrés Pérez's performance on electoral choice in the 1978 presidential election were analyzed, as well as the effects of evaluations of Herrera Campins's performance on electoral choice in the 1979 municipal elections. These presidents were the respective incumbents at the time of these elections. Additionally, assessments of expected future social mobility and perceived past mobility were also analyzed in order to determine if workers are sensitive to personal economic conditions when deciding for which party to vote.[14] Also included in the regression analysis were a broad range of other possible determinants of voting behavior in order to avoid specification problems.[15]

The purpose of the regression analyses is to assess how performance satisfaction shapes working-class support for hegemonic parties. Additionally, it was necessary to find out if worker discontent with the performance of hegemonic parties leads to support for leftist parties. Thus, two important facets of political control can be investigated: (1) the extent to which satisfaction with regime performance accounts for electoral support for hegemonic parties and (2) the extent to which leftist parties can capitalize on working-class discontent with incumbent hegemonic parties.

Tables 28 and 29 show beta coefficients for retrospective evaluations of incumbent performance and for perceived social mobility. First, it should be noted that perceived social mobility, whether perceptions of past mobility or expected future mobility, did not influence how either Venezuelan or Mexican workers voted in the 1978 and 1979 elections. These findings are consistent with previous research that shows perceptions of personal economic conditions to have little influence on voting behavior.[16] These findings are inconsistent with the "labor aristocracy thesis" that industrial workers in third-world capitalist countries tend to support hegemonic parties because of satisfaction with their own personal economic situation.

The next item to examine is how retrospective evaluations of performance affect working-class voting behavior. Tables 28 and 29 reveal rather dramatic differences between Mexican and Venezuelan workers. Note that Mexican workers satisfied with government performance were not necessarily prone to support the PRI in the 1979 elections. The only variable that achieves statistical significance is evaluation of urban services (beta = .10). Discontent with performance is, at best, weakly converted into electoral support for opposition parties. As we have seen, workers were discontent with government performance at the time of the interviewing, yet this discontent did not lead to significant voting for either the PAN or for leftist parties.

Unfortunately, the 1976 presidential election in Mexico cannot be used for reasons previously discussed. Hence, it is impossible to assess whether these results are simply an artifact of using a low-stimulus legislative election in the analysis. Fortunately, the Venezuelan data provide a usable high-stimulus and low-stimulus election.

The results in table 29 show that evaluations of incumbent performance significantly affect the voting behavior of Venezuelan workers. Note that how workers evaluated the performance of the AD incumbent, Carlos Andrés Pérez, strongly influenced whether or not they voted for AD in the 1978 presidential election (beta = .38). Similarly, how workers evaluated the performance of the COPEI administration of Luis Herrera Campins significantly influenced whether or not a ballot was cast for COPEI candidates in the 1979 municipal elections (beta = .21). Clearly, performance evaluation is a stronger de-

Table 28. Perceived Social Mobility, Retrospective Evaluation of
          Government Performance, and Electoral Choice in the
          1979 Mexican Legislative Races: Standardized Regression
          Coefficients

	Voted for		
	PRI	PAN	Left
Evaluation of urban services	.10[a]	− .03	− .05
r^2 change	(.01)[a]	(.00)	(.00)
Evaluation of public education	.06	.03	− .04
r^2 change	(.00)	(.00)	(.00)
Evaluation of economic performance	.04	.04	− .09
r^2 change	(.00)	(.00)	(.01)
Expected future mobility	− .02	.00	− .02
Perceived past mobility	− .09	.03	.05
r^2 change for two mobility			
indicators	(.01)	(.00)	(.00)

Note: Each evaluation of performance variable was entered in separate equations to avoid any multicolinearity problems. The r^2 value for social mobility indicators is based on equation in which evaluation of urban services was entered. Type of union, socio-economic status, age, and ideological identification (left, center, or right) were used as controls. Partisanship was not used, because of multicolinearity problems that were particularly severe in the case of Venezuelan workers.

[a]Significant at the .05 level.

terminant of electoral choice in a high-stimulus presidential race, but even in municipal races, these assessments influence how workers vote.

Let us next examine how Venezuelan workers tend to express political discontent. For both the 1978 and 1979 elections, discontented Venezuelan workers were more prone to vote for the "out" hegemonic party rather than for a leftist party (table 29). The left was clearly better able to capitalize on discontent in the more visible presidential election of 1978 than in the 1979 municipal elections, though ironically the left fared better nationally in the 1979 than in the 1978 elections.

What do these findings reveal about how working-class political mobilization is controlled? Clearly, performance satisfaction is not a reliable mechanism for generating electoral support for incumbent parties in either country. Performance satisfaction has little effect on how Mexican workers vote. It does influence whether Venezuelan workers support the incumbent party. However, performance satisfaction must generate only limited electoral support for an incumbent

Table 29. Perceived Social Mobility, Retrospective Evaluation of
Incumbent Performance, and Electoral Choice in
the 1979 Municipal Elections and 1978 Presidential
Election in Venezuela: Standardized Regression
Coefficients

	Voted for					
	AD		COPEI		Left	
	1978	1979	1978	1979	1978	1979
Evaluation of performance of Andrés Pérez	.38[a]	——	−.17[a]	——	−.12[a]	——
r² change	(.12)[a]	——	(.03)[a]	——	(.01)[a]	——
Evaluation of performance of Herrera Campins	——	−.19[a]	——	.21[a]	——	−.05
r² change	——	(.03)[a]	——	(.04)[a]	——	(.00)
Expected future mobility	−.01	.11	.07	−.02	−.04	−.03
Perceived past mobility	−.02	.07	.04	.00	−.04	−.00
r² change for two mobility indicators	(.00)	(.02)	(.01)	(.00)	(.00)	(.00)

Note: Controlling for socioeconomic status, age, type of union, and ideological identification (left, center, right). See note in table 23 as to rise of ediological identification.
    [a]Significant at the .05 level.

party among these workers given that discontent with performance
is pervasive.

    These results are revealing as to why leftist parties in both coun-
tries confront difficulty in capitalizing on working-class discontent
with state capitalism. Discontent is high but not strongly converted
into electoral support for the left.[17] In the case of Venezuelan workers,
there is a tendency to convert discontent into support for the "out"
hegemonic party rather than into support for the left. This pattern
observed among workers in this sample has likely been repeated on
the national level where the "out" hegemonic party has defeated the
incumbent party in all presidential elections since 1963.[18] In the case
of Mexican workers, discontent is simply not channeled into the electoral arena. Workers in both countries are not likely to convert discontent into leftist voting since the left does not provide a viable
alternative to hegemonic parties.

    Before leaving this topic, one should recognize that these results

Table 30. Percentage of Mexican Workers Identifying Parties with Correct Spatial Label

Identifying Socialist Party with Left	
Mexican Communist Party (PCM)	76.2
Socialist Workers Party (PST)	68.8
Mexican Workers Party (PMT)	38.2
Popular Socialist Party (PPS)	54.8
Identifying Center/Right Party with Right	
Party of the Institutional	
Revolution (PRI)	76.8
National Action Party (PAN)	61.4
Authentic Party of the Mexican	
Revolution (PARM)	67.6
Mexican Democratic Party (PDM)	38.0

are not simply an artifact of partisanship. While partisanship could not be controlled because of multicolinearity problems, ideological identification, a variable that is highly correlated with partisanship, could be controlled.[19] Thus, the study has indirectly controlled for partisanship. The findings reported are not a result of partisans reacting favorably to their party and adversely to other parties.

Additionally, it should be noted that the failure of discontented workers to vote for the left is not simply a result of their lack of political sophistication. Sophistication is shown by comprehension of spatial labels and capacity to apply them to political parties.

To assess comprehension of spatial labels, workers were asked to explain the meaning of "left" and "right." Responses were dichotomized as either comprehensible or incomprehensible (including don't-know responses). *Comprehensible* does not mean that workers impart well-developed abstract ideological content to those labels. Few citizens anywhere exhibit this ability.[20] Rather, a response was considered comprehensible if respondents accorded some meaning to the term that accorded with conventional usage. For example, if the respondent defined "left" as being against the government or pro-workers, the response was considered comprehensible.

Using this criterion, 64.7 percent of the Venezuelan sample could impart comprehensible meaning to the label "left." Seventy-two percent of this sample could impart meaning to the label "right." An equally high percentage of Mexican workers could impart meaning to these terms: 75.8 percent of the Mexicans understood the term *left* and 72.6 percent understood the meaning of *right*.

Table 31. Percentage of Venezuelan Workers Identifying Parties with Correct Spatial Label

Identifying Socialist Party with Left	
Electoral Movement of the People (MEP)	75.5%
Movement toward Socialism (MAS)	86.7%
Movement of the Revolutionary Left (MIR)	91.7%
Venezuelan Communist Party (PCV)	91.3%
Identifying Center/Right Party with Right	
Democratic Action Party (AD)	88.8%
Christian Democratic Party (COPEI)	89.8%

Turning next to the capacity of workers to apply spatial labels to parties, tables 30 and 31 show that Venezuelan laborers are clearly more able than Mexican workers to label correctly various parties representing different positions on the ideological continuum. This is not unexpected, given differences in political contexts and in the history of recognition of opposition parties.[21] Only two Mexican parties were not recognized correctly by a majority of Mexican workers: the Mexican Workers Party and the Mexican Democratic Party. The latter is a small, right-wing party whose influence is largely restricted to a small geographic area. The former is a small, then recently formed, left-wing party that did not field candidates in the 1979 legislative races.[22] Overall, the percentages are relatively high for both samples. Indeed, the results are comparable to those reported for advanced industrial countries.[23]

Not only do workers in this sample tend to comprehend generally what leftist parties are about but also to adopt points of view compatible with the left. Elsewhere we have shown that only a very few of these workers adopt a *laissez-faire* view of government regulation, and most favor either government ownership of industry or else government regulation of industry.[24] In sum, the data suggest that the structural weakness of leftist parties and their competitive disadvantage *vis-à-vis* hegemonic parties better accounts for the lack of working-class support for the left. It is clearly not a case of working-class conservatism or the presence of a "working-class culture" that stymies industrial workers from supporting the left in Venezuela and Mexico.

Many political analysts, including Lenin, have recognized the dual role of labor unions in capitalist economies. Labor unions can assume a short-term economistic role in seeking to maximize labor's immediate benefits through collective bargaining. They can also perform a longer-term political role by seeking to maximize the collective political power of labor. Political power permits labor to influence electoral outcomes (or nonelectoral processes of leadership selection), thereby structuring the public-policy choices made by political leaders.[25] This distinction in union roles corresponds to what William Form labels job unionism versus political unionism.[26] Political unionism may be manifested in a highly militant or more moderate form, depending on attitudes toward the existing sociopolitical system. Juan Felipe Leal, for example, differentiates "anti-capitalist unionism" from "conciliatory unionism." The former seeks the elimination of capitalism via the "socialization of the means of production." The latter seeks "the defense of the interests of the workers . . . from a base of collaboration with employers and with the state."[27]

Left-wing parties in Western Europe have traditionally depended on formal and informal ties with organized labor in order to maximize their electoral strength.[28] Their electoral success often hinges on the capacity of the union movement to turn out the vote. The literature on corporatism in Latin America[29] provides an explanation as to why unions have not served a similar function in this region of the world. Presumably, the union movement has been captured by hegemonic parties or else is controlled by the bureaucratic state,[30] all of whom are committed to delivering the union vote to hegemonic parties. The literature thus suggests that incorporated unions engage in a type of "political unionism" that is basically "conciliatory" in nature, designed to prevent system-challenging mobilization. By contrast, "anti-capitalist" political unionism ought to be found only among autonomous unions. Presumably, the leadership of these unions ought to be more militant and sympathetic toward labor's national allies on the left as these leaders have not been coopted or incorporated into structures of control. Thus, one would expect to find evidence of greater leftist voting among members of autonomous unions.

This section of the chapter analyzes (1) the extent to which incorporated unions deliver the vote to hegemonic parties and (2) the extent to which autonomous unions deliver the vote to leftist or other opposition parties. The data analysis will show that neither type of union decisively influences how rank-and-file workers vote. Therefore, I shall discuss reasons for these findings, drawing both from qualitative interviews[31] conducted among leaders of unions used for this study and from survey data on rank-and-file perceptions of their unions and their leaders.

In assessing how unions influence voting behavior, one must be cautious in using only raw percentages because these tell nothing about the extent of actual union influence on voting behavior. A particular distribution of electoral preferences within a given union may be an artifact of self-selection or of a particular distribution of individual characteristics within the union population. To illustrate, leftist workers might conceivably seek out employment in industries organized by left-wing organizers. Unions might conceivably recruit a particular type of worker who is disposed to support leftist parties. Such unions might well produce a strong leftist vote without the union leadership undertaking to deliver the union vote to the left. Regression analysis allows one to avoid the problem with using raw percentages by holding constant individual characteristics in assessing the effects of union membership on voting behavior.[32]

The first point to examine is how unions influenced voting behavior in the 1979 legislative elections in Mexico. The raw percentages in table 32 indicate that support for the PRI tends to be higher in incorporated unions than in either autonomous unions or nonunionized workplaces. However, the regression analysis in which individual characteristics are controlled show that these unions exert minimal effect on worker support for the PRI (beta = .02, table 33). It is plausible that incorporated unions could exercise a strong indirect effect on voting behavior by shaping the attitudes and beliefs of workers. However, the qualitative interviews with union leaders in Mexico suggest otherwise as does the data analysis reported in chapter 6.

In like manner, the data provide no indication that autonomous unions deliver the vote to the left. The beta coefficient for the relationship between an autonomous union and leftist voting in the 1979 elections is a weak .04, the same as for incorporated unions (table 33). Table 32 does suggest, nevertheless, that Mexican unions may generally exercise a slight depressing effect on leftist voting. Notice that with one exception, the percentage of leftist voting is lower in all unionized settings than it is in the nonunionized setting. The one exception is the autonomous union in a strategic industry where the leftist vote is slightly higher than for nonunionized workers. In no case is there evidence that any of the Mexican unions deliver a significant vote to leftist parties as commonly found in Western Europe.

The Mexican data do provide one case in which unions clearly influence the voting behavior of rank-and-file workers. That case is the autonomous union in a nonstrategic industry (the shoe factory of León). Both tables 33 and 34 show that a sizable portion of this vote in the 1979 elections was delivered to PAN. The previous chapter sug-

Table 32. Type of Union Membership and Electoral Choice in the 1979 Mexican Legislative Races

| | | Type of Union Membership | | | |
| | | Incorporated Union | | Autonomous Union | |
	Non-unionized	Nonstrategic Industry	Strategic Industry	Union/ Nonstrategic Industry	Strategic Industry
Electoral choice					
PRI	56.5%	67.6%	81.1%	51.9%	61.4%
PAN	17.6	14.8	10.4	39.5	18.2
Minor rightist parties	10.6	1.4	0.0	0.0	3.4
Left	14.1	12.2	7.7	8.6	15.9
Null	1.2	4.0	3.9	6.0	1.1
N	85	74	77	81	88

Table 33. Union Membership and Electoral Choice in the 1979 Mexican Legislative Elections: Standardized Regression Coefficients

| | Membership | | |
Voted for	Incorporated Union	Autonomous Union	R^2 Change
PRI	.02	−.14[b]	.02[a]
PAN	−.04	.20[b]	.05[b]
Left	.04	.04	.00

Note: Controlling for retrospective evaluations of performance, socioeconomic status, social mobility, age, and ideological identification.

[a]R^2 value represents the percentage of variance explained by the union membership variables.

[b]Significant at the .05 level.

gested that the FAT union may well maintain informal ties with PAN as both the union and party retain close ties with the Christian Democratic movement.

Next, the influence of Venezuelan unions on the electoral choice of rank-and-file workers in the 1978 presidential race and 1979 municipal races is examined. Particularly noticeable about the raw percentages shown in table 34 is the greater dispersion of electoral choice among nonunionized workers than among unionized workers. This would suggest union influence on individual electoral choice, leading

Table 34. Type of Union Membership and Electoral Choice in the 1978
and 1979 Venezuelan Elections

	Type of union membership								
	Nonunionized		Nonstrategic Industry		Strategic Industry		Strategic Industry		Strategic Industry	
	1978	1979	1978	1979	1978	1979	1978	1979	1978	1979
AD	24.2%	28.3%	8.6%	6.3%	18.6%	18.2%	12.9%	12.3%	25.9%	9.3%
COPEI	31.8	39.1	53.1	58.3	52.9	38.2	50.6	53.2	19.8	18.8
Left	31.8	26.1	25.9	31.2	24.3	27.3	24.7	31.9	50.6	62.5
Others	4.5	0.0	1.2	0.0	2.8	12.7	5.9	2.9	0.0	6.3
Null	7.5	6.5	11.1	4.2	1.4	3.6	5.9	0.0	3.7	1.5
N	66	46	81	48	70	55	85	47	81	64

Note: 1978 presidential election; 1979 municipal election.

to greater homogeneity in voting behavior within unions. However,
the regression analysis shows that union influence on voting behavior
is slight, though clearly present. Table 35 shows that members of
incorporated unions were likely persuaded to vote for COPEI. However, this factor does not account well for COPEI electoral support in
either the 1978 or 1979 elections, as shown by the weak r^2 values.

Leftist electoral strength is found only in the autonomous unions
in the strategic oil industry (table 34). However, the regression analysis (table 35) suggests that autonomous unions do not have a strong
effect on rank-and-file voting behavior. These results suggest then
that other factors might better account for strong electoral support
for the left by petroleum workers in Venezuela's autonomous unions.

In sum, Venezuela's unions do not appear to exert a strong influence on how rank-and-file workers vote. The data reveal that
unions exercise some limited influence on voting behavior but clearly
other factors are more important in explaining how Venezuelan workers vote. Indeed, partisan and ideological identifications as well as
evaluations of government performance are more decisive in determining how Venezuelan workers vote than is the type of union to
which they belong.

How might the incapacity of local unions in Mexico and Venezuela
to influence voting behavior be explained? Interviews with local union
leaders in Venezuela and Mexico reveal that greater priority is given
to job unionism than to political unionism. This was the case for all
union officials who were interviewed for this study. As will be shown,
the primary mission of the union movement was seen to be the maxi-
mization of economic benefits. The leadership may have been reflect-

Table 35. Union Membership and Electoral Choice in the 1978 and 1979 Venezuelan Elections: Standardized Regression Coefficients

| | Membership | | |
| | Incorporated | Autonomous | R^2 |
Voted for	Union	Union	Change[a]
AD			
1978	−.06	−.01	.01
1979	−.13	−.13	.01
COPEI			
1978	.13	.03	.01
1979	.13	.06	.01
Left			
1978	−.05	.03	.01
1979	−.04	.09[b]	.01

Note: Controlling for retrospective evaluations of performance, SES, social mobility, age, and ideological identification.

[a]R^2 represents the percentage of variance explained by the union membership variables.

[b]Significant at the .05 level.

ing not only the larger political environment, in which anticapitalist political unionism is risky, but also the wishes of rank-and-file workers.[33] In fact, unionized workers in both countries overwhelmingly perceived the primary mission of their union in terms of strictly short-term economistic goals. These attitudes are clearly shown in response to an open-ended question about the principal struggle of the union.

A total of 91.4 percent of the Mexican workers mentioned either salaries or benefits; 67.4 percent of the Venezuelan workers mentioned these goals as the principal struggle of the union movement. Virtually no workers mentioned broad public policy objectives (0.3 percent for both samples), and relatively few even mentioned contract negotiations (7.3 percent for the Mexican sample; 16.0 percent for the Venezuelan sample) or violations that involve government arbitration boards (1.0 percent for the Mexican sample; 14.9 percent for the Venezuelan sample). It is interesting to note, however, that contract negotiations are more salient to workers in Venezuela than in Mexico. This may reflect less paternalistic labor relations in Venezuela.

The presence of job unionism among both local union elites and rank-and-file workers helps to account for the lack of a strong union influence on voting behavior. The primary attention of rank-and-file workers is not focused on politics. The same appears to be largely true for local union leaders, as will be demonstrated, first for Mexico, then for Venezuela.

In the two incorporated unions that were examined in Mexico, leaders viewed political mobilization as serving strictly short-term, utilitarian goals. The leaders of both unions admitted to seeking electoral support for the PRI. However, in neither union was there any formal mechanism for ideological indoctrination, nor was there any systematic effort to shape political consciousness. The tie that bound, as is so often the case in Mexican politics, was instrumental rather than ideological. One of the members of the executive committee of the textile workers' union put it this way. "More participation is needed. It benefits the workers because they become familiar with those elements that represent them. Thus it is possible to propose things, to mention needs. On the other hand, one can be burned principally by supporting the wrong party."[34] In both unions workers are cued by leaders to support the PRI for instrumental reasons. The ties seem more subtle and implicit in the textile workers' union and quite overt in the case of the *petroleros*. Officials of both unions emphasized the absence of compulsion at the local level. They pointed out that some workers vote for opposition parties, principally for the National Action Party. Moreover, the leaders at Ayotla Textiles alleged that, in contrast to many other PRI unions, workers were not mobilized for participation in progovernment demonstrations.

Still, the Ayotla union was certainly partisan. A few low local union officials held ranking positions in the PRI-dominated local *municipio*. These positions are not likely to be important policy-making positions.[35] Rather, they are more likely to be positions offered with a cooptative purpose in mind, that is, relatively minor positions allocated by the PRI to interest group leaders so as to keep them in line. The effect of this cooptation pattern is that union leaders are not likely to align with opposition parties but rather to support the PRI so as to maintain access to privilege. Accordingly, they are highly unlikely to try to align their union with a leftist party.

By contrast, Section 24 of the STPRM in Salamanca does formally endorse PRI candidates from the local to the national level. Section 24 leaders dutifully support the official endorsements made at the national level of the union. With the STPRM strict, centralized control is exercised by a union leadership that maintains a tightly symbiotic relationship with the PRI-government hierarchy. As noted in chapter 2, the leadership does not hesitate to use repression and to impose strict control from above but combines the stick with very juicy carrots.

On the surface it would appear that the sTPRM local would possess a high capacity for external mobilization. However, the data analysis indicates that this capacity may not be as effective as generally assumed.

Both of the Mexican incorporated unions limit their political role to conciliatory unionism. They give greater priority to job unionism than to political unionism in that they accept the existing distributional parameters within society and seek to maneuver for improvements within those limits. Political activity is only encouraged when needed to gain access to short-term benefits.

But how about the autonomous unions that have recently received so much attention in Mexico? Do they seek to align with Socialist and Marxist parties or movements? Do they seek to become the vanguard of the working class? To the contrary, Mexico's autonomous unions, including those that were studied,[36] exhibit a tendency to shun formal entry into partisan politics.[37] While they may be militant and strike over local issues, they nonetheless engage primarily in job unionism. They may, as in the case of the Nissan union, challenge local representatives of the political elite in order to attain autonomy for a local union. However, they generally eschew any permanent alliances with external organizations. Their only links are with independent labor confederations, which themselves eschew overt partisan connections. At most, the independent local unions engage in sporadic solidarity strikes with other unions or in demonstrations sponsored by leftist parties.[38]

The reasons given by autonomous union leaders for eschewing partisan politics are that workers' interests would not be well served. The union delegate in the leather-goods local in Leon stated: "We believe that politics should not be mixed with unionism. We think it is prejudicial for the workers. Take the case of what is occurring in Poland as evidence."[39] A similar view was expressed by a union official at the Nissan plant in Cuernavaca. "Parties are not beneficial for the unions. They should not be inside of unions because they would handle grievances for political motives instead of protecting the interests of the workers."[40]

Mexico's autonomous unions are willing to forego political unionism for enhanced job unionism. This implicit bargain implies that they are seeking autonomy from the state but not autonomy to transform the state. Their bargain is consistent with the leadership's stated view that improvement in the short-term conditions of employment is the primary purpose of the union movement. Alignment with the left offers little or nothing for achieving these goals. Leftist parties are in no position to deliver on material benefits. They are also unlikely to produce systemic transformation. Therefore, autonomous union leaders see the possibility of alignment with the partisan left as only risking disunity among their followers. Such disunity could only undermine the collective bargaining power of the union. Leaders of autonomous unions are also likely to be aware of the severe costs imposed on dissident unions that have overstepped the boundary of permissible behavior in the past. So while their conciliatory unionism may be more militant than that of the leaders of incorporated unions, they are not really seeking to supplant Mexican state capitalism, nor are they challenging the nature of the Mexican polity itself.

Before turning to Venezuelan leaders, we should note the special case of the FAT union in Leon. As shown, union leaders denied any mixing of partisan politics and union affairs. However, the data analysis indicated that this union clearly influenced workers to vote for the PAN. While one can only conjecture, it appears that ties between the union and PAN are largely covert and informal. Indeed, the leaders may perceive greater security in this arrangement than in more formal links to the PAN. Here it should be noted that labor ties are not with the left but with a center-right opposition party. Furthermore, this union is located in a small, nonstrategic industry and in a provincial city. Thus, no threat is posed to PRI hegemony in this isolated case of limited political unionism.

The local Venezuelan labor leaders who were interviewed were also more attuned to job unionism than to political unionism. Their primary concerns were with collective bargaining and with obtaining improved benefits for workers. In contrast to Mexican leaders, however, they tended to see partisan activity as normal activity for labor leaders and for workers. As a general rule, Venezuelan leaders tended to be skeptical of the value of overtly political activity by unions. They did not see politics as highly useful in generating material benefits for workers or in improving other working conditions. Indeed, overtly political activity on the job was viewed as being potentially divisive and a threat to unity that was necessary in collective bargaining.

Nonetheless, in twelve of thirteen Venezuelan unions, leaders acknowledged that they do work actively in political campaigns. They claimed to do so as individuals. The contrast with the Mexican unions is striking. In Mexico only the leaders of the petroleum workers union openly acknowledged campaign involvement (on behalf of the PRI). Interestingly, while Venezuelan union leaders acknowledged working actively for their respective parties, their unions generally do not officially endorse candidates. Only in a communist-dominated union in a plastics company in Barquisimeto were formal endorsements made. Nonendorsement of candidates seems to be a practice by which to avoid inflaming partisan divisions within the union.

Furthermore, union leaders generally drew a sharp distinction between their *politico* and *sindical* roles. Proselytizing for parties is carried out as an *adeco* or as a *mepista*, not as a part of one's union responsibilities. This role differentiation seems to be related to a belief that the material defense of workers' interests can be weakened by political involvement. Leaders in five Venezuelan unions saw political activity to be a *dis*advantage because of potential partisan divisiveness. In three cases union leaders acknowledged advantages in partisan activity but believed that the benefits accrued only to union leadership, not to the rank and file. Only one union leader interviewed saw political activity as opening up any benefits to rank-and-file workers. That leader, a *mepista* union official in the liquor company at La Miel, viewed politicized unions as effective pressure groups on behalf of working-class interests.[41]

What mobilizing strategies, then, might Venezuelan union leaders employ? The data provide few hints that there is any reciprocal exchange of votes or campaign support for material benefits for workers. There may well be some implicit understandings that were uncovered. Many Venezuelan union leaders admitted to propagandizing on behalf of parties with which they are affiliated. These activities may indicate efforts at external mobilization via symbol manipulation. But no evidence of clientelist-exchange relationships was found.

Venezuelan union leaders are frequently committed to a brand of conciliatory unionism, even when they are members of socialist parties. The following quotation, from a nominally socialist union leader, illustrates that conciliatory attitude. The individual was asked to define the term *class struggle*. We have to defend the workers, of course, but we are not only leaders of industrial workers, we are also leaders who need to serve the popular classes when they are in need. The union has to contribute something to the community, in the social and recreational fields. "We have to struggle on behalf of the dispossessed in the community—to help the poor (reconstruct their housing) when there are floods, to support the students in their causes, etc."[42] While displaying an admirable sense of class solidarity with those who are less well off, this "socialist" expressed little sense of conflict with higher social classes. His views reflect the conciliatory perspective of many Venezuelan Socialists.

By way of contrast, a communist labor leader did express a more combative view when defining the term *class conflict*. "Class struggle is the history of humanity; as long as exploiters and exploited exist, the confrontation of social classes is inevitable. The struggle begins when the worker arrives at the company and says 'I would like to earn 40 *bolivares*' and the company says 'You are going to earn 35 *bolivares*.' The class struggle ends when the workers take power."[43]

The leader who uttered this statement, an almost eloquent expression of militant class consciousness, heads a union that has *never* gone out on strike. His union had existed for only seven years, but it remained quite unclear that the leader's rhetorical commitment to a socialist transformation was matched by any corresponding behavioral patterns as a union tactician.[44]

These two individuals represent the range of variation one finds among leftist labor leaders in Venezuela. While less conciliatory at the rhetorical level than are the autonomous labor leaders in Mexico, the Venezuelan leaders generally fall short of having well thought-through strategies for long-range political action. In some cases they are Socialists who seem to deemphasize class conflict, to have little idea of how socialism might be instituted in Venezuela and who might well be satisfied with a "responsive" populist government. In other cases they are rhetorically militant Marxists but militants who fail to connect their long-term vision of societal reconstruction to short-term tactics. While the Venezuelan leftist union leaders may approximate anticapitalist, political unionists more than do the Mexican leaders of autonomous unions, it seems that Venezuelan union leaders, at most, occupy a midpoint on the continuum between ideal types. They are at least as they are conciliatory as they are anticapitalist and remain heavily oriented toward job unionism, whatever the veneer of political unionism that they might exhibit. The difference between Mexican and Venezuelan union leaders is only one of degree, not of kind.

Given the restraint exhibited by union leaders in the two countries, a crucial factor in explaining the mobilizational incapacity of unions has to be related to the nature of the union leadership. Leaders such as those who were interviewed cannot be expected to mobilize workers effectively for political action. Unions are a natural constituency of leftist parties. If the union leadership fails to mobilize workers effectively, leftist parties will suffer.

In democratic Venezuela, where bipartisanship is firmly entrenched and minor parties are well represented via the mechanisms of proportional representation, most union leaders express considerable reticence about engaging in explicitly partisan activity. Even fewer indicate a belief that protests, demonstrations, or other forms of demonstrative political action are useful. These leaders operate within a set of norms that constrain them to using less of the mobilizational space than the system would seem to afford.

Why do autonomous union leaders in Venezuela eschew mobilizing workers for system-challenging political action? Several factors come to mind. At the local level, Venezuela's leftist union officials might see very little to be gained in turning out a strong vote for the left or in more militant forms of political action. The position of AD and COPEI as hegemonic parties will clearly not be threatened by local electoral activism. But strong efforts on behalf of the left may provoke disunity within the local union. Furthermore, the preservation of Venezuela's democratic system is a value for most of Venezuela's socialist union leaders.[45] Many of these leaders witnessed severe repression of the labor movement under Gen. Marcos Pérez Jiménez.[46] Consequently, they use the available mobilizational space with restraint.

In Mexico the political space for citizen-initiated political action is considerably more constrained than in Venezuela. As Susan Purcell has observed, the leaders of Mexico's authoritarian regime are always loathe to let citizens believe that they can set the agenda for public discussion.[47] Leaders of autonomous unions in Mexico are capable of analytical sophistication; they reflect consciously on just how far they can go. The limits of union autonomy preclude both overt system-challenging action and explicit partisan activity. Indeed, to engage in opposition partisanship is to challenge the very nature of the regime. To challenge the nature of the Mexican regime is to invite repression.

Yet left-wing partisanship, as the data have shown, can generate both participatory motivations and political participation itself. The apolitical autonomous union of Mexico is a less-than-efficient tool for political mobilization. Similarly, the muted partisanship of Venezuela's leftist union leaders can also impede the political mobilization of working-class Venezuelans.

It is time to review why industrial workers in state-capitalist regimes are prone to support hegemonic parties rather than leftist parties. Lack of more widespread electoral support for the left cannot be explained by attitudinal or cognitive factors. There is nothing in the cognitive or attitudinal profile of workers in this sample that would suggest cultural or ideological constraints on electoral support for the left. To the contrary, a high aggregate level of political sophistication and discontent with the performance of incumbent parties would suggest a ready pool of leftist supporters.

The nature of the union movement in these two countries does not account for the electoral strength of hegemonic parties. No evidence was uncovered that incorporated unions strongly influence workers to vote for hegemonic parties. Nor did incorporated or autonomous unions in either country deliver a sizable vote to leftist parties. In general, the most striking feature of unions in Mexico and Venezuela is their relative incapacity to deliver the vote to either hegemonic or opposition parties. The pervasive apolitical unionism found in both autonomous and incorporated unions at the local level serves as a control mechanism over working-class mobilization, preventing unions from fully utilizing their political power. Certainly, apolitical unionism can be seen as a realistic adaptation to a political system where it is difficult for unions at the local level to influence national decision makers.

The one case where a manifestation of political unionism at the local level was found is instructive for understandng the other cases of apolitical unionism. The one exception to apolitical unionism at the local level was found in the FAT union in the leather-goods factory in Leon where the union apparently had formed ties with the PAN. In contrast to Venezuela's partisan-penetrated unions, there appears to be only a single party that has penetrated this union. Thus, PANistas within the local union leadership need not fear partisan divisiveness that seems to inhibit local Venezuelan union leaders from more aggressive political involvement. Furthermore, because of its small size and relative geographic isolation, this union may be able to get by with what larger unions cannot. The Mexican state would not likely tolerate electoral mobilization within large unions by opposition parties. Even in the case of the FAT union, the ties between the union and opposition parties appear to have been kept covert and informal rather than open and formal.

In sum, corporatist interest intermediation helps little to explain why workers support hegemonic parties. Restricted partisan competition explains far better why workers tend to support hegemonic rather than leftist parties. The willingness of workers to deviate from their party loyalty depended in part on the opportunity of their preferred party to gain power. Thus, deviations from party loyalty occurred less frequently among partisans of hegemonic parties than among partisans of opposition parties. Furthermore, deviations from opposition party loyalties were more likely to occur among Mexican workers than among Venezuelan workers as opposition parties in Mexico have less opportunity to win power. Additionally, deviant voting by opposition partisans was more likely to benefit hegemonic

Table 36. Determinants of Leftist Voting among Venezuelan and
Mexican Workers

Determinant	Beta Coefficient[a]
Socioeconomic status	.10
Age	−.12
Critical Consciousness	.14
Membership, autonomous union	.10
Psychological involvement in politics	.18
Performance evaluation	−.18
Electoral system (semi-competitive vs. competitive)	.24
Multiple r	.47
r^2	.22

[a]All coefficients are statistically significant at the .01 level. N = 806.

parties in Mexico than in Venezuela. All these findings can be explained by rational choice theory. Voters are prone to consider as options only parties that have a realistic chance of gaining power.

Restricted partisan competition also helps to account for the nature of the partisanship exhibited by these workers. The data suggested a disengaged partisanship among PRI supporters in Mexico. This type of partisanship is characterized by relatively low interest in politics and a cognitive disassociation of incumbent performance from partisanship. Voting, therefore, takes on a perfunctory character for PRIistas. By contrast, hegemonic partisans in Venezuela tend to be more interested in politics than nonpartisans and to relate their partisan loyalties to assessments of incumbent performance.

Restricted partisan competition also helps to explain why opposition parties cannot readily capitalize on working-class political discontent. Workers do not consider as a viable option opposition parties that have little or no chance of capturing political power. Thus, discontented Mexican workers are not prone to support any of the opposition parties. Indeed, they are prone to sit out elections (chapter 7). In the case of Venezuelan workers, the discontented are prone to vote for the "out" hegemonic party rather than for a leftist party. The former party is capable of capturing control of the national executive and legislative branches of government; the latter parties lack such capabilities.

It follows that the degree of partisan competition will significantly influence whether industrial workers will likely support leftist parties.

Workers will look for other options if they do not believe that the left can win. The impact of the larger electoral system on working-class support for the left is graphically illustrated in table 36. The regression analysis from a pooled sample of Venezuelan and Mexican workers shows that the type of electoral system in which workers are located better predicts electoral support for the left than do attitudes, type of union affiliation, and individual characteristics. This table illustrates the major point developed in this chapter—namely, that perceptions of the opportunity structure provided by elections more than any other factor shape working-class voting behavior in these two state-capitalist regimes.

Chapter Nine

Beyond Controlled Mobilization

Chapter 1 explained how Latin American inclusionary regimes use social pacts to incorporate various social sectors. Incorporation came about through social pacts in which economic benefits and other public goods were extended to various societal groups in exchange for their expected support of the existing state. The nature of the pact depended on the group's political power and control of investable capital. More privileged groups could negotiate more favorable bargains than less privileged groups.

Pact-constructed states, like Mexico and Venezuela, are designed to integrate all sectors of society into the state without disrupting economic development via a state-capitalist strategy. Private capital accumulation is protected by pacts with privileged groups. To paraphrase Terry Karl, capitalists are guaranteed the right to make money.[1] The support of less privileged groups is retained by granting access to limited public goods and services in ways that do not threaten capital accumulation.

The underlying social pacts have served the interests of privileged groups in these societies far more than the lower classes. This study has questioned why less privileged groups in Mexico and Venezuela have not mobilized to seek a different, more equitable strategy of economic development. In fact, it has shown that lower-class political mobilization has posed little threat to underlying social pacts or to the prevailing economic-development strategy. In other words, lower-class mobilization in these inclusionary regimes has not produced what Antonio Gramsci labeled a "hegemonic crisis" in which subordinate classes reject the terms of their incorporation into the existing political economy.[2]

On a theoretical level, patterns of controlled political mobilization were identified and contrasted with demobilization and patterns of autonomous mobilization (chapter 1). Then, this study analyzed the extent to which a sample of Mexican and Venezuelan industrial workers exhibited patterns of controlled rather than autonomous political mobilization. The analysis then focused on how working-class mobilization is controlled in these two political systems.

Data analysis, based on samples of industrial workers, revealed that some conventional explanations of how political control is maintained may be suspect. No evidence was found that these workers are crippled by a lack of political sophistication or by an authoritarian culture that would preclude them from self-directed political participation. For the most part, these workers appear to be capable of self-directed political activism without guidance from political parties or interest associations with which they are affiliated. Nor was support found for the "labor aristocracy thesis" according to which the more privileged sector of the lower classes, namely industrial workers, remains basically content with the status quo and, therefore, is unlikely to mobilize to bring about change. The data show that these workers generally believe their interests are ill-served by the existing state or by management and that they are dissatisfied with the performance of recent administrations. Surprisingly, little support was found for the explanation that attributes control to corporatist interest intermediation. There is no convincing evidence from these data that incorporated unions, in contrast to autonomous unions, defuse participatory motivations and generate electoral support for hegemonic parties.

How might one account for the absence of stronger guidance within the incorporated unions used for this study? One factor is clearly the tendency of local union leaders to shun political activism, as discussed in chapter 8. Another factor might be related to the nature of the formal proletariat in these unions. The formal proletariat may not be as dependent on external guidance as the informal sector of the lower class. The relatively high political sophistication of the formal sector (chapter 5), combined with a modicum of economic security, may increase the independence of these workers from organizational control. Similar observations have been made about organized labor in the United States.[3] Far greater organizational guidance of political participation might have been found had the study employed a sample of peasants or urban workers in the informal service or manufacturing sector. Even if the findings are partially an artifact of the unions sampled, these findings still highlight the need for a more refined explanation of how incorporated unions shape working-class political behavior. Clearly, guided political participation is not the norm in all Venezuelan and Mexican incorporated unions.

The possibility cannot be dismissed that incorporation of unions into hegemonic parties might provide an effective mechanism to control the union leadership even if the rank-and-file are not so easily controlled. Indeed, the leadership of incorporated unions used for this study was uniformly accommodative and compliant, though the same was generally true for leaders of autonomous unions.

The data do provide, however, reason to view the labor union movement as politically consequential. Both incorporated and autonomous unions in Mexico tend to defuse participatory motivations among rank-and-file workers. Both types of unions in Venezuela facilitate voting. More significantly, the priorities of the union movement in both countries minimize labor's political power. In all local unions examined for this study, higher priority was given to "job unionism" than to "political unionism." It cannot be determined if these priorities are a cause or a consequence of political powerlessness. Nevertheless, it can be asserted that existing priorities are related to organized labor's political weakness in these two countries.

Restricted partisan competition better explains how political mobilization is controlled than does union incorporation. Restricted party competition, as found in Mexico, clearly aids the hegemonic party in defusing political attentiveness and *concientización* among its working-class supporters, while enhancing its capacity to guide electoral mobilization and prevent short-term defections. Furthermore, leftist political parties in both countries cannot capitalize on working-class political discontent because of their competitive disadvantage with hegemonic parties. The left is not viewed as a viable alternative by workers in either country. This factor, rather than performance satisfaction, corporatist interest intermediation, or a working-class political culture, best explains why industrial workers in Venezuela and Mexico generally vote for hegemonic parties.

Restricted partisan competition by itself, however, fails to fully explain why industrial workers in these two countries do not devise strategies to create new electoral options. The study has suggested a rational utility explanation. Simply stated, if the left cannot win, why vote for it? As with demand protest or revolutionary activity, workers conclude that a system-challenging electoral strategy is no option, given the realities of the established electoral system.

Adam Przeworski's discussion of why some groups do not actively seek regime liberalization is useful for understanding why Venezuelan and Mexican workers are unlikely to opt for system-challenging political activity. Basically, Przeworski's argument is that the decision of a given group or actor to join a movement for liberalization depends not only on considerations of interests but also on calculations of likelihood of success. To determine likely success, the

individual (or group) calculates the likely number of other participants.[4] As Przeworski explains:

> Let k be the number of actors necessary and sufficient to make a move toward
> liberalizations successful. The strategic situation is then as follows. If I move
> and fewer than (k-1) others join, then I am likely to suffer unpleasant con-
> sequences. If I move and (k-1) others join, I will belong to a victorious move-
> ment and can expect to be rewarded appropriately. If I do not move and fewer
> than k others do, I will remain on the side of power and benefit from it.
> Finally, if I do not move, but more than (k-1) others do, I will again find
> myself on the losing side. Note that the value of the outcome increases as
> the number of actors making a move approaches k, from both sides.
>
> Without making specific assumptions about the value of the particular
> outcomes, one cannot make any predictions about strategic behavior. But
> what is apparent is the importance of expectations of success. Neither position
> is safe under the circumstances: to make a precipitous move is as dangerous
> as not joining in a movement that is successful. What this analysis implies,
> therefore, is that interests may be quite stable throughout the process but
> that they will be a poor predictor of behavior when expectations of success
> shift rapidly. Consequently, group analysis may generate weak predictions
> when groups are identified only by their interests, and therefore particular
> strategic postures may be embraced at particular moments by the same
> groups.[5]

These considerations might apply to the case of industrial workers
in Latin America. While workers may perceive their interests to
be better served by leftist parties, they are not likely to support
them unless they believe these parties can be successfully elected.
Voting for hegemonic parties might be a "risk aversive" strategy for
workers in electoral systems where competition is restricted. One does
not jeopardize one's standing with those in and likely to remain in
power. To support the left, on the other hand, is to be "on the losing
side."[6]

To understand why industrial workers in these countries and
elsewhere in Latin America perceive success for the left as unlikely,
one should compare their situation with that of industrial workers in
Western European countries. In the latter countries, it is far easier
than in Latin America to build a winning leftist multiclass coalition.
In Sweden, for example, over 70 percent of the nonmanual employees
were organized by 1970, principally in the Tjanstemannens Central-
organisation (Central Organization of Salaried Employees, or TCO).
When salaried employees are added to the very high percentage of
manual employees organized in the Landsorganisationen (Swedish

Federation of Trade Unions or LO),[7] the strength of the Swedish Social Democratic party/labor movement is considerable. In cases like Sweden and Norway, the basis of a dominant center-left political coalition is an organized formal industrial proletariat in league with an organized corps of middle-class service workers and intellectuals.

In Latin America the class structure is greatly different than Sweden's.[8] The *formal industrial proletariat*, while substantial in countries like Venezuela and Mexico, does not even approach being a majority of the urban population, let alone of the total national population. Alejandro Portes estimates the formal proletariat as around 22 percent for Latin America as a whole.[9] There is also a sizable *informal petty bourgeoisie* (very small merchants or manufacturers, poorly capitalized, using simple technologies of manufacture or merchandising), estimated at around 10 percent, and a much larger *informal proletariat* (self- or family-employed individuals or workers in the poorly capitalized small enterprises noted above). The latter constitutes somewhere between 30 percent and 60 percent of the population in Latin American countries. The well-paid service sector workers constitute what Portes denotes as the *bureaucratic-technical class*, which averages about 6 percent of the population in Latin America and rarely surpasses 10 percent.

Consider the implications. In Northern European countries, such as Sweden and Norway, the formal proletariat and the middle class (which Portes calls the bureaucratic-technical class) can easily constitute an electoral majority. Strong incentives exist to build an electoral coalition capable of sustaining power through an alliance of proletarians and progressive middle-class elements. But in Latin America the numbers are just not there. Those social classes in Northern Europe that can comprise a "majority coalition" capable of dominating the political process through a political party/labor union alliance cannot do so in Latin America. If one accepts Portes's estimates of class structures, the total of the formal proletariat and the whole of the middle classes (including both the bureaucratic-technical class and the informal bourgeoisie) would not on an average surpass 38 percent. Defections of certain middle class groups from progressive causes could be expected and would reduce the percentage.[10]

Hence, building a progressive alliance with any hope of attaining power and of transforming Latin American societies through electoral means, as has been attempted in Scandinavia and was attempted in Chile before 1973, would require a wider coalition. The organizational effort would have to extend into the informal proletariat and peasants. These groups comprise the most sizable segment of Latin American populations. Yet formidable barriers exist to creating such a leftist coalition.

The dispersion of these groups into multiple work sites with multiple employers is problematic. In small enterprises and in rural areas, paternalistic labor relations are the norm. Dispersion and the prevailing paternalistic authority structures create problems for leftist organizers seeking to form horizontal class loyalties transcending the immediate workplace. Furthermore, leftist parties often lack the resources to deal with the immediate problems of the poor. Such groups' grievances may have as much to do with urban housing, sanitation, or tenure as with classwide conditions.[11]

Another problem involves the nature of leftist party leadership in Venezuela, Mexico, and elsewhere in Latin America. The leadership, as well as the mass base of these parties, has come overwhelmingly from progressive elements of the middle and upper classes. Consequently, most members of these parties are not "well grounded" in the realities of life in impoverished communities. Furthermore, these parties often engage in arcane ideological debates among themselves and are hurt by cognitive associations with totalitarianism, violence, the Soviet Union, and atheism. These factors help to create a popular lower-class image of the left as being irrelevant and even dangerous.

The existing state also poses a barrier to expanding the base of support for Venezuelan and Mexican leftist parties. Leaders of autonomous unions, peasant associations, and other possible target groups may be fully aware of limits to the possible. It is doubtful that leaders of hegemonic parties in either country would permit the radical shift in power resources implied by a left-labor-peasant alliance. The PRI has recently employed electoral fraud and intimidation to put down the challenge to its hegemony by the PAN in some northern states.[12] This example, as well as others discussed in chapter 4, shows that the PRI is not likely to acquiesce easily to strong challenges from the left. Similarly, leaders of Venezuelan hegemonic parties would be likely to see a broad-based leftist movement as a threat to the social pacts by which the Venezuelan state was constituted. Leaders of interest associations linked to the lower classes, therefore, might see explicitly political strategies as self-defeating or as unrealistic, given the uneven distribution of power resources. For this reason they may well focus on more modest goals rather than seek to transform the existing sociopolitical order via political strategies.

Both the Movement toward Socialism (MAS) in Venezuela and the Mexican Communist party have recently sought to expand their mass

base beyond middle-class intellectuals to include workers and peasants.[13] Their attempts have met with little success in either country,
despite severe economic crises and unpopular austerity programs in
the eighties. In Mexico the left lost ground to the PRI and to the PAN
in every election since 1979,[14] while the Venezuelan left has experienced similar erosion of its strength throughout the eighties.[15]

These developments suggest that a left-labor-peasant alliance will
not easily be forged in either country. The results of this study show
why lower-class discontent is not likely to be converted into electoral
support for the left. So long as the left is perceived as incapable of
winning, it is likely to remain incapable of building a larger lower-
class support base. Consequently, the lower classes cannot utilize
their most potent political resource—their size—to bring to power a
government more responsive to their interests.[16]

A review of the consequences of controlled mobilization for economic development in Venezuela and Mexico and a discussion of the
potential of the union movement as a vanguard in forming a left-
labor-peasant alliance will conclude this study.

In much of Latin America, economic growth has been sustained
and dramatic throughout the twentieth century. As noted in chapter
3, both Venezuela and Mexico have industrialized rapidly in the post-
World War II era.[17] Yet four decades of industrial transformation have
not produced dramatic changes in national distributions of income,
which often remain essentially static. The possibility that the Latin
American poor might have improved in absolute terms while re-
maining far behind in relative terms is a subject of continuing debate
among scholars, but most scholars agree that Latin American income-
distribution profiles have not changed dramatically in the post-World
War II era, except for countries undergoing revolutionary change.[18]
Attempts to diagnose the causes of distributional stasis have provoked
even more disagreement.[19] That complicated empirical dispute cannot
be resolved in this volume. Yet it is clear that labor movements must
surely have profound consequences for the distribution of income in
society and for the type of development to which society can aspire.[20]

The Venezuelan economist, Asdrubal Baptista, noted recently
that "the distribution of income [in Venezuela] has not followed the
usual tendency in other [European] countries and, more importantly,
has moved in the opposite direction in recent years, exhibiting a decrease in salaries as a percentage of national income." This author
concludes that "the internal market is very limited, and worse yet,
its growth has been very slow in comparison with the demands imposed by the growth in productive activity in Venezuela. Internal

demand for national production, in view of the distribution of income, has been less than it should have been in order to promote an harmonic and equilibrated development of the economy."[21]

Similar observations are made by domestic economists in most of Latin America, including Mexico. While this study does not suggest that the condition of labor movements can explain all distortions of national development in Latin American state-capitalist regimes, labor union performance may well be related to distributional outcomes. Not only the amount of economic growth experienced but also the type of development experienced, if genuine development occurs at all, may well depend on the success of low-income classes in pressing for improvements in economic distributions. Such improvements do not happen automatically.[22]

Perhaps, it is unrealistic to expect organized labor ever to lead in the formation of a left-labor-peasant alliance that might lead to the reorientation of development policy. Yet this sector might better take the lead than other groups. Unfortunately, existing leftist parties are weak and highly fragmented and comprised of a leadership with few roots in the lower classes. Peasant organizations and the few organizations of informal sector workers would suffer from problems already mentioned, particularly geographic dispersion and existing paternalistic labor relations. In addition, rank-and-file members of such organizations might lack the political sophistication and economic security to mobilize for autonomous political action independent of ruling parties.

The data analysis presented in this study suggests that existing levels of consciousness and clientelist controls might prove less than formidable barriers for mobilizing rank-and-file industrial workers. The prerequisite union leadership might prove a more formidable barrier. This is true because the union leadership must overcome such problems as internal fragmentation of the union movement and ideological diversity among union leaders, as well as be willing to accept the risks of "political unionism." Some union leaders have been willing to lead insurgent movements seeking autonomy from official control. However, the purpose has more often been to achieve more effective "job unionism" than to promote "political unionism."[23] Even if such a commitment were made, the task of forging a left-labor-peasant alliance would remain formidable for reasons already discussed.

It would be unrealistic to expect union leaders to accept the risks of forming a broad-based political alliance unless the state and privileged groups were willing to tolerate such developments. Past history in both countries suggests that privileged groups would resort to repression in such instances (chapter 4). More than one Latin American military coup has been justified to the middle and upper classes by invoking the specter of uncontrolled mass mobilization and alleged radicalism of labor leaders.[24]

Yet there are costs with imposing political control over working-class political mobilization. These costs include (1) prolongation of economic policies that do not lead to national economic integration and (2) accumulation of social tensions that may make social peace difficult to sustain over the longer term. Failure to attain national economic integration may well mean that the society loses because the growth rate becomes less than what it could be and the growth that occurs will benefit fewer people than it could.[25] Moreover, there is always the possibility that accumulated social tensions will find outlets in crime and that social violence may erupt into political violence after years of apparent peace.[26]

This study has shown that labor's failure to play a more creative role in building a more socially just and democratic society in these two countries is not likely the fault of rank-and-file industrial workers. They remain politically silent because they cannot envision new alternatives to hegemonic parties and existing social pacts. To create new alternatives would be a Herculean and, perhaps, an impossible task for Mexican and Venezuelan labor leaders. However, such a task might be perceived as more tenable by labor elites in the late eighties than at the time of inverviewing for this study in 1979 and 1980. Workers interviewed for this study were generally supportive of their unions.[27] However, the economic crisis of the eighties has likely weakened the capacity of union leaders to build support among rank-and-file workers by delivering material benefits and protecting real wages.[28] Therefore, a political strategy centered on building a broad-based progressive alliance could become attractive to union leaders in the future if economic stagnation continues. As this study has shown, rank-and-file industrial workers ought to be amenable to the creation of such a left-labor-peasant alliance, just as Western European workers favored the creation of leftist alternatives.

Data Base for Study of Venezuelan and Mexican Workers

Sampling Criterion	Geographic Location	Type of Unions Sampled	Dominant Partisan Tendency of Union Leadership[a]	Number of Cases
Venezuela				
(1) Non-Unionized, Non-Strategic Industries	Barquisimeto	None (workers from various small industries and shops)	Not Applicable	120
(2) Incorporated Unions, Non-Strategic Industries	Barquisimeto	Five unions representing metal fabrication workers, textile workers, graphic arts workers, dairy workers, and soft drink bottling workers, respectively	Either AD(1) or COPEI(1) or an AD/COPEI coalition(3)	128
(3) Incorporated Unions, Strategic Industries	Punto Fijo	Four unions of petroleum workers	COPEI(2) or URD(2)	99
(4) Autonomous Unions, Non-Strategic Industries	A) La Miel B) Barquisimeto	Two unions, one representing a soft drink factory and another representing plastics workers	MEP and the Venezuelan Communist Party	72
(5) Autonomous Unions, Strategic Industries	Punto Fijo	Two unions of petroleum workers	Left Coalition and MEP	100
Mexico				
(1) Non-Unionized, Non-Strategic Industries	Mexico City	None (workers from various small industries and shops)	Not Applicable	100
(2) Incorporated Unions, Non-Strategic Industries	Ayotla, Puebla	Union of textile workers	Confederation of Mexican Workers, (CTM) PRI Affiliated	100
(3) Incorporated Unions, Strategic Industries	Salamanca, Guanajuato	Union of petroleum workers	Confederation of Mexican Workers (CTM)	100
(4) Autonomous Unions, Non-Strategic Industries	León, Guanajuato	Union of leather goods workers	Frente Autentico de Trabajo (FAT)	100
(5) Autonomous Unions, Strategic Industries	Cuernavaca, Morelos	Automobile workers' union	Unidad Obrera Independente (UOI)	100

[a]Determination of dominant partisan tendency of Venezuelan union leadership based on elite interviews with union leaders. AD Acción Democrática; COPEI Social Christian Party; MEP Movimiento Electoral del Pueblo; URD Union Republicana Democratica.

Source: Charles L. Davis, "Political Regimes and the Socioeconomic Resource Model of Political Mobilization: Some Venezuelan and Mexican Data," *Journal of Politics* 45, no. 2 (May 1983): 444–45.

Measurement and Scaling of Independent and Control Variables

As a general introduction to our scaling decisions, it ought to be noted that the study sought to develop equivalent measures for the Venezuelan and Mexican samples. Usually, this implied the use of identical or analogous items, although sometimes functionally equivalent items were employed. Dependent variables are not presented because frequency distributions are presented in chapter 5 and factor scales are described in Appendix C.

ISSUE-BASED MOTIVATIONS

Evaluation of Government Performance, Mexico

Respondents were asked to evaluate the performance of the then current president, José López Portillo (1976-82) and his predessor, Luis Echeverría (1970-76) in the following areas: public transportation, police protection, housing for the poor, public education, jobs creation, and income redistribution. Respondents evaluated performance on a five-point scale. A varimax rotated factor analysis of all items revealed a three-dimensional solution. The three factors are labeled as follows: Evaluation of Urban Services, Evaluation of Public Education, and Evaluation of Economic Redistribution. The respective factor scales follow.

Evaluation of Urban Services

Police protection:	López Portillo	.73
	Echeverría	.65
Public transportation	López Portillo	.57
	Echeverría	.54
Housing for the poor:	Echeverría	.36
Eigenvalue		4.40
Percentage of variance explained by factor		36.6%

Evaluation of Public Education

López Portillo	.56
Echeverría	.79
Eigenvalue	1.33
Percentage of variance explained by factor	11.1%

Evaluation of Economic Redistribution

Income redistribution:	López Portillo	.52
Jobs creation:	Echeverría	.57
Income redistribution:	Echeverría	.62
Eigenvalue		1.17
Percentage of variance explained by factor		9.8%

Evaluation of Government Performance, Venezuela

The same items were used in the Venezuelan survey instrument with the exception of the items for income redistribution. Thus, five items were used to assess how Venezuelan workers in the sample evaluated the performance of the then incumbent Luis Herrera Campins (1987-83) and his predecessor, Carlos Andrés Pérez (1973-78). A varimax rotated factor analysis revealed that Venezuelan workers are prone to organize their assessments of performance around discrete presidential administrations rather than around general policy areas as found to be the case for Mexican workers. The data analysis uses only the assessment scale of Andrés Pérez because Herrera Campins was still early into his administration at the time of interviewing.

	Rotated Factor Loading
Evaluation of Performance of Andrés Pérez	
Public transportation	.75
Police protection	.77
Housing for the poor	.73
Public education	.75
Jobs creation	.60
Eigenvalue	4.52
Percentage of variance explained by factor	45.2%

Critical Consciousness (concientización)

This factor scale was constructed from three independently derived factor scales: (1) class consciousness, (2) structure-blaming attitudes, and (3) class solidarity. A master scale was formed via factor analysis in both the Venezuelan and Mexican samples. Class consciousness (or perceptions of labor-management relations) is based on the following items: (1) whether workers receive appropriate salaries *vis-à-vis* work done; (2) whether workers; salaries are high or low; (3) extent to which owners and managers truly care about workers; (4) extent to which owners earn too much or too little; and (5) extent to which company profits benefit workers. Structure-blaming attitudes are inferred from two items and follow-up probes. One item dealt with whether the majority of Mexicans/Venezuelans received their fair share of the good things in life; a second item dealt with whether the individual received a fair share of the good things in life. In the follow-up probes, those who attributed the existence of "unfairness" to social structures (such as, lack of educational opportunity, the power of the upper classes, political corruption that reinforces existing conditions) were assigned a higher value than those who interpreted existing inequities as a result of personal deficiencies of the deprived (such as lack of effort and lack of training). Both groups received a higher score than those who perceived no inequities. Class solidarity was operationally measured as the product of three items, including (1) endorsement of local unions joining general strikes, (2) abstract endorsement of idea of general strikes, and (3) endorsement of interenterprise strikes.

The varimax rotated factor scales for critical consciousness as formed from the three subscales follow.

Critical Consciousness
Rotated Factor Loading
Mexico
Class consciousness	.39
Class solidarity	.32
Structure-blame	.61
Eigenvalue	1.37
Percentage of variance explained by factor	45.8%

Venezuela
Class consciousness	.32
Class solidarity	.53
Structure-blame	.47
Eigenvalue	1.38
Percentage of variance explained by factor	46.1%

ISSUE-NEUTRAL MOTIVATIONS

Psychological Involvement in Politics

For both samples a similar procedure was followed in constructing this scale. A political interest and political information scale were formed. Scores on these two scales were standardized and then summed. The political interest scale was formed from items that loaded on a separate factor dimension in the analysis of the structure of political participation as reported in table 8. To measure the political information available to the respondent, a wide array of items in which respondents were asked the more obvious (name of current president) to the more esoteric (major national export) was used. A selection of items was culled to form acceptable Guttman scales for both national samples (for Mexico, coefficient of reproducibility = .95, coefficient of scalability = .73; for Venezuela, coefficient of reproducibility = .92, coefficient of scalability = .68).

RESOURCE VARIABLES

Age

The actual age in years as reported by the respondent during the interview was used to measure age.

Socioeconomic Status

A three-item factor scale was employed. The items used and the factor scores from a rotated varimax factor analysis are reported below.

Socioeconomic Status
Factor Loading
Mexico

Number of years of formal education	.31
Weekly family income	.78
Job skill level (unskilled, semiskilled, skilled)	.34
Eigenvalue	1.42
Percentage of variance explained by factor	47.4%

Venezuela

Number of years of formal education	.36
Weekly family income	.67
Job skill level (unskilled, semiskilled, skilled)	.70
Eigenvalue	1.66
Percentage of variance explained by factor =	55.3%

MEASUREMENT OF EXTERNAL MOBILIZATION

Strength of Institutional Affiliation

To measure strength of institutional affiliation, researchers devised an ordinally ranked typology similar to that used by Verba, Nie, and Kim in *Participation and Political Equality*, 106-11. However, this study did not use their distinction between politicized and nonpoliticized interest groups and focused entirely on membership in labor unions, the only type of politicized organization with which our respondents tended to be affiliated. Similar to Verba, Nie, and Kim, the typology here is formed by combining strength of party loyalty with union membership. The four categories in the institutional affiliation typology are defined as follows:

(1) Nonpoliticals. These individuals have no political institutional affiliation. They are neither members of labor unions nor do they identify with political parties.

(2) Weakly affiliated. These individuals are either nonidentifiers with a party who are members of a union or else moderately weak party identifiers who are nonunion members.

(3) Moderately affiliated. These individuals are either union members who are moderate/weak party identifiers or else nonunion members who strongly identify with a political party.

(4) Strongly affiliated. These are union members who are strong party identifiers.

Partisan Identification

Dichotomized dummy variables were created to measure (1) identification with hegemonic parties and (2) identification with leftist parties. Hegemonic parties in Venezuela included COPEI and Acción Democrática (AD). The hegemonic party in Mexico is the Partido Revolucionario Institucional (PRI). Identification with the following Mexican parties was treated as leftist sympathy: the Popular Socialist Party (PPS), the Party of Mexican Workers (PMT), the Socialist Workers Party (PST), and the Mexican Communist Party (PCM). Venezuelan leftist parties included the Electoral Peoples' Movement (MEP), the Movement toward Socialism (MAS), the Revolutionary Leftist Movement (MIR), and the Venezuelan Communist Party (PCU).

Union Membership

Dichotomized, dummy variables were created to measure (1) membership in autonomous unions and (2) membership in incorporated unions. The incorporated and autonomous unions used for this study are listed in Appendix A.

Modes of Political Activity:
A Varimax Factor Analysis

	Political Interest	Campaign Activity	Voting	Communal Activity
Venezuelan Workers				
Discuss politics at home	.647	.340	.067	− .131
Discuss politics at work	.495	.407	.018	.062
Read news in paper	.754	.202	.105	.321
Pay attention to news:				
TV or radio	.716	.175	.111	.310
Attend political meetings	.297	.602	.059	.214
Participate in campaign activities	.159	.816	.071	.278
Discuss politics in organizations	.402	.681	.086	.140
Generally vote	.155	.057	.249	.129
Generally vote in national elections	.068	.040	.808	.043
Vote in 1973 election	− .008	− .051	.611	.086
Vote in 1978 election	− .039	− .019	.609	− .006
Vote in 1979 election	.128	.145	.415	.070
Member:				
Parents' association	.017	.089	.084	.391
Cooperative	.139	.101	.161	.456
Neighborhood organization	.102	.178	− .073	.243
Eigenvalue	4.28	2.13	1.19	1.00

	Voting	Political Interest	Campaign Activity	Communal Activity
Mexican Workers				
Discuss politics at home	.018	.482	.259	− .012
Discuss politics at work	.004	.562	.204	.000
Read news in paper	− .074	.865	.114	.154
Pay attention to news:				
TV or radio	− .032	.732	.164	.093

	Voting	Political Interest	Campaign Activity	Communal Activity
Attend political meetings	− .108	.324	.639	− .040
Participate in campaign activities	− .047	.232	.920	.005
Discuss politics in organizations	.042	.244	.704	.179
Generally vote	.846	.012	− .012	− .035
Generally vote in national elections	.768	− .016	− .045	− .018
Vote in 1970 election	.574	− .041	.009	.133
Vote in 1976 election	.722	− .045	− .058	.075
Vote in 1979 election	.695	.010	.002	− .056
Member:				
Parents' Association	.068	.105	.093	.614
Cooperative	− .018	.017	.003	.383
Neighborhood Organization	.035	.015	.000	.530
Eigenvalue	3.59	3.04	1.52	1.24

Notes

CHAPTER ONE

1. Richard Couto, "Political Silence and Appalachia," *Appalachian Journal* 5, no. 1 (Autumn 1977): 116-23.

2. For an excellent overview of social and economic problems in Appalachia, see David Whisnant, *Modernizing the Mountaineer: People, Power, and Planning* (Boone, N.C.: Appalachian Consortium Press, 1982).

3. Political silence does not imply political inactivity but rather a lack of political activity designed to challenge existing policy priorities and to bring about sociopolitical reform. In fact, as recent empirical studies have shown, lower-class populations in Latin America do engage in political activity usually for short-term instrumental purposes and in a nonthreatening way. This literature is further discussed in chapter 5.

4. Among the earlier formulations of dependency theory were those by Fernando Henrique Cardoso and Enzo Faletto in *Dependency and Development* (Berkeley: Univ. of California Press, 1979, English language version of work first published in Spanish in 1969); and by Theotonio dos Santos, "The Structure of Dependence," *American Economic Review* 60, no. 9 (May 1970): 231-36. Later, numerous empirically grounded investigations have specified more exactly the mechanisms by which external constraints operate. See, for example, Gary Gereffi, *The Pharmaceutical Industry and Dependency in the Third World* (Princeton: Princeton Univ. Press, 1983).

5. On the central role of the state in late capitalist industrializing nations, see Sylvia Ann Hewlett and Richard S. Weinert, "Introduction: The Characteristics and Consequences of Late Development in Brazil and Mexico," in Hewlett and Weinert, eds., *Brazil and Mexico: Patterns in Late Development* (Philadelphia: Institute for the Study of Human Issues, 1982), 2-4.

6. Wayne A. Cornelius, "Immigration, Mexican Development Policy, and the Future of U.S.–Mexican Relations," *Working Papers in U.S.–Mexican Studies*, no. 8 (La Jolla, Calif. Center for U.S.–Mexican Studies, Univ. of California, San Diego, 1980): 32-33.

7. For an analysis of a specific case of capital flight in the face of a populist regime seeking only "quasi-comprehensive reforms," see Soledad Loaeza, "La política del rumor: México, Noviembre-Diciembre de 1976," *Foro Internacional* 17, no. 4 (Abril-Junio 1977): 557-86.

8. Anderson has identified three approaches to economic development: the *conventional* approach, the *democratic reform* approach, and the *revolutionary socialist* approach. See Charles W. Anderson, *Politics and Economic Change in Latin America* (New York: VanNostrand Reinhold Co., 1967), 163-99.

9. For a discussion of the concept of preemptive reform, see Kenneth M. Coleman and Charles L. Davis, "Preemptive Reform and the Mexican Working Class," *Latin American Research Review* 18, no. 1 (1983): 3-31.

10. Alain de Janvry, *The Agrarian Question and Reformism in Latin America* (Baltimore: John Hopkins Univ. Press, 1981).

11. James M. Malloy, "Generation of Political Support and Allocation of Costs," in Carmelo Mesa-Lago, ed., *Revolutionary Change in Cuba* (Pittsburgh: Univ. of Pittsburgh Press, 1970), 26.

12. Ibid., 26.

13. See Robert R. Kaufman, "Democratic and Authoritarian Responses to the Debt Problem: Argentina, Brazil, and Mexico" (paper presented at the 1983 annual meeting of the American Political Science Association, Washington, D.C.).

14. This point is developed in Evelyne Huber Stephens, *The Politics of Workers' Participation: The Peruvian Approach in Comparative Perspective* (New York: Academic Press, 1980), 31-37. Stephens notes: "Ownership can be conceptualized as a bundle of rights, the two basic types being the right to control the use of property (control rights) and the right to appropriate profits generated by its use (income rights). . . . Either or both of these . . . rights can be transferred in varying degrees from the holder of the legal title of ownership to other actors" (10).

15. Anderson, *Politics and Economic Change*, 97-104.

16. See Guillermo O'Donnell, "Reflections on the Patterns of Change in the Bureaucratic-Authoritarian State," *Latin American Research Review* 13, no. 1 (1978): 6.

17. See Edward C. Epstein, "Legitimacy, Institutionalization, and Opposition in Exclusionary Bureaucratic-Authoritarian Regimes: The Situation of the 1980s," *Comparative Politics* 17, no. 1 (Oct., 1984): 37-54.

18. See Fernando Henrique Cardozo, "On the Characterization of Authoritarian Regimes in Latin America," in David Collier, ed., *The New Authoritarianism in Latin America* (Princeton: Princeton Univ. Press, 1979), 38-40.

19. See Ieda Siqueira Wiarda, "Venezuela: The Politics of Democratic Developmentalism," in Howard J. Wiarda and Harvey F. Kline, eds., *Latin American Politics and Development*, 2d ed. (Boulder, Colo.: Westview Press, 1985), 309.

20. Daniel Levy and Gabriel Szekely, *Mexico: Paradoxes of Stability and Change* (Boulder, Colo.: Westview Press, 1983), 69.

21. See table 1 in José A. Silva Michelena and Heinz Rudolf Sonntag, *El Proceso Electoral de 1979* (Caracas: Editorial Ateneo de Caracas, 1979), 159.

22. See James M. Malloy, "The Politics of Transition in Latin America," in Malloy and Mitchell A. Seligson, eds., *Authoritarians and Democrats: Regime Transition in Latin America* (Pittsburgh: Univ. of Pittsburgh Press, 1987), 239-40.

23. Malloy, "Politics of Transition," 240-41.

24. On the role of "power capabilities" in negotiating entry into the political arena, see Anderson, *Politics and Economic Change*, 87-101.

25. For supporting data see Alejandro Portes, "Latin American Class Structures: Their Composition and Change during the Last Decades," *Latin American Research Review* 20, no. 3: 7-40.

26. For data on working-class electoral support for the left in Western Europe, see tables 1 and 2 in Brian H. Smith and José Luis Rodriguez, "Comparative Working-Class Political Behavior," *American Behavioral Scientist* 18, no. 1 (Sept. 1974): 62-63.

27. The research design is explained in more detail later on in the chapter.

28. Among other things, see Wayne A. Cornelius, *Politics and the Migrant Poor in Mexico City* (Stanford: Stanford Univ. Press, 1975).

29. Among many recent studies on organized labor in Latin America, see John Humphrey, *Capitalist Control and Workers' Struggle in the Brazilian Auto Industry* (Princeton: Princeton Univ. Press, 1982); and Jennifer L. McCoy, "From Party to State: Inducements, Constraints, and Labor in Venezuela," *Latin American Research Review* (forthcoming).

30. The lack of adequate survey data on organized workers in the industrial sector in Latin America has sometimes necessitated the use of secondary data sources. See, for example, Howard Handleman, "Unionization, Ideology, and Political Participation within the Mexican Working Class," in Mitchell A. Seligson and John A. Booth, eds., *Political Participation in Latin America*, 2 (New York: Holmes and Meier, 1979): 154-68.

31. This interpretation is often found in studies that emphasize organized labor as a privileged stratum of the lower class.

32. This point is cogently argued in the case of Chilean, Colombian, Argentine, and Venezuelan labor in Charles Bergquist, *Labor in Latin America: Comparative Essays on Chile, Argentina, Venezuela, and Colombia* (Stanford: Stanford Univ. Press, 1986).

33. On the *Coordinadoras* in Mexico, see Barry Carr, "The Mexican Left, the Popular Movements, and the Politics of Austerity, 1982-1985," in Carr and Ricardo Anzaldua Montoya, eds., *The Mexican Left, the Popular Movements, and the Politics of Austerity*, Monograph Series 18 (La Jolla, Calif.: Center for U.S.–Mexican Studies, Univ. of California, San Diego, 1986), 1-18. On the *nuevo sindicalismo* in Venezuela, see Daniel Hellinger, "Venezuelan Democracy and the Challenge of 'Nuevo Sindicalismo' " (Paper presented at the 1986 Meeting of the Latin American Studies Association, Boston).

34. See Elizabeth Jelín, *La Protesta Obrera: Participación de Bases y Sindicato* (Buenos Aires: Ediciones Nueva Visión, 1974), 77-94.

35. Cornelius, *Politics and the Migrant Poor*, 109-34.

36. See Raymond B. Pratt, "Community Political Organizations and Lower-Class Politicization in Two Latin American Cities," *Journal of Developing Areas* 5 (July 1971): 523-42.

37. See Karen L. Remmer, "Military Rule and Political Demobilization in Latin America" (Paper delivered at the 1979 Meeting of the American Political Science Association, Washington, D.C.), 3.

38. Remmer, "Military Rule and Political Demobilization," 7-12, passim.

39. Remmer recognizes other interpretations of Chilean politics that emphasize greater state control over political mobilization.

40. See Evelyne Huber Stephens and John D. Stephens, "The Transition to Mass Parties and Ideological Politics: The Jamaican Experience since 1972," *Comparative Political Studies* 19, no. 4 (Jan. 1987): 443-83.

41. See Kenneth Paul Erickson, *The Brazilian Corporative State and Working-Class Politics* (Berkeley: Univ. of California Press, 1977).

42. See Henry Dietz, "Some Modes of Participation in an Authoritarian Regime," *Journal of Political and Military Sociology* 3 (Spring 1977): 63-77.

43. See Guillermo O'Donnell, *Modernization and Bureaucratic-Authoritarianism: Studies on South American Politics* (Berkeley: Institute of International Studies, Univ. of California, 1972).

44. See various articles in David Collier, ed., *The New Authoritarianism in Latin America* (Princeton: Princeton Univ. Press, 1979).

45. For empirical support of this proposition, see Sidney Verba, Norman H. Nie, and Jae-On Kim, *Participation and Political Equality: A Seven-Nation Comparison* (Cambridge: Cambridge Univ. Press, 1978), 112-43.

46. See Ronald Inglehart, "Changing Paradigms in Comparative Political Behavior" (Paper presented at the 1982 Annual Meeting of the American Political Science Association, Denver, Colo.), 12.

47. Ibid., 13.

48. See Kay Lehman Schlozman and Sidney Verba, *Injury to Insult: Unemployment, Class, and Political Response* (Cambridge: Harvard Univ. Press, 1979), 103-38.

49. Philippe C. Schmitter, "Still the Century of Corporatism?" in F.B. Pike and T. Stritch, eds., *The New Corporatism: Social-Political Structures in the Iberian World* (Notre Dame: Univ. of Notre Dame Press, 1974), 93-94.

50. See Seymour Martin Lipset and Stein Rokkan, *Party Systems and Voter Alignments* (New York: Free Press, 1967).

51. See Lawson's discussion of alternative linkage mechanisms in Kay Lawson, "Political Parties and Linkage," in Lawson, ed., *Political Parties and Linkage: A Comparative Perspective* (New Haven: Yale Univ. Press, 1980), 3-24.

52. John G. Corbett, "Linkage as Manipulation: The *Partido Revolucionario Institutional* in Mexico," in Lawson, *Political Parties,* 328-29.

53. See Kevin J. Middlebrook, "Corporatism and the Political Economy of Organized Labor in Colombia, Brazil, and Mexico" (Paper prepared for delivery at the 1979 meeting of the Latin American Studies Association, Pittsburgh, Pa).

54. Robert Kaufman, "Corporatism, Clientelism, and Partisan Conflict: A Study of Seven Latin American Countries," in James M. Malloy, ed., *Authoritarianism and Corporatism in Latin America* (Pittsburgh: Univ. of Pittsburgh Press, 1977), 112.

55. Benjamin Ginsberg, *The Captive Public: How Mass Opinion Promotes State Power* (New York: Basic Books, 1986), 48-49.

56. See the definition for this concept that is provided in chapter 6.

57. See Portes, "Latin American Class Structures," 7-40.

58. See Cornelius, *Politics and the Migrant Poor*, 201-25.

59. See David Felix, "Income Distribution and the Quality of Life in Latin America: Patterns, Trends, and Policy Implications," *Latin American Research Review* 18, no. 2 (1983): 3-34. See also Portes, "Latin American Class Structures," 22-27.

60. For further elaboration of the "labor aristocracy thesis," see Charles L. Davis, "The 'Labor Aristocracy Thesis' and the Political Quiescence of Labor," *Social Science Quarterly* 67, no. 2 (June 1986): 419-31.

61. The term *participant citizenship* comes from Alex Inkeles, "Participant Citizenship in Six Developing Countries," *American Political Science Review* 63, no. 4 (Dec. 1969): 1120-41. The concept of "participant," "subject," and "parochial" political cultures was developed by Almond and Verba, *The Civic Culture*: chap. 1.

62. See Charles L. Davis, "The Persistence and Erosion of a Legitimating Revolutionary Ideology among the Lower Class in Mexico City," *Journal of Political & Military Sociology* 7, no. 1 (Spring 1979): 35-51.

63. Susan K. Purcell, *The Mexican Profit-Sharing Decision: Politics in an Authoritarian Regime* (Berkeley: Univ. of California Press, 1975), 3-4.

64. In Mexico Prof. Kenneth M. Coleman and I worked with Tecnia, S.A. de C.V., a firm headquartered in Mexico City and directed by Manuel Cosio. In Venezuela we contracted with Multianalisis, C.A., a survey research firm located in Barquisimeto in the state of Lara. Multianalisis was then headed by Dr. Fausto Izcaray, who is now a professor of research methodology at the Instituto Pedagogico Experimental de Barquisimeto.

65. Kenneth M. Coleman, the principal investigator for this project, participated in all such interviews jointly with native Spanish-speaking collaborators in each country. The unions studied are described in Charles L. Davis, "Political Regimes and the Socio-Economic Resource Model of Political Mobilization: Some Venezuelan and Mexican Data," *Journal of Politics* 45, no.2 (May 1983): 444.

66. See J. Samuel Valenzuela and Arturo Valenzuela, "Modernization and Dependency: Alternative Perspectives in the Study of Latin American Underdevelopment," *World Politics*, July 1987, 535-53. Also see Samuel P. Huntington, "The Change to Change: Modernization, Development, and Politics," *Comparative Politics* 3 (April 1971): 283-322.

67. For a good discussion of how comparison across samples can be confounded by compositional differences in samples, see M. Kent Jennings, "The Variable Nature of Generational Conflict: Some Examples from West Germany," *Comparative Political Studies* 9, no. 2 (July 1976): 171-88.

68. Four females were interviewed. Given the small n, one can assume, in effect, that gender is constant. There are too few females to attempt to partial out whatever minimal effects exist.

69. A *tabulador* is a position-by-position listing of all jobs available in a firm, with pay scale attached. *Tabuladores* are negotiated by labor unions and management in contract discussions. Not all firms have elaborate *tabuladores*.

CHAPTER TWO

1. See William H. Form, *Blue-Collar Stratification: Autoworkers in Four Countries* (Princeton: Princeton Univ. Press, 1976), 136-80.

2. See Cornelius, *Politics and the Migrant Poor*, 109-34.

3. As reported by Luis Fernando Talavera Aldana, "Organizaciones sindicales: obreros de la rama textil: 1935-1970," *Revista Mexicana de Ciencias Politicas y Sociales* 83 (Jan.-March 1976): 246.

4. By contrast, in 1940 textiles and leather employed more than 25 percent of all industrial workers and accounted for 17.6 percent of the value added in manufacturing. Source: Direccion General de Estadistica, Secretaria de la Economia Nacional *Compendio Estadistico, 1947* (Mexico, D.f.): 322-37; and United Nations, *General Industrial Statistics*, vol. 1 of the *Yearbook of Industrial Statistics, 1979* (New York, 1981), 350-57.

5. In an interview on Feb. 27, 1981. Francisco Zapata and Kenneth Coleman, interviewers; various members of the union directorate were the interviewees, including the secretary of claims, the secretary of education and social welfare, and the director of housing.

6. For details see George Grayson, *The Politics of Mexican Oil* (Pittsburgh: Univ. of Pittsburgh Press, 1980), 95.

7. See Grayson, *Politics of Mexican Oil*, 99.

8. See Lourdes Orozco, "Explotación y fuerza de trabajo en México: los trabajadores transitorios," *Cuadernos Politicos* 16 (April-June 1978): 68-72.

9. This is a closed-shop provision that can be used by union leaders, who have the power to expel members.

10. See Ian Roxborough, *Unions and Politics in Mexico: The Case of the Automobile Industry* (Cambridge: Cambridge Univ. Press, 1984), 132-44.

11. A pseudonym has been adopted here.

12. See Minerva Villanueva Olmedo, "Sindicatos y negociación colectiva: Los trabajadores del calzado en León, Guanajuato," Tésis de grado, Univ. of Veracruz, 1980.

13. See Juana Valenti Nigrini, "Empresa, sindicato y conflicto: El caso de Nissan," Tésis de grado, FLACSO, 1978, 109.

14. Villanueva Olmedo, "Sindicatos," 102-3.

15. Roxborough, *Unions and Democracy*, passim.

16. Ibid., 101.

17. Valenti Nigrini, "Empresa," 133.

18. Juan Ortega Arenas, "Interview," *Expansión* (April 16, 1980): 47-50.

19. Valenti Nigrini, "Empresa," 40-42.

20. Such was done by the UOI faction after gaining control of the Nissan union used for this study. See Valenti Nigrini, "Empresa," 110-17.

21. Roughly, U.S. $2,225 for a natural death, U.S. $4,450 for an accidental death, and U.S. $355 for funeral expenses.

22. That is, having at least 51 percent Mexican capital.

23. In fact, Nissan workers in this sample tend to vote against leftist parties.

24. See Kevin J. Middlebrook, "The Political Economy of Mexican Organized Labor, 1940-1978" (Ph.D. diss., Harvard University, 1982), 380-81.

25. For an excellent extended description of one of these neighborhoods, El Centro, see Susan Eckstein, *The Poverty of Revolution: The State and the Urban Poor in Mexico* (Princeton: Princeton Univ. Press, 1977), 41-53.

26. When asked, in the abstract, how well unions work in protecting the interests of workers, 33 percent thought that they worked "very well" and another 47 percent thought that they worked "sometimes" to protect workers. This compares favorably with the assessments of their own unions rendered by the unionized workers.

27. Where there has been any reason to suspect that the unions exposed to identical structural environments would vary among themselves, a separate analysis has been conducted. Results will be reported should those analyses vary. In general, they do not.

28. At least, as of the 1971 census, Barquisimeto ranked fourth with a population of 334,333. See Leonidas Pérez Pérez, *Espacio y demografía en la sub-región Barquisimeto* (Barquisimeto: Department of Regional Urban Studies, Office of Urban Planning, 1979). All population, employment, and income data cited in the paragraph that follows come from the same (unpaginated) source.

29. Oficina Central de Estadistica e Informatica, Bariquisino, Venguela (1981).

30. Data on employment generated in field interviews in Punto Fijo with union leaders.

31. SINTRAPETROL: Sindicato Autonomo de Trabajadores Petroleros, Petroquimicos y Derivados del Estado de Falcón.

32. STOPPS: Sindicato de Trabajadores Organizados del Petroleo, Petroquimicos y Similares del Estado del Falcón.

33. STIP: Sindicato de Trabajadores de la Industria Petrolera del Estado Falcón. OSMPM: Organizacion Sindical de Marineros, Petroleros y Mercantes del Estado Falcón.

34. On the discrepancy in wages between unionized industrial workers and unorganized workers in the service sector, see Andreas Boeckh, "Organized Labor and Government under Conditions of Economic Scarcity: The Case of Venezuela" (Ph.D. diss., University of Florida, 1972), 52-79.

35. Dissatisfaction was universal over inadequate housing for *petroleros*.

36. For a review of early research on Venezuelan migration, see Daniel Levine, "Urbanization, Migrants, and Politics in Venezuela, A Review Essay," *Journal of Inter-American Studies and World Affairs* 17, no. 3 (July 1975): 358-72.

37. Thirty of the 46 workers sampled at La Miel were born in La Miel itself; most of the rest were born in surrounding small towns.

38. Following the proportional representation scheme typically employed in Venezuela, the MEP was awarded five of seven seats on the directorate for having won upward of 70 percent of the vote in the most recent elections. The fact of having three competing slates, an AD slate, a COPEI slate, and a MEP slate, is typical of Venezuela's more democratic union elections.

39. At least in terms of their ability to employ common ideological symbols in accord with conventional interpretations, the union leaders at La Miel seem "sophisticated." They were, for example, among the few union leaders who imparted any coherent content to the concept of "the class struggle" when asked to explain what, if anything, that concept meant to them. See Kenneth M. Coleman and José Gonzalez, Field Notes of Interviews with Venezuelan Labor Leaders, May 11, 1981, p. 16. There are, of course, other definitions of ideological sophistication.

40. SUOEP: Sindicato Unificado de Obreros y Empleados Petroleros del Estado Falcón.

41. MIR: Movimiento Izquierdista Revolucionario. MAS: Movimiento al Socialismo.

42. UNMPM: Unión Nacional de Marineros, Petroleros y Mercantes del Estado Falcón.

43. For example, SUOEP leaders weere displeased that they had asked for a 25 to 30 *bolivar* increase but got only a 15 *bolivar* increase in weekly wages.

44. See John A. Peeler, *Latin American Democracies: Colombia, Costa Rica, Venezuela* (Chapel Hill: Univ. of North Carolina Press, 1985), chap. 3.

45. In Venezuela a small sample (n = 35) of nonunionized workers in unionized plants was also drawn. These individuals were even more poorly paid: 69 percent had incomes less than 800 bolivares per month. They were likely to be temporary employees who were not subject to provisions of the labor law. Unless otherwise noted, these individuals have not been included in the nonunionized worker category.

46. Weekly incomes for both the Mexican and Venezuelan samples were grouped into equal interval categories and then converted into U.S. currency (circa 1980). The per capita category was calculated simply by dividing the average household size (national average) into the high and low point of the mean category of income.

47. Per capita income in Venezuela was estimated by the World Bank to have been U.S. $3,120 in 1979; the comparable estimate for Mexico was U.S. $1,973. Thus, in both relative and absolute terms, the Mexican workers appear to be better off than do the Venezuelan workers.

48. On the availability of public services to squatter settlements in Mexico City, see Cornelius, *Politics and the Migrant Poor*, 213-15.

49. The differences between wage levels might also be related to differences in industry.

50. Whether these findings reveal more about low profit margins in nonstrategic industries or about the relative weakness of unions in nonstrategic industries, it is difficult to say.

51. For a reinterpretation of Latin America labor history based on a similar premise, see Bergquist, *Labor in Latin American*, 1-19.

CHAPTER THREE

1. See the discussion of Venezuelan *caudillismo* in Terry Karl, "The Political Economy of Petrodollars: Oil and Democracy in Venezuela, vol. 1" (Ph.D. diss., Stanford University, 1983), 74-76.

2. John D. Martz, "The Evolution of Democratic Politics in Venezuela," in Howard R. Penniman, ed., *Venezuela at the Polls: The National Election of 1978* (Washington: American Enterprise Institute, 1980), 3.

3. John V. Lombardi, *Venezuela: The Search for Order, The Dream of Progress* (New York: Oxford Univ. Press, 1982), 189-90.

4. Ibid., 172, passim.

5. Ibid., 14-15.

6. Karl, "Political Economy of Petrodollars," 78-80.

7. Ibid., 80.

8. See Jorge Salazar-Carrillo, *Oil in the Economic Development of Venezuela* (New York: Praeger, 1976), 71-127.

9. See Steven Ellner, *Los Partidos Politicos y su Disputa por el Control del Movimiento Sindical en Venezuela, 1936-1948* (Caracas: Universidad Catolica Andres Bello, 1980), 95-144.

10. Karl, "Political Economy of Petrodollars," 100-107.

11. Peter H. Smith, *Labyrinths of Power: Political Recruitment in Twentieth-Century Mexico* (Princeton: Princeton Univ. Press, 1979), 28-29.

12. Susan Kaufman Purcell, "Mexico: Clientelism, Corporatism, and Political Stability," in S.N. Eisenstadt and Rene Lemarchand, eds., *Political Clientelism, Patronage and Development, Contemporary Political Sociology*, vol. 3 (Beverly Hills: Sage Publications, 1981), 195.

13. Smith, *Labyrinths of Power*, 30.

14. On the role of the state in late industrialization, see Douglass Bennett and Kenneth Sharpe, "The State as Banker and Entrepreneur: The Last Resort Character of the Mexican States' Economic Intervention, 1917-1970," in Hewlett and Weinert, *Brazil and Mexico*, 169-212.

15. Lorenzo Meyer, "Historical Roots of the Authoritarian State in Mexico," in José Luis Reyna and Richard S. Weinert, eds., *Authoritarianism in Mexico* (Philadelphia: Institute for the Study of Human Issues, 1977), 16.

16. For an elaboration of this point, see Daniel H. Levine,"Venezuela since 1958: The Consolidation of Democratic Politics," in Juan J. Linz and Alfred Stepan, eds., *The Breakdown of Democratic Regimes: Latin America* (Baltimore: Johns Hopkins Univ. Press, 1978), 82-109.

17. Meyer, "Historical Roots," 19.

18. See Peeler, *Latin American Democracies*, 76-93.

19. See Levine, "Venezuela since 1958," 82-109.

20. Karl, "Political Economy of Petrodollars," 111-12. See also Bergquist, *Labor in Latin America*, 4-7.

21. See Charles L. Davis and Kenneth M. Coleman, "Political Control of Organized Labor in a Semi-Consociational Democracy: The Case of Vene-

zuela," in Edward Epstein, ed., *Labor in Latin America* (Boston: Allen & Unwin, forthcoming).

22. Karl, "Political Economy of Petrodollars," 113-14.

23. See Margarita López and Nickolaus Werz, "El estado venezolano y el movimiento sindical (1958-1980)," *Revista Relaciones de Trabajo* 2 (April 1983): 660.

24. Karl, "Political Economy of Petrodollars," 115.

25. Susan Kaufman and John F.H. Purcell, "State and Society in Mexico: Must a Stable Polity Be Institutionalized?" *World Politics* 32, no. 2 (Jan. 1980): 195.

26. In this case the pact was based on implicit understandings rather than reflecting a formal, contractual agreement as was negotiated in Venezuela in 1958.

27. See Arnaldo Cordova, "La Transformación del PNR en PRM: El Triunfo del Corporativismo en Mexico," in James W. Wilkie, Michael C. Meyer, and Edna Monzón de Wilkie, eds., *Contemporary Mexico: Papers of the IV International Congress of Mexican History* (Berkeley: Univ. of California Press, 1976), 204-27.

28. Manuel Camacho, *Las clase obrera en la historia de México: El futuro inmediato* (México: Siglo 21, 1980), 31-35.

29. Middlebrook, "Political Economy of Mexican Organized Labor," 48-58.

30. Nora Hamilton, *The Limits of State Autonomy: Post-Revolutionary Mexico* (Princeton: Princeton Univ. Press, 1982), 104-137.

31. Cordova, "La transformación del PNR en PRM," 204-27.

32. Hamilton, *Limits of State Autonomy*, 124-28, 148-52.

33. The peasant confederation is the National Confederation of Peasants (CNC); the labor confederation is the Confederation of Mexican Workers (CTM).

34. Hamilton, *The Limits of State Autonomy*, 267-70.

35. Manuel Comacho, "Los Trabajadores y el Régimen Mexicano," manuscript (1979), 13. Published as *La Cluse Obrera en la Historia de México: El Futuro Immediato* (Mexico City: Siglo XXI, 1980).

36. Hamilton, *Limits of Autonomy*, 279.

37. This categorization derives from Frederick S. Weaver, *State, Class, and Industrial Structure: Historical Process of South American Industrial Growth* (Westport, Conn.: Greenwood Press, 1980), 16-22, and from sources cited therein.

38. See Juan Pablo Pérez Sáinz and Paul Zarembka, "Accumulation and the State in Venezuelan Industrialization," *Latin American Perspectives* 6, no. 3 (Summer 1979): 5, 8.

39. Julio Godio, *El movimiento obrero venezolano, 1850-1944* (Caracas: Editorial Ateneo, 1980), 48.

40. Godio, *El movimiento*, 48.

41. Daniel Levine, *Conflict and Political Change in Venezuela* (Princeton: Princeton Univ. Press, 1973), 17.

42. Anderson, *Politics and Economic Change*, 282-83.

43. Perez Sainz and Zarembka, "Accumulation and the State," 10.

44. Anderson, *Politics and Economic Change*, 285.

45. Peter Evans and Gary Gereffi, "Foreign Investment and Dependent Development: Comparing Brazil and Mexico," in Hewlett and Weinert, *Brazil and Mexico*, 122-23.

46. On the political formula, see Levine, *Conflict and Political Change*, 41-61, 231-54.

47. For a definition of the term, see Gene E. Bigler, "State Economic Control vs. Market Expansion: The Third Sector in Venezuelan Politics" (Ph.D. diss., Johns Hopkins University, 1980), 8.

48. Ibid., 193.

49. The ratios of units produced per capita in 1978 were .0135 in Venezuela; .0092 in Brazil; and .0057 in Mexico. Authors' calculation from data presented in Motor Vehicles Manufacturers Association, *Facts and Figures, 1979*, 16; and World Bank, *World Development Report, 1981* (Oxford, New York, and elsewhere: Oxford Univ. Press and the World Bank, 1981), 134.

50. Perez Sainz and Zarembka, "Accumulation and the State," 14.

51. Three major types of imports continued to exist: (1) foodstuffs, which increased in response to declining domestic consumption, (2) capital goods, and (3) raw materials or other components of goods manufactured in Venezuela. On the first point, see Reinaldo Reina Cordero, *Al final de la inflacion* (Barquisimeto, Edo. Lara: Ediciones de la Universidad Central Occidental Lisandro Alvarado, 1981); and on the second two points, see Perez Sainz and Zarembka, "Accumulation and the State," 5-29.

52. On the capital-intensive character of industrialization in Venezuela, see Pérez Sáinz and Zarembka, "Accumulation and the State," 10-18.

53. Many industrial workers in Venezuela earn at least twice as much as typical service sector workers. See Juan Buttari, "Diferencias salariales en los sectores manufactureros de Venezuala y de Uruguay," in Jorge Salazar-Carrillo, ed., *Estructura de los salarios industriales en America Latina* (Buenos Aires: Ediciones SIAP, 1979), 175.

54. See Jennifer L. McCoy, "The Politics of Adjustment: Labor and the Venezuelan Debt Crisis," *Journal of Interamerican Studies and World Affairs* (forthcoming).

55. See Roger Hansen, *The Politics of Mexican Development* (Baltimore: Johns Hopkins Univ. Press, 1974), 13-23.

56. See Hamilton, *Limits of State Autonomy*, 110.

57. Ibid., 186.

58. See Frederick Turner, *The Dynamics of Mexican Nationalism* (Chapel Hill: Univ. of North Carolina Press, 1970), 154.

59. See Bennett and Sharpe, "State as Banker and Entrepreneur," 169-212.

60. See Hansen, *Politics of Mexican Development*, 83-85; and Leopoldo Solis, *Economic Policy Reform in Mexico: A Case Study for Developing Countries* (New York: Pergamon Press, 1981), 19-25.

61. Solis, *Economic Policy Reform*, 19-25.

62. Hansen, *Politics of Mexican Development*, 87.

63. Bennett and Sharpe, "State as Banker and Entrepreneur," 170.

64. Robert E. Looney, *Mexico's Economy: A Policy Analysis with Forecasts to 1990* (Boulder, Colo.: Westview Press, 1978), 14.

65. The consumer price index increased by an average of 13 percent annually from 1940 through 1955. Looney, *Mexico's Economy*, 15.

66. Rene Villareal, "The Policy of Import-Substituting Industrialization, 1929-1975," in Reyna and Weinert, *Authoritarianism*, 73.

67. José Luis Reyna, "Redefining the Authoritarian Regime," in Reyna and Weinert, *Authoritarianism*, 163.

68. Richard S. Graham, "Mexican and Brazilian Economic Development: Legacies, Patterns, and Performance," in Hewlett and Weinert, *Brazil and Mexico*, 33.

69. See Hansen, *Politics of Mexican Development*, 41-70.

70. Cited in ibid, 57-58.

71. Evans and Gereffi, "Foreign Investment and Dependent Development," 122-25, 143ff.

72. Salazar-Carrillo, "Estructura," 138.

73. David Felix, "Income Distribution Trends in Mexico and the Kuznets Curve," in Hewlett and Weinert, *Brazil and Mexico*, 285.

74. Ibid., 282. The category of household software includes clothing, shoes, draperies, laundry and cleaning materials, personal grooming articles, etc.

75. Solis, *Economic Policy Reform*, 30.

76. Solis, *Economic Policy Reform*, 67ff.

77. Ibid., 187.

78. See James D. Cockcroft, *Mexico: Class Formation, Capital Accumulation, and the State* (New York: Monthly Review Press, 1983): 178-85.

79. O'Donnell, *Modernization and Bureaucratic-Authoritarianism*.

80. Coleman and Davis, "Preemptive Reform," 3-32.

81. This represents a major contrast with the Venezuelan situation of 1973 to 1977 because Venezuela had to make no new investments to profit immensely from the radically changed post-1973 price structure of petroleum.

82. Conditions of poverty in Venezuela are reported in Asdrúbal Baptista, "Más alla del optimismo y del pesimismo: las transformaciones fundamentales del país," in Moises Naim and Ramon Piñango, eds., *El caso venezolano: Una illusión de armonía* (Caracas: Ediciones IESA, 1984), 20-41. On Mexican poverty, see Hansen, *Politics of Mexican Development*, 21-95.

83. Peter Ward, *Welfare Politics in Mexico: Papering Over the Cracks* (Boston: Allen & Unwin, 1986), 8.

CHAPTER FOUR

1. See Hamilton, *Limits of State Autonomy*, 104-41; and Middlebrook, "Political Economy of Mexican Organized Labor," 58-98.

2. Wayne A. Cornelius and Ann L. Craig, "Politics in Mexico," in Gabriel

A. Almond and G. Bingham Powell, Jr., eds., *Comparative Politics Today: A World View* (Boston: Little, Brown & Co., 1984), 447.

3. Middlebrook, "Political Economy of Mexican Organized Labor," 97.

4. The largest union in terms of membership is the union of government workers (FSTSE). Middlebrook,"Political Economy of Mexican Organized Labor," 97.

5. See Ilan Bizberg, "Las perspectivas de la oposicion sindical en Mexico," *Foro Internacional* (April-June 1983): 336; and Barry Carr, "The Mexican Economic Debacle and the Labor Movement: A New Era or More of the Same?" in Donald L. Wyman, ed., *Mexico's Economic Crisis: Challenges and Opportunities*, monograph series 12 (La Jolla, Calif.: Center for U.S.–Mexican Studies, Univ. of California, San Diego, 1983), 106.

6. See Susan Kaufman Purcell and John F.H. Purcell, "State and Society in Mexico: Must a Stable Polity Be Institutionalized?" *World Politics* 32, no. 2 (Jan. 1980): 194-227.

7. Middlebrook, "Political Economy of Mexican Organized Labor," 129-30.

8. See Smith, *Labyrinths of Power*, 224.

9. Middlebrook, "Political Economy of Mexican Organized Labor," 230.

10. See Carr, "Mexican Economic Debacle," 98.

11. According to the 1970 census, 16.4 percent of the economically active population was unionized. See Francisco Zapata, "Afiliación y organización sindical en México," in José Luis Reyna et al., *Tres estudios sobre el movimiento obrero en México* (Mexico City: Centro de Estudios Sociologicos, El Colegio de México, 1976), 109-30.

12. Middlebrook, "Political Economy of Mexican Organized Labor," 109-16.

13. See Evelyn P. Stevens, *Protest and Response in Mexico* (Cambridge: MIT Press, 1974), 99-126. Also, Mary Kay Vaughan and Leonardo Ramirez, "The Resurgence of Popular Democracy in Mexico in the 1970s" (Paper presented at the 1980 meeting of the Latin American Studies Association, Bloomington, Indiana), 9-16.

14. Middlebrook, "Political Economy of Mexican Organized Labor," 116-20.

15. Larissa Lomnitz, "Horizontal and Vertical Relations and the Social Structure of Urban Mexico," *Latin American Research Review* 17, no. 2 (1982): 57-58.

16. Roxborough, *Unions and Politics in Mexico*, 159, 167.

17. Ibid., 111.

18. Stuart I. Fagan, "The Venezuelan Labor Movement: A Study in Political Unionism" (Ph.D. diss., University of California at Berkeley, 1974), 145.

19. Ibid., 120.

20. Ibid., 121-22.

21. See Boeckh, "Organized Labor and Government" 212-17.

22. Boeckh points out numerous problems with using official estimates of the unionized work force. Around three quarters of all legalized unions

are agrarian unions that do not negotiate collective contracts. Also, defunct unions are not always removed from the records. Finally, before general union elections, there is a proliferation of phony unions in order to strengthen various unions factions. For these reasons Boeckh discounts the Labor Ministry estimate of the number of unionized workers in Venezuela in 1970 to be 43 percent of the economically active population. Uning the number of workers covered by collective contracts, he estimates 20.9 percent of the economically active work force was unionized in 1969. See Boeckh, "Organized Labor and Government, 132-33.

23. Ibid., 152-54.

24. At the plant level, union leaders told researchers that these ties are problematic for maintaining worker unity.

25. Daniel H. Levine, "Venezuelan Politics: Past and Future," in Robert D. Bond, ed., *Contemporary Venezuela and Its Role in International Affairs* (New York Univ. Press, 1977), 14-15.

26. See Donald L. Herman, *Christian Democracy in Venezuela* (Chapel Hill: Univ. of North Carolina Press, 1980), 76-77.

27. Formally the Comite Popular Electoral Independiente but in reality the Christian Democratic party.

28. See Herman, *Christian Democracy*, 76-82.

29. Karl, "Political Economy of Petrodollars," 122.

30. On the use of state repression to control Venezuelan unions, see Boeckh, "Organized Labor and Government," 205-6.

31. Reasons for the weakness of the left in Mexico are discussed below.

32. To go too far down the road toward explicit indentification with the left might also stimulate more conservative workers to return to the CTM-PRI fold.

33. On the protracted legal battle over "state intervention" of the union at the SIDOR steel mill in Ciudad Guyana, see "Venezuela: Union Bosses under Fire," in *Latin America Regional Reports: Andean Group* 82-103 (April 2, 1982): 4.

34. See Daniel Hellinger, "Venezuelan Democracy and the Challenge of 'Nuevo Sindicalismo' " (Paper delivered at the 1986 Meeting of the Latin American Studies Association, Boston, Massachusetts).

35. See John d. Martz, "The Minor Parties," in Penniman, *Venezuela at the Polls*, 155-69.

36. See Wiarda, "Politics of Democratic Developmentalism," 309.

37. David J. Myers, "The Acción Democrática Campaign," in Penniman, *Venezuela at the Polls*, 106.

38. Henry Wells, "The Conduct of Venezuelan Elections: Rules and Practice," in Penniman, *Venezuela at the Polls*, 46-47.

39. See Enrique A. Baloyra and John D. Martz, *Political Attitudes in Venezuela: Societal Cleavages and Political Opinion* (Austin: Univ. of Texas Press, 1979), 46-49.

40. David J. Myers, "Venezuela's MAS," *Problems of Communism* 29, no. 5 (Sept.-Oct. 1980): 16-27.

41. See Levy and Szekely, *Paradoxes of Stability and Change*, 65-75.

42. In 1981 the Mexican Communist Party (PCM) formed the Unified Socialist Party (PSUM) with four minor leftist parties. However, three leftist parties refused to join.

43. See Davis, "Persistence and Erosion," 35-51.

44. See Kevin J. Middlebrook, "Political Change and Political Reform in an Authoritarian Regime: The Case of Mexico," in Jack W. Hopkins, ed., *Latin America and the Caribbean Contemporary Record* (New York: Holmes and Meier, 1983), 149-61.

45. See Charles L. Davis and Kenneth M. Coleman, "Electoral Change in the One-Party Dominant Mexican Polity, 1958-1973: Evidence from Mexico City," *Journal of Developing Areas* 16, no. 4 (July 1982): 523-42.

46. On the selective inclusion of the masses in Cuba, see Eldon Kenworthy, "Dilemmas of Participation in Latin America," *Democracy* 3, no. 1 (Winter 1983): 72-83.

47. Cornelius and Craig, "Politics in Mexico," 436-37.

48. Ibid., 427.

49. See Purcell and Purcell, "State and Society in Mexico," 205-6. Still policies might be sabotaged in the implementation process by politically powerful groups or by bureaucratic resistance.

50. Cornelius and Craig, "Politics in Mexico," 428.

51. Ibid., 428-29.

52. See Susan Kaufman Purcell, "Decision-Making in an Authoritarian Regime: Theoretical Implications from a Mexican Case Study," *World Politics* 26 (Oct. 1973): 28-54.

53. Stevens, *Protest and Response*, 277.

54. See various chapters in Wyman, *Mexico's Economic Crisis*.

55. See Coleman and Davis, "Preemptive Reform," 3-32.

56. Cornelius and Craig, "Politics in Mexico," 433-34.

57. See Steven E. Sanderson, "Presidential Succession and Political Rationality in Mexico," *World Politics* 35, no. 3 (April 1983): 315-34.

58. Romulo Betancourt was elected the first president (1958-63) after the restoration of competitive democracy in 1958.

59. See Gene E. Bigler, *La politica y el capitalismo del estado en Venezuela* (Madrid: Editorial Tecnos, 1981) for an analysis of the Andrés Pérez presidency (1973-78).

60. "Ex-President Gains in Struggle within Venezuelan Party," *Miami Herald*, April 5, 1987, 26a.

61. Wells, "Conduct of Venezuelan Elections," 43.

62. See R. Lynn Kelley, "Venezuelan Constitutional Forms and Realities," in John D. Martz and David J. Myers, eds., *Venezuela: The Democratic Experience* (New York: Praeger, 1986), 32-53.

63. It is also worth anticipating the argument below that the two dominant parties share a commitment to state-capitalist development and to a sizable private sector.

64. See Martz, "Evolution of Democratic Politics," 7-16.

65. Karl, "Political Economy of Petrodollars," 2: 348-443.

66. Levine, "Venezuelan Politics," 14.

67. See Purcell and Purcell, "State and Society in Mexico," 194-227.

68. Ibid, 198.

69. Levine, "Venezuela since 1958," 93.

70. That is, conflict given effective expression within the system does not reflect fundamental ideological issues. Some political actors do raise such issues.

71. For an examination of three possible explanations of why social conflict has *not* been worse under no-growth conditions, see Juan Carlos Navarro, "Por qué no ha habido una 'explosión social' en Venezuela," *SIC* 475 (Mayo 1985): 203-5.

72. See Bo Anderson and James D. Cockcroft, "Control and Cooptation in Mexican Politics," in James D. Cockcroft, Andre Gunder Frank, and Dale L. Johnson, *Dependence and Underdevelopment: Latin America's Political Economy* (New York: Doubleday and Co., 1972), 219-44.

73. Some scholars, particularly neo-Marxists, emphasize the centrality of repression on a mechanism of control in Mexico. See Juan Felipe Leal, *México: Estado, Burocracía y sindicatos* (Mexico, D.F.: Ediciones "El Caballito," 1975). Other scholars do not dismiss the use of repression but emphasize the cooptative capacity of the Mexican state. See Anderson and Cockcroft, "Control and Cooptation," 219-44; and Purcell and Purcell, "State and Society in Mexico," 194-227.

74. See Collier, *New authoritarianism in Latin America.*

75. See Boeckh, "Organized Labor and Government," 204-6.

76. David E. Blank, *Venezuela: Politics in a Petroleum Republic* (New York: Praeger, 1984), 109.

77. See Hellinger, "Venezuelan Democracy," 14-21.

78. See Orozco, "Explotacion," 65-74.

79. Blank, *Politics in a Petroleum Republic,* 101.

80. Boeckh, "Organized Labor and Government," 204.

81. Notably in Ciudad Guyana.

82. See Levine, "Venezuela since 1958." 82-109.

83. See Arturo Valenzuela, "Party Politics and the Failure of Presidentialism in Chile: A Proposal for a Parliamentary Form of Government" (paper prepared for delivery at the 1987 annual meeting of the American Political Science Association, Chicago, Ill.), 20-26.

84. Vaughan and Ramirez, "Resurgence of Popular Democracy."

85. Ibid., 14.

86. Ibid., 15.

87. Purcell and Purcell, "State and Society in Mexico," 200.

88. For other examples see Stevens, *Protest and Response,* 99-240.

89. See also Boeckh, "Organized Labor and Government," 206-8.

90. See Middlebrook, "Political Economy of Mexican Organized Labor," 76-91.

CHAPTER FIVE

1. On the failure of PAN to nominate a presidential candidate in the 1976 election, see Levy and Szekely, *Paradoxes of Stability and Change*, 71-72.

2. An argument to this effect is developed in Middlebrook, "Political Change and Political Reform," 149-61.

3. The 1976 election is excluded from consideration here because of the absence of a PAN presidential candidate.

4. For the 1970 election, see table 6 and for the 1958 and 1964 elections, see table 4 in Smith and Rodriguez, "Comparative Working-Class Political Behavior," 66, 69. The data for Chile is limited to residents of the greater Santiago area.

5. See table 1 in ibid., 62.

6. See Sidney Verba, Norman H. Nie, and Jae-on Kim, *The Modes of Democratic Participation: A Cross-National Comparison* (Beverly Hills, Calif.: Sage Professional Papers in Comparative Politics, 2, no. 01-013, 1971), 44-45.

7. See Norman H. Nie, Sidney Verba, and John R. Petrocik, *The Changing American Voter* (Cambridge: Harvard Univ. Press, 1979), 15-18.

8. See ibid., 272-80.

9. See Henry S. Kariel, ed., *Frontiers of Democratic Theory* (New York: Random House, 1970).

10. The Nie, Verba, and Petrocik study also reports that a substantial majority of the U.S. population follows presidential campaigns in the media. See Nie, Verba, and Petrocik, *Changing American Voter*, 274. By contrast, only very distinct minorities of the sample reported being attentive to media coverage of politics.

11. See Verba, Nie, and Kim, *Participation and Political Equality*, 310-39.

12. Ibid., 46-62.

13. See John A. Booth, "Political Participation in Latin America: Levels, Structure, Context, Concentration, and Rationality," *Latin American Research Review* 14, no. 3 (1979): 29-60.

14. See Richard J. Moore, "The Urban Poor in Guayaquil, Ecuador: Modes, Correlates, and Context of Political Participation," in Seligson and Booth, *Political Participation*, 198-217.

15. Verba, Nie, and Kim, *Participation and Political Equality*, 58-59.

16. Booth, "Political Participation in Latin America," 32-34.

17. See Mitchell A. Seligson and John A. Booth, "Development, Political Participation, and the Poor in Latin America," in Seligson and Booth, *Political Participation*, 3-8.

18. See Edward N. Muller, *Aggressive Political Participation* (Princeton: Princeton Univ. Press, 1979), 51-54.

19. See Monte Palmer and William Thompson, *The Comparative Analysis of Politics* (Itasca, Ill.: F.E. Peacock Publishers, 1978, chap. 7.

20. Cornelius, *Politics and the Migrant Poor*, 184.

21. See Jelín, *La Protesta Obrera*, 77-94.

22. Sigelman has shown that relationships of various predictor variables

with turnout are not distorted by overreporting in survey data. See Lee Sigelman, "The Non-Voting Voter in Voting Research," *American Journal of Political Science* 26 (Feb. 1982): 47-56.

23. See table 3-2 in Verba, Nie, and Kin, *Participation and Political Equality*, 58-59.

24. See Galen Irwin, "Compulsory Voting Legislation: The Impact on Voter Turnout in the Netherlands," *Compatative Political Studies* 7 (Oct. 1974): 292-315.

25. On the 1978 reforms, see David J. Myers, "The Elections and the Evolution of Venezuela's Party System," in Penniman, *Venezuela at the Polls*, 226-28.

26. On the 1977 political reform, see Middlebrook, "Political Change and Political Reform," 149-61.

27. See Baloyra and Martz, *Political Attitudes in Venezuela*, 46-52. By contrast, Mexicans are quite aware of the limited impact that voting has. See Cornelius, *Politics and the Migrant Poor*, 79.

28. See note 25.

29. Some studies have shown higher levels of campaign involvement. However, these studies have measured interest in campaigns rather than actual involvement. See Enrique A. Baloyra and John D. Martz, "Dimensions of Campaign Participation," in Mitchell A. Seligson and John A. Booth, eds., *Political Participation in Latin America*, vol. 1 (New York: Holmes and Meier, 1979), 68-69.

30. While there is significant variation in campaign activism across the nations studied by Verba, Nie, and Kim, the level tends to be low—much more so than for voting. See Verba, Nie, and Kim, *Participation and Political Equality*, 58-59.

31. Robert E. O'Connor, "The Media and the Campaign," in Penniman, *Venezuela at the Polls*, 181.

32. They do not do so through campaign advertisements but rather through special programming set aside for all political parties.

33. See Muller, *Aggressive Political Participation*, 37-68.

34. Booth, "Political Participation in Latin America," 33.

35. Norbert S. Relenberg, Harmut Karner, and Volkmar Kohler, *Los Pobres de Venezuela: Autoorganizacion de los Probladores: Un Informe Critico* (Caracas: El Cid, N.d.), 114-15.

36. Cornelius, *Politics and the Migrant Poor*, 179.

37. Ibid., 83, 179.

38. See chapter 4. These patterns are generally found throughout Latin America. See Portes, "Latin American Class Structures," 7-40.

39. None of the respondents reported contacting officials about status of land tenure. Fully 97.8 percent of the Mexican workers reported having piped water, whereas only 29.7 percent of Cornelius's migrant sample so reported. See Cornelius, *Politics and the Migrant Poor*, 179-82.

CHAPTER SIX

1. See Verba, Nie, and Kim, *Participation and Political Equality*, 1-22.

2. Verba, Nie, and Kim report that this type of mobilization is most likely to occur with voting.

3. See Russell J. Dalton, "Cognitive Mobilization and Partisan Dealignment in Advanced Industrial Democracies," *Journal of Politics* 46, no. 1 (Feb. 1984): 264-85.

4. See Verba, Nie, and Kim on this point.

5. See Coleman and Davis, "Preemptive Reform," 11.

6. See Inkeles, "Participant Citizenship," 1120-41.

7. An example is provided by the criticisms by the labor wing of AD and the Confederation of Venezuelan Workers of government's policies to manage the economic crisis of the eighties. See Hector Lucena, "El papel del sindicalismo venezolano ante la crisis economica," *Revista Relaciones de Trabajo* 6 (Sept. 1985): 123-44.

8. On this point in the case of the Venezuelan labor movement, see McCoy, "Politics of Adjustment." In the case of Mexican labor, see Francisco Zapata, "El sistema politico mexicano y el conflicto sindical," mimeo (Mexico City: El Colegio de México, 1987).

9. The allegation has been made against Juan Ortega Arenas, the head of the UOI independent labor confederation in Mexico.

10. See Stephens and Stephens, "Transition to Mass Parties," 443-44.

11. Verba, Nie, and Kim noted that these motivations were not converted into actual participation at an equal rate in all polities.

12. The study has controlled for partisanship, performance satisfaction, *concientización*, socioeconomic status, and age.

13. This is true for workers employed in the state-operated PEMEX, petroluem industry, as well as for workers employed in the Nissan plant. Clearly, in the case of Mexico, employment in a state enterprise is not a sufficient condition for workers to become attentive to politics.

14. In the case of representative institutions at the local level in Cuba, see Kenworthy, "Dilemmas of Participation," 72-83. The workers' participation scheme of the Velasco government in Peru was intended for a similar purpose of containing worker mobilization at the local level. See Stephens, *Politics of Workers' Participation*, 89-92.

15. See Bergquist, *Labor in Latin America*, 191-273.

16. Age and socioeconomic status are adjusted. It seems more realistic to assume that differences between parties on issues (and performance evaluations) should be taken into account rather than held constant. It is simply not realistic to statistically manipulate the data so as to remove these differences. Thus, MCA analysis provides a more realistic assessment of differences between partisan groups than does regression analysis.

17. See Lester W. Milbrath and M.L. Goel, *Political Participation: How and Why Do People Get Involved in Politics?* (Chicago: Rand McNally College Publishing Co., 1977), 83-86.

18. The parties are identified in figure 4.

19. The policy areas included public transportation, law enforcement, housing for the poor, public education, jobs creation, and, for the Mexican sample, economic redistribution.

20. Though less discontent was noted among petroleum workers in Venezuela. See Davis, " 'Labor Aristocracy Thesis' " 419-31.

21. See Coleman and Davis, "Preemptive Reform," 3-32.

22. On political secrecy in Mexico, see Stevens, *Protest and Response*, 21-64.

23. On the role of rumors in Mexican politics, see Loaeza, "La politica rumor," 557-86.

24. See Charles L. Davis, "Political Regimes," 421-47.

25. See Wayne A. Cornelius, "The Political Economy of Mexico under de la Madrid: The Crisis Deepens, 1985-1986," *Research Report* 43 (La Jolla, Calif.: Center for U.S.–Mexican Studies, Univ. of California, San Diego, 1986).

26. The study assumes that political sophistication was at least indirectly controlled by partialing out the effects of age and socioeconomic status.

CHAPTER SEVEN

1. See Cornelius and Craig, "Politics in Mexico," 446-48, as cited in chapter 4. Also, Evelyn P. Stevens, "Mexico's PRI; The Institutionalization of Corporatism?" in Malloy, *Authoritarianism and Corporatism*, 227-58. In the case of Venezuelan politics, see Alan Gilbert and Peter M. Ward, *Housing, the State, and the Poor: Policy and Practice in three Latin American Cities* (Cambridge: Cambridge Univ. Press, 1985), 130-73.

2. Verba, Nie, and Kim, *Participation and Political Equality*, 112-42.

3. The union and party affiliation variables were analyzed in a separate regression equation.

4. Our measure of strength of institutional affiliation (see Appendix B) is similar to that used by Verba, Nie, and Kim, *Participation and Political Equality*, 106-11.

5. The point is explored more fully in Charles L. Davis and Kenneth M. Coleman, "Who Abstains? The Situational Meaning of Nonvoting," *Social Science Quarterly* 64, no. 4 (Dec. 1983): 764-76.

6. Note in particular that affiliation with any type of union increases the probability of voting (beta = +.18 for incorporated unions; +.13 for autonomous unions), as does identification with leftist parties (beta = +.12).

7. As will be shown, the leadership of this union disavowed formal ties with all parties. However, informal ties with the local PAN organization may have developed because of similar Christian Democratic backgrounds. Certainly, these data are suggestive of this interpretation.

8. See chapter 2 for more information on this point.

9. See John A. Booth and Mitchell A. Seligson, "The Political Culture

of Authoritarianism in Mexico: A Reexamination," *Latin American Research Review* 19, no. 1 (1984): 106-24.

10. The same point is made about urban squatters in Mexico City. See Cornelius, *Politics and the Migrant Poor*, 182-84.

11. As chapter 8 will show, PRI loyalists are similar to the "habitual voters" in Japan that Richardson analyzes. They vote consistently for the PRI but without a strong emotional commitment to the party. See Bradley M. Richardson, "Japan's Habitual Voters: Partisanship on the Emotional Periphery," *Comparative Political Studies* 9, no.3 (Oct. 1986): 356-84.

CHAPTER EIGHT

1. The classic study of voting behavior by the University of Michigan team is Angus Campbell et al., *The American Voter* (New York: John Wiley Press, 1960).

2. See Charles H. Franklin, "Issue Preferences, Socialization, and the Evolution of Party Identification," *American Journal of Political Science* 28, no. 3 (Aug. 1984): 459-78.

3. Ian Budge, Ivor Crewe, and Dennis Fairlie, eds., *Party Identification and Beyond* (New York: John Wiley, 1976).

4. The terminology is borrowed in part from Bruce Campbell, "Patterns of Change in Partisanship of Native Southerners: 1952-1972," *Journal of Politics* 39 (Aug. 1977): 730-61.

5. This view is developed in regard to the poor in Venezuela by Talton F. Ray, *The Politics of the Barrios of Venezuela* (Berkeley: Univ. of California Press, 1969), 98-138. On the tendency of the Mexican poor to petition government bureaucrats rather than party officials, see Cornelius, *Politics and the Migrant Poor*, 182-84.

6. This view of decision making in the Mexican political system is developed in Stevens, *Protest and Response.*

7. See Stanley Feldman and Alan S. Zuckerman, "Partisan Attitudes and the Vote: Moving beyond Party Identification," *Comparative Political Studies* 15, no. 2 (July 1982): 211-12.

8. The rationale for using particular elections is explained later.

9. All beta coefficients for partisanship are greater than .50.

10. for an overview of this literature, see Heinz Eulau and Michael S. Lewis-Beck, "Introduction: Economic Conditions and Electoral Outcomes in Trans-National Perspective," in Eulau and Lewis-Beck, *Economic Conditions and Electoral Outcomes: The United States and Western Europe* (New York: Agathon Press, 1985), 1-14.

11. Ibid.

12. See, in particular, Michael Lewis-Beck, "Comparative Economic Voting: Britain, France, Germany, Italy," *American Journal of Political Science* 30, no. 2 (May 1986): 315-46.

13. See Levy and Szekely, *Paradoxes of Stability and Change*, 71.

14. It is assumed that perceptions of social mobility are closely linked to perceptions of personal economic condition.

15. The need to consider simultaneously a broad range of possible determinants of electoral choice is emphasized in Lewis-Beck, "Comparative Economic Voting," 326-33.

16. See ibid. for documentation of this point, 328.

17. Similar findings are reported in David J. Myers and Robert E. O'Connor, "The Undecided Respondent in Mandatory Voting Settings: A Venezuelan Exploration," *Western Political Quarterly* 36, no. 3 (Sept. 1983): 420-33.

18. See Charles L. Davis and Scott Turner, "The Impact of Continuing Economic Crisis in Latin America on Electoral Support for the Incumbent Party: The Case of Mexico and Venezuela" (paper prepared for the 1987 meeting of the Kentucky Political Science Association, Centre College, Danville, Kentucky), 11-13.

19. The data show a strong relationship between ideological self-label and partisan identification. For Venezuelan workers ideological identification (right, center, or left) is correlated with dichotomous measures of party identification as follows: with identification with a leftist party, $r = .56$; with identification with AD, $r = -.37$; with identification with COPEI, $r = .46$. Strong correlations are also found for the Mexican sample. Ideological identification is correlated as follows: with identification with a leftist party, $r = .41$; with identification with PAN, $r = .20$; with identification with PRI, $r = -.54$.

20. See Pamela Johnston Conover and Stanley Feldman, "The Origins and Meaning of Liberal/Conservative Self-Identification," *American Journal of Political Science* 25, no. 4 (Nov. 1981): 617-45.

21. On the status of the Mexican Communist party, see Cornelius and Craig, "Politics in Mexico," 441.

22. On the Mexican Democratic party and the Mexican Workers party, see Levy and Szekely, *Paradoxes of Stability and Change*, 75-76.

23. See Hans D. Klingemann, "Measuring Ideological Conceptualization," in Samuel Barnes and M. Kaase, eds., *Political Action: Mass Political Participation in Five Western Democracies* (Beverly Hills, Calif.: Sage Publications, 1979), 215-54.

24. See tables 8 and 9 in Charles L. Davis, Kenneth M. Coleman, et al., "Ideology and Belief Systems: Social and Political Structures as Determinants of Working-Class Politicization in Venezuela and Mexico" (Paper prepared for presentation at the 1980 Latin American Studies Association, Indiana University, Bloomington, Indiana).

25. These political efforts have been most successful in the northern tier of European industrial democracies (Sweden, Norway, etc.) where a very high percentage of the work force is unionized. See Stephens, *Politics of Workers' Participation*, 16-25.

26. William H. Form, "Job Unionism vs. Political Unionism in Four Countries," in Irving L. Horowitz, John C. Leggett, and Martin Oppenheimer,

eds., *The American Working Class: Prospects for the 1980s* (New Brunswick: Transaction, 1979), 214-30.

27. Felipe Leal, *Estado, burocracía y sindicatos*, 127-28.

28. See note 26.

29. See James M. Malloy, "Authoritarianism and Corporatism in Latin America: The Modal Pattern," in Malloy, ed., *Authoritarianism and Corporatism in Latin America* (Pittsburgh: Univ. of Pittsburgh Press, 1977), 3-22.

30. On the distinction between "social corporatist organizations" and "corporatist state administrative structures," see Middlebrook, "Political Economy of Mexican Organized Labor," 387-400.

31. Kenneth M. Coleman participated in all such interviews, which corresponded to union leaders in the eight unionized cells in table 1. The interviews were conducted in February and March of 1981 in Mexico and in May of 1981 in Venezuela.

32. Obviously, one cannot rule out other individual characteristics.

33. This possibility is explored in Form, "Job Unionism," 216.

34. Ilan Bizberg and Kenneth M. Coleman, field notes of interview with leaders of Ayotla Textile workers' union, Ayotla, Mexico, Feb. 24, 1981, 14.

35. Local *municipios* generally have almost no policy-making autonomy from state and national control.

36. Recall that the study included the Nissan union in Cuernavaca, which has attained considerable notoriety inside Mexico as a classic case of a militant, independent union. See Roxborough, *Unions and Politics in Mexico*, 99-102, 104-6.

37. Among the total array of autonomous unions in Mexico, there are a few exceptions to this generalization, generally unions of highly skilled, professional workers. See Carr, "Mexican Economic Debacle," 85.

38. See Middlebrook, "Political Economy of Mexican Organized Labor," 272-76.

39. The emergence of *Solidarnosc* in 1981 was not necessarily detrimental to Polish workers. What is important, however, is this leader's understanding of events in Poland.

40. Ilan Bizberg and Kenneth M. Coleman, field notes of interview with leaders of Sindicato Independiente de Trabajadores de Nissan, Cuernavaca, March 3, 1981.

41. Interestingly, there appeared to be little actual political mobilization in this union.

42. José Gonzalez and Kenneth M. Coleman, field notes of interview with leaders of the Sindicato Unificado de Obreros y Empleados Petroleros del Estado Falcon, Punto Fijo, May 13, 1981.

43. José Gonzalez and Kenneth M. Coleman, field notes of interview with leaders of Sindicato de Trabajadores de la Industria Plastica y sus Similares del Estado Lara, Barquisimeto, May 17, 1981, 16.

44. Dissatisfaction with the moderation of traditional leftist union leaders in Venezuela accounts, in part, for the emergence of a more militant *nuevo sindicalismo* in the eighties. See Hellinger, "Venezuelan Democracy," 5-9.

45. Some leftist leaders, including leaders of the Revolutionary Leftist Movement (MIR) and the Socialist League (LS), had been revolutionary insurrectionists in the early sixties before accepting an amnesty offered by Christain Democratic president Rafael Caldera in 1968. The MAS and the MEP have different origins, however, and are always at pains to dissociate themselves from other leftist parties that were born in the guerrilla movement of the sixties.

46. For labor leaders concern over the fragility of democracy is not a wholly irrational perspective, given the repression that was directed toward the labor movement under the dictatorship of Marcos Pérez Jiménez (1952-58). See Levine, *Conflict and Political Change*, 231-54.

47. Purcell, *Mexican Profit-Sharing Decision*, 38-41.

CHAPTER NINE

1. See Terry Lynn Karl, "Petroleum and Political Pacts: The Transition to Democracy in Venezuela," *Latin American Research Review* 22, no. 1 (1987): 85.

2. Such a crisis can be provoked through the electoral process as events in Chile in the late sixties and early seventies and in Guatemala in the fifties illustrate. For an application of Gramsci's concept to events in Chile, see Atilio A. Boron, "Notas sobre las raices historico-estructurales de las movilización politica en Chile," *Foro Internacional* 16, no. 1 (1975): 64-121.

3. For example, Reagan drew significant support from rank-and-file union members in both the 1980 and 1984 presidential elections despite strong endorsements for the opposition candidates by the union leadership. See Gerald Pomper et al., *The Election of 1984: Reports and Interpretations* (Chatham: Chatham House Publishers, 1985), 67, table 3-2.

4. See Adam Przeworski, "Some Problems in the Study of the Transition to Democracy," in Guillermo O'Donnell, Philippe C. Schmitter, and Laurence Whitehead, eds., *Transitions from Authoritarian Rule: Comparative Perspectives* (Baltimore and London: Johns Hopkins Univ. Press, 1986), 53-56.

5. Ibid., 55.

6. In like manner Browning et al. show that minority groups in the United States are not likely to mobilize to gain access to white-dominated power structures in city governments unless they have the numbers—i.e., the size—to prevail. See Rufus P. Browning, Dale Rogers Marshall, and David H. Tabb, *Protest Is Not Enough: The Struggle of Blacks and Hispanics for Equality in Urban Politics* (Berkeley: Univ. of California Press, 1984).

7. See John D. Stephens, *The Transition from Captialism to Socialism* (Atlantic Highlands, N.J.: Humanities Press, 1980), 180ff.

8. For an elaboration of those differences, see Hewlett and Weinert, "Introduction," 8-10.

9. See Portes, "Latin American Class Structures," 22-23 and passim. Portes's estimates of the industrial proletariat for Mexico and Venezuela are

somewhat smaller than estimates made in other sources, perhaps because he separates the formal from the informal proletariat.

10. Kenneth M. Coleman's assistance in the preparation of the above three paragraphs for an earlier version is gratefully acknowledged.

11. See Alan Gilbert and Peter M. Ward, *Housing, the State and the Poor: Policy and Practice in Three Latin American Cities* (Cambridge: Cambridge Univ. Press, 1985), 13-16.

12. See Wayne A. Cornelius, "Political Liberalization and the 1985 Elections in Mexico," in Paul W. Drake and Eduardo Silva, eds., *Elections and Democratization in Latin America, 1980-85* (La Jolla, Calif.: Center for U.S.–Mexican Studies and Institute of the Americas, Univ. of California, San Diego, 1986), 122-37.

13. See Barry Carr, *Mexican Communism, 1968-1983: Eurocommunism in the Americas?* Research Report 42 (La Jolla, Calif.: Center for U.S.–Mexican Studies, Univ. of California, San Diego, 1985), 11-17; and Myers, "Venezuela's MAS," 16-27.

14. See Cornelius, "Political Liberalization," 122.

15. Enrique A. Baloyra, "Public Opinion and Support for the Regime: 1973-1983," in John D. Martz and David J. Myers, eds., *Venezuela: The Democratic Experience*, 2d ed. (Westport, Conn.: Praeger/Greenwood Press, 1986), 54-71.

16. Browning et al. show a high correlation between minority group size and incorporation into the majority coalition that controls city government. See Browning, Marshall, and Tabb, *Protest Is Not Enough*, 46-138.

17. Bitar and Troncoso estimate that Mexico's industrial product grew at an average annual rate of 7.3 percent between 1950 and 1979, while in Venezuela, which started from a lower degree of industrialization, the average annual rate was 7.9 percent over the same period. See Sergio Bitar and Eduardo Troncosco, *El desafío industrial de Venezuela* (Buenos Aires: Editorial Pomaire, 1983), 51.

18. Among nonrevolutionary states the distribution of income in Costa Rica may have improved slightly, from an already preferable profile.

19. See Mitchell Seligson, *The Gap between Rich and Poor: Contending Perspectives on the Political Economy of Development* (Boulder, Colo.: Westview Press, 1984).

20. Stephens, *The Politics of Workers' Participation*, 1-37.

21. Baptista, "Más alla del optimismo y del pesimismo," 20-41.

22. Kenneth M. Coleman prepared the above three paragraphs for an earlier version of this volume.

23. These concepts are defined in chapter 8.

24. Among such instances were the Brazilian coup of 1964, the Guatemalan coup/CIA sponsored invasion of 1954, and the annulment of the 1972 elections in El Salvador.

25. It is possible that a more equitably distributed style of growth could produce even higher rates of growth.

26. Albert O. Hirschman, "The Changing Tolerance for Income Inequality

in the Course of Economic Development," *Quarterly Journal of Economics* 87 (Nov. 1973): 544-66.

27. For supportive data see table 9 in Kenneth M. Coleman and Daniel N. Nelson, "State Capitalism, State Socialism, and the Politicization of Workers," in *Carl Beck Papers in Soviet and East European Studies* (Pittsburgh: Univ. of Pittsburgh, 1983).

28. The inability of labor leaders to deliver goods and protect wages is already a serious problem in Mexico. See Alejandro Alvarez, "Crisis in Mexico: Impacts on the Working Class and the Labor Movement," in Carr and Anzaldua Montoya, *Mexican Left*, 47-58.

Index